Recontextualizing Indian Shakespeare Cinema in the West

GLOBAL SHAKESPEARE INVERTED

Global Shakespeare Inverted challenges any tendency to view Global Shakespeare from the perspective of 'centre' versus 'periphery'. Although the series may locate its critical starting point geographically, it calls into question the geographical bias that lurks within the very notion of the 'global'. It provides a timely, constructive criticism of the present state of the field and establishes new and alternative methodologies that invert the relation of Shakespeare to the supposed 'other'.

SERIES EDITORS
David Schalkwyk, Queen Mary, University of London, UK
Silvia Bigliazzi, University of Verona, Italy
Bi-qi Beatrice Lei, National Taiwan University, Taiwan

ADVISORY BOARD
Douglas Lanier, University of New Hampshire, USA
Sonia Massai, King's College London, UK
Supriya Chaudhury, Jadavpur University, India
Ian Smith, Lafayette College, USA

Eating Shakespeare: Cultural Anthropophagy as Global Methodology, Edited by Anne Sophie Refskou, Marcel Alvaro de Amorim and Vinicius Mariano de Carvalho

Shakespeare in the Global South: Stories of Oceans Crossed in Contemporary Adaptation, Sandra Young

Migrating Shakespeare: First European Encounters, Routes and Networks, Edited by Janet Clare and Dominique Goy-Blanquet

Shakespeare's Others in 21st-century European Performance: The Merchant of Venice and Othello, Edited by Boika Sokolova and Janice Valls-Russell

Disseminating Shakespeare in the Nordic Countries: Shifting Centres and Peripheries in the Nineteenth Century, Edited by Nely Keinänen and Per Sivefors

FORTHCOMING TITLES
Reconstructing Shakespeare in the Nordic Countries: National Revival and Interwar Politics, 1870–1940, Edited by Nely Keinänen and Per Sivefors

Recontextualizing Indian Shakespeare Cinema in the West

Familiar Strangers

Edited by
Varsha Panjwani and
Koel Chatterjee

THE ARDEN SHAKESPEARE
LONDON • NEW YORK • OXFORD • NEW DELHI • SYDNEY

THE ARDEN SHAKESPEARE
Bloomsbury Publishing Plc
50 Bedford Square, London, WC1B 3DP, UK
1385 Broadway, New York, NY 10018, USA
29 Earlsfort Terrace, Dublin 2, Ireland

BLOOMSBURY, THE ARDEN SHAKESPEARE and the Arden Shakespeare logo are trademarks of Bloomsbury Publishing Plc

First published in Great Britain 2023
This paperback edition published 2024

Copyright © Varsha Panjwani, Koel Chatterjee and contributors, 2023

Varsha Panjwani and Koel Chatterjee have asserted their right under the Copyright, Designs and Patents Act, 1988, to be identified as editors of this work.

For legal purposes the Acknowledgements on p. xiv constitute an extension of this copyright page.

Cover design by Maria Rajka
Cover image: 36 Chowringhee Lane (1981 India) Directed by Aparna Sen Shown: Jennifer Kendal (right) © Film-Valas/Photofest

All rights reserved. No part of this publication may be reproduced or transmitted in any form or by any means, electronic or mechanical, including photocopying, recording, or any information storage or retrieval system, without prior permission in writing from the publishers.

Bloomsbury Publishing Plc does not have any control over, or responsibility for, any third-party websites referred to or in this book. All internet addresses given in this book were correct at the time of going to press. The author and publisher regret any inconvenience caused if addresses have changed or sites have ceased to exist, but can accept no responsibility for any such changes.

A catalogue record for this book is available from the British Library.

Library of Congress Cataloging-in-Publication Data

Names: Panjwani, Varsha, editor. | Chatterjee, Koel, editor.
Title: Recontextualizing Indian Shakespeare cinema in the West : familiar strangers / Varsha Panjwani, Koel Chatterjee.
Description: London ; New York : The Arden Shakespeare 2023. | Series: Global Shakespeare inverted | Includes index.
Identifiers: LCCN 2022034948 | ISBN 9781350168657 (hardback) | ISBN 9781350361263 (paperback) | ISBN 9781350168664 (epub) | ISBN 9781350168671 (ebook) | ISBN 9781350168688
Subjects: LCSH: Shakespeare, William, 1564–1616–Film adaptations. | Motion pictures–India–History and criticism. | Film adaptations–India–History and criticism. | Motion pictures–Political aspects–India.
Classification: LCC PR3093 .R4393 2023 | DDC 791.43/6—dc23/eng/20221003
LC record available at https://lccn.loc.gov/2022034948

ISBN:	HB:	978-1-3501-6865-7
	PB:	978-1-3503-6126-3
	ePDF:	978-1-3501-6867-1
	eBook:	978-1-3501-6866-4

Series: Global Shakespeare Inverted

Typeset by RefineCatch Limited, Bungay, Suffolk

To find out more about our authors and books visit www.bloomsbury.com and sign up for our newsletters.

CONTENTS

List of Illustrations viii
Notes on Contributors ix
Acknowledgements xiv
Foreword: On Reading the Indian Shakespeare Film xvi
Poonam Trivedi

Introduction: Indian Shakespeare Cinema in the West: Past, Present and Future Directions A Conversation between *Varsha Panjwani* and *Koel Chatterjee* 1

PART ONE: Dismantling the Familiar

1. Re-generation: Remapping the Screenscape in Fractious Times 29
   Diana E. Henderson

2. Two Indian Film Offshoots of *Twelfth Night* 55
   Robert White

3. 'For never was a story of more woe': Dialogic Telling and Global Interchange in *Qayamat se Qayamat Tak*, a 'Bollywood' Film Adaptation of *Romeo and Juliet* 79
   Mark Thornton Burnett

4 'Indian' Independent Cinema and Shakespeare 99
Sharat Katariya and *Vandana Kataria* in conversation with *Tula Goenka*

5 Vandana Kataria's *Noblemen*: Global Frames of Interpretation 121
Taarini Mookherjee

6 Chutzpah: The Politics of Bollywood Shakespeare Subtitles 135
Varsha Panjwani

PART TWO: Recontextualizing the Stranger

7 Curating Indian Shakespeares at the BFI in 2016 157
Helen de Witt in conversation with *Anne Sophie Refskou*

8 'Travelling' with Shakespeare through Bhardwaj's *Haider*: From US Classrooms to the Global Shakespeare Movement 167
Jyotsna G. Singh

9 Understanding Nimmi: Tracing Interpretations of Vishal Bhardwaj's *Maqbool* 183
Ana Laura Magis Weinberg

10 '*Nainā ṭhaga leṃge*': Visual Uncertainty in *Othello* and Vishal Bhardwaj's *Omkara* 203
   Shani Bans

11 A Pair of Homotextual Lovers: Bhansali's *Ram-Leela* and Shakespeare's *Romeo and Juliet* 225
   Amritesh Singh

12 'All the world's a stage': The Participatory Indian Cinema Audience and its Impact on Indian Shakespeare Films 253
   Koel Chatterjee

Afterword 271
Sonia Massai

Index 279

ILLUSTRATIONS

6.1	Film still: 'Netflix Subtitles', *Haider* (2014), Dir. Vishal Bhardwaj, India: UTV Motion Pictures.	137
6.2	Film still: 'Mirrors in Leela's Bedroom', *Goliyon Ki Rasleela: Ram-Leela* (2013), Dir. Sanjay Leela Bhansali, India: Eros International.	145
6.3	Film still: 'Haider's Chutzpah', *Haider* (2014), Dir. Vishal Bhardwaj, India: UTV Motion Pictures.	148
11.1	Film still: 'Hand-in-hand: *Ramayana* and *Romeo and Juliet*', *Goliyon Ki Rasleela: Ram-Leela* (2013), Dir. Sanjay Leela Bhansali, India: Eros International.	234
11.2, 11.3	Film stills: 'Not kissing by the book', *Goliyon Ki Rasleela: Ram-Leela* (2013), Dir. Sanjay Leela Bhansali, India: Eros International.	238
11.4, 11.5	Film stills: 'Apt and proportionate "meuynge"', *Goliyon Ki Rasleela: Ram-Leela* (2013), Dir. Sanjay Leela Bhansali, India: Eros International.	241
11.6	Film still: 'A story of woe', *Goliyon Ki Rasleela: Ram-Leela* (2013), Dir. Sanjay Leela Bhansali, India: Eros International.	244

CONTRIBUTORS

Shani Bans is a PhD Candidate at University College London, UK. Her thesis, 'Optics in Shakespeare's Tragedies', explores Shakespeare's use of optics as a metaphor for the relativity of human perception in *Hamlet*, *Othello*, *Macbeth* and *King Lear*.

Mark Thornton Burnett is Professor of Renaissance Studies at Queen's University Belfast. He is the author of *Masters and Servants in English Renaissance Drama and Culture: Authority and Obedience* (1997), *Constructing 'Monsters' in Shakespearean Drama and Early Modern Culture* (2002), *Filming Shakespeare in the Global Marketplace* (2007; 2nd ed. 2012), *Shakespeare and World Cinema* (2013) and *'Hamlet' and World Cinema* (2019). His co-edited collection, *Women and Indian Shakespeares*, was published by Bloomsbury Academic in 2022.

Koel Chatterjee is Lecturer in Integrated English at Trinity Laban Conservatoire of Dance and Music, London. Her essays have been published in collections such as *Shakespeare and Indian Cinemas*, *Eating Shakespeare*, *Shakespeare's Audiences* and *Shakespeare and Accentism*. She conceived the 'Indian Shakespeares on Screen' project in 2016 while completing her PhD on the same subject and is currently the curator of www.shakespop.co.uk, an online space for academic and general interest discussions of Shakespeare in pop culture.

Tula Goenka is a Professor of Television, Radio & Film at S.I. Newhouse School of Public Communications, Syracuse University, USA. She began her filmmaking career at Lintas Bombay and MTV Networks in New York City. She then transitioned to editing feature films for Mira Nair, Spike Lee and

James Ivory, among others. She uses the power of storytelling to illuminate oppression, heal trauma and create positive change, and teaches fiction and nonfiction production. Her book of conversations with twenty-eight filmmakers across the spectrum of Indian cinema, '*Not Just Bollywood: Indian Directors Speak*', was published by Om Books in 2014.

Diana E. Henderson, the Arthur J. Conner Professor of Literature at the Massachusetts Institute of Technology (MIT), is the author of *Collaborations with the Past: Reshaping Shakespeare Across Time and Media* and *Passion Made Public: Elizabethan Lyric, Gender, and Performance*. She edited *Alternative Shakespeares 3*, *A Concise Companion to Shakespeare on Screen*, and co-edited *The Arden Handbook to Shakespeare and Adaptation*, *Shakespeare and Digital Pedagogy*, and the annual *Shakespeare Studies* (Volumes XLII–). She works as a professional dramaturg, has produced a documentary based on MIT's participation with the Compagnia de' Colombari *Merchant in Venice*, and created the MITx/edX course 'Global Shakespeares: Re-Creating *The Merchant of Venice*'.

Sonia Massai is Professor of Shakespeare Studies at King's College London, UK. Her publications include her books on *Shakespeare's Accents: Voicing Identity in Performance* (2020; CHOICE Outstanding Book of 2021) and *Shakespeare and the Rise of the Editor* (2007), her collections of essays on *Hamlet* (Bloomsbury 2021), *Ivo van Hove* (Bloomsbury 2018), *Shakespeare and Textual Studies* (2015) and *World-Wide Shakespeares* (2005), and critical editions of *The Paratexts in English Printed Drama to 1642* (2014) and John Ford's *'Tis Pity She's a Whore* (Bloomsbury 2011). She is Principal Investigator of 'Wartime Shakespeare', co-organizer of the exhibition 'Shakespeare at War' (National Army Museum, 2023–4) and co-editor of the accompanying exhibition book (2023). She is currently preparing a new Shakespeare Arden edition of *Richard III*, and she has recently been appointed as one of the General Editors of the New Cambridge Shakespeare (CSE) series.

Taarini Mookherjee is a Lecturer at Columbia University, New York, where she teaches Literature Humanities, a required course in the Core Curriculum. She previously taught British and Transnational Literature at the State University of New York (SUNY), New Paltz. She received her PhD in English and Comparative Literature from Columbia University and holds a Masters in Shakespeare Studies from King's College London. Her current book project, *'Desifying* Shakespeare: Performing Contemporary India in Adaptations', focuses on contemporary Indian adaptations of Shakespeare in film and theatre. Her broader research and teaching fields include early modern drama, global Shakespeare, translation theory, post-colonial theory, and theatre and performance studies.

Varsha Panjwani teaches Shakespeare at New York University, London, UK. She is the author of *Podcasts and Feminist Shakespeare Pedagogy* (2022) and creator of the podcast series, *Women & Shakespeare* (www.womenandshakespeare.com). Her essays have been published in edited collections such as *Shakespeare, Race and Performance*, *Shakespeare and Indian Cinemas* and *Eating Shakespeare*, and in journals such as *Shakespeare Survey* and *Shakespeare Studies*. She was one of the principal organizers of 'Indian Shakespeares on Screen' – an international conference, film festival and exhibition in collaboration with the BFI Southbank and Asia House.

Anne Sophie Refskou teaches comparative literature at Aarhus University, Denmark and works on early modern drama and Shakespearean afterlives. Her publications include *Eating Shakespeare: Cultural Anthropophagy as Global Methodology*, co-edited with Vinicius Mariano de Carvalho and Marcel Alvaro de Amorim (Arden Shakespeare, Bloomsbury 2019). She is currently completing a monograph on Shakespeare and compassion in early modern culture.

Amritesh Singh is an Associate Lecturer at the International Education Institute, the University of St Andrews, UK. His research interests are diverse, ranging from Bollywood Studies to Critical Pedagogy and Academic English to constructions of gender in early modern England, all of which are informed by his expertise in queer theory.

Jyotsna G. Singh is a Professor in Early Modern Studies at Michigan State University. Her research interests include Shakespeare, travel writing, postcolonial theory, histories of Islam, and gender and race studies. Her major publications include: *The Weyward Sisters: Shakespeare and Feminist Politics* (co-authored, Callaghan and Helms); *Colonial Narratives/ Cultural Dialogues: 'Discovery' of India in the Language of Colonialism*; *Travel Knowledge: European 'Discoveries' in the Early Modern Period* (co-ed. Ivo Kamps); *A Companion to the Global Renaissance: English Literature and Culture in the Era of Expansion, 1559–1660*, ed.; *The Postcolonial World* (co-ed. David D. Kim); Routledge; *Shakespeare and Postcolonial Theory* (Arden 2019), and a second, expanded edition of *A Companion to the Global Renaissance: Literature and Culture in the Era of Expansion, 1500–1700* (2021). (She is currently co-editing (with Matthew Dimmock) Shakespeare's *The Tempest*, under contract with Cambridge University Press.

Poonam Trivedi taught at Indraprastha College, University of Delhi. She has co-edited books on Indian and Asian Shakespeare: *Asian Interventions in Global Shakespeare: 'All the World's his Stage'* (2020), *Shakespeare and Indian Cinemas: 'Local Habitations'* (2019), *Shakespeare's Asian Journeys: Critical Encounters, Cultural Geographies, and the Politics of Travel* (2017), *Re-playing Shakespeare in Asia* (2010) and *India's Shakespeare: Translation, Interpretation and Performance* (2005) and has authored a CD 'King Lear *in India*' (2006). Her latest articles are in the *Cambridge Companion to Shakespeare on Screen* and in *Cahiers Elizabethans*. She is on the editorial board of the Shakespeare on Screen series.

Ana Laura Magis Weinberg is an early career scholar. She holds a BA in English Literature from the National Autonomous University of Mexico, and a PhD in Adaptation Studies from

De Montfort University, UK. She has written extensively on Shakespeare in Bollywood and *The Three Musketeers* on screen. She also works outside of academia as a critically acclaimed translator and a published author, and has received multiple awards.

Robert S. White (FAHA) is Emeritus Winthrop Professor of English at the University of Western Australia and a Chief Investigator in the Australian Research Council Centre of Excellence in the History of Emotions. He has held an Australian Research Council Professorial Fellowship and Visiting Professorships at Oxford. His publications are mainly in the field of Shakespeare, and also Romantic literature. They include *Pacifism in English Literature: Minstrels of Peace* (2008), and most recently *Avant-Garde Hamlet* (2015), *Shakespeare's Cinema of Love* (2016), *Ambivalent Macbeth* (2018), *A Midsummer Night's Dream: Language and Writing* (2020), and *Keats's Anatomy of Melancholy* (2020).

ACKNOWLEDGEMENTS

The questions that propel this edited collection began to form during the 2016 'Indian Shakespeares on Screen' international conference and film festival. The co-editors of this volume were two of the four principal organizers of this all-women team. We would like to thank the other half of our crew – Preti Taneja and Thea Buckley – who contributed valuable funding, time, energy, ideas and lots of verve! The team at the British Film Institute (BFI Southbank) especially Helen de Witt and Aga Baranowska, was instrumental in believing in the project and giving us the space for screenings. Asia House, with the wonderful Pamela Kember and Jemimah Steinfeld at the helm, was the perfect home for discussions that have made their way into the book. Funding from The Queen Mary University Centre for Public Engagement and from Royal Holloway, University of London allowed us to plan big, and Dr Deana Rankin's guidance and mentorship was invaluable. INOX India (especially Siddharth Jain), Mama India Clothing (especially Neelam Bhasin), and the National Film Archive of India (NFAI) also have our gratitude. Last but not least our appreciation is owed to Vishal Bhardwaj, Abbas Tyrewala, and Robin Bhatt who will always be celebrities to us despite their absolutely humble un-celebrity-like behaviour when they spoke at our events. Their Indian Shakespeare films are a gift and extensively discussed in this collection. We also want to express our deepest thanks to our excellent conference and film festival contributors, some of whom developed their papers for this volume and others who are not in the volume but cheered and supported us all the way, especially Kinga Földváry, Rosa Maria García-Periago, Madhavi Menon, Jonathan Gill Harris, Timo Uotinen, and Vikas Wadhwani.

The audiences at these events indicated a need and appetite for this work as well as challenging us with thoughtful comments and questions.

This book has had every manner of personal and professional crises thrown at it, as well as a global pandemic. The reason why it has proved resilient is due to the immense support it has received from our extremely patient contributors who believed in the project and had faith in us. We hope that they share our joy in completing this publication. We are grateful to the series editors, especially David Schalkwyk, who provided invaluable support right from the proposal stage and the anonymous reviewers, both at the proposal and submission stage, who encouraged us to sharpen and focus our ideas. Big shoutouts to Mark Dudgeon, Lara Bateman, and Ella Wilson of the Arden Shakespeare team for their flexibility, patience, and ingenuity.

Our family and friends who let us talk about this edited collection endlessly and forgave us when we cancelled plans with them to work on this are the true force behind the publication. Varsha would like to thank her family – Sushma Panjwani, Rajkumar Panjwani, and Chirag Panjwani – and two friends in particular – Delia Jarrett-Macauley and Benjamin Poore – for their wicked sense of humour and endless cheerleading capabilities. Koel would like to thank her husband, Alexander Bradley, and her new son Rohan, though it must be admitted that this book would probably have been finished a lot earlier if not for them.

Last but not least, we are always ever so grateful for our students whose curiosity always hones our thinking. We consider them our collaborators as they teach us so much.

FOREWORD
On Reading the Indian Shakespeare Film
Poonam Trivedi

The globalization of Shakespeare into a world icon, invested with a certain cultural capital, has seen a proliferation of Shakespeare on film from outside the Europhone world in the twenty-first century. Indian, Chinese, Japanese, Taiwanese, Korean, Thai, Malaysian, Indonesian, Tibetan, African, Maori, Latin American, Mexican and more cinemas have turned to Shakespeare to express themselves. And these 'rich and strange' creations have thrown a challenge to critical regimes largely emerging from the West: such as the intercultural stage productions of Shakespeare from the late 1970s onwards which generated a subversive shift of critical attention towards the non-Europhone. Likewise the intercultural Shakespeare film too has disturbed the status quo on what it means to be Shakespeare. All these films, acutely localized, engage with Shakespeare's plays and meanings in diverse and unconventional but compelling ways, overturning the critical epistemes of reading Shakespeare on film. Even though the medium of film is more accessible than that of live theatre, and the transnational nature of the technologies of film as well as the practice of subtitling facilitates cross-cultural viewing, yet the non-Europhone film, particularly the Shakespeare film, suffers from a lack of legibility and consequent pleasure, especially in the West. The intercultural Shakespeare film which needs must work with a translated Shakespeare, changes not just language, but also locations, and often character and narrative too to fit the new setting. It may interpolate to refine localization in a culture which might be totally unfamiliar. Its language may not translate well, subtitling being a poor substitute, and the specificity of its *mis-en-scène* and performative practice again might be alien to that of the Europhone. Film criticism determined by the dominant Western model of cinematic aesthetics and narrative is all too often at odds with intercultural differences which are apt to be viewed askance.

Within such a scenario, it is not surprising that the Indian Shakespeare film has had until recently very little exposure or academic attention even though it goes back almost a hundred years. As a matter of fact, Indian cinema as a whole has lacked scholarly estimation being largely considered escapist, populist and commercial. Further, unlike many other cinemas, Indian cinema, from the very beginning, has charted its own idiosyncratic track, different to the *cinema verité* developed in the West, with its trademark modes of overlapping narratives, intense emotionality and stylized song and dance, features which have not found favour with Western audiences whose viewing tastes have evolved along different trajectories. Indian film distributors too did not make special efforts to circulate their films with subtitles and it is only in the last few decades, with increasing Indian diasporic audiences in different parts of the world, that Indian films have found any kind of a notable presence in the West, even though they have always been popular in the Middle East, many parts of Africa, Central, South East and Far East Asia. Early Indian film critics too, under a colonial hangover, were apologetic and undermined their own cinema which has only begun to garner critical attention with the development of film and cultural studies. Within the massive enterprise that is the Indian cinemas (almost 2,000 films a year), if the Indian Shakespeare film has suddenly acquired a crossover kind of appeal and circulation, it is not only due to the Shakespearean brand value, but also to Bollywood being increasingly recognized as a brand in itself. And if today Vishal Bhardwaj's tragic trilogy is the best-known face of the Indian Shakespearean cinema, it is not a flash in the pan, but rather a culmination of a long history.

It is not common knowledge that the Indian cinematic engagement with Shakespeare starts quite early, with silent cinema (1923, *Champraj Hado*, dir. Nanubhai Desai), nor that the world's first full-length talkie of *Hamlet* (1935, *Khoon ka Khoon*, dir. Sohrab Modi) was produced in India, as also was the first feature film of the *Comedy of Errors* (1963, *Bhranti Bilas*, dir. Manu Sen). A recent filmography lists 140 titles of feature films in which Shakespeare appears, variously, as the full play, as scenes, characters, direct quotations, inspirational citations, resonances or parodic afterlives, performed in thirteen Indian language cinemas and incorporated in an almost staggering range of film genres, a variety as vast as the industry itself.[1] Hence it is evident that no one paradigm will do: definitions and taxonomies of the 'Indian Shakespeare film' become inadequate and redundant as soon as they are formulated; not only has the evolving technological dynamics of the industry triggered shifts in the deployment of Shakespeare, but regional and local differences of language, taste and tradition within genres, the practice of 'remakes' from one language to another and socio-economic changes affecting patterns of viewership, all create a vast and intricate web of variants and tendencies spread over almost a hundred years which are almost impossible to enumerate and illustrate in full. Added to this is the political milieu in which the Indian engagement with Shakespeare has evolved over almost two and a half centuries, from colonial imposition, mimicry, post-colonial resistance and adaptation, to now a globalized freedom to play around with his texts. Within this paradigm, the popular spheres of public theatre and cinema in India have always been more openly subversive taking the liberty to borrow, change and mash up the plays.

Moreover, 'Bollywood', the shorthand for the Hindi film industry from Mumbai, and which is popularly reckoned as the face of all Indian cinemas, is currently changing rapidly: a newer generation of directors targeting a multiplex stratified audience is creating shorter, 'content driven' films, with socially relevant themes and fewer, more integrated, songs which have found favour at the box-office. The niche film is challenging Bollywood's masala mainstream now. Regional cinemas which have not only their own linguistic but also cultural identities are now contesting and overtaking the Hindi film industry, e.g. Telugu cinema's unprecedented success with the *Baahubali* films (2015, 2017) which are said to have grossed $270 million worldwide. Further, the development of OTT (over-the-top) platforms which have enabled the streaming of a hitherto unimaginable range of world cinema have impacted the formulation of new productions, many of which are now being targeted for the small screen. In this fluid and dynamic setup of the many Indian cinemas, detailed micro, rather than macro, analyses are the only viable ones. Pre-fabricated models of 'Bollywood' types and their characteristics, unfortunately prevalent in the West, can be superficial and misleading.

A more generalized recognition of Bollywood, one finds, relates more to the appeal of a particular lush visual culture, of sumptuous ornate costuming, choric dances and choreographic moves with their hybridized music. The prevalent cinematic conventions of Bollywood, its prioritization of the emotive, the immersive 'psychological realism', its stylizations which produce narrative discontinuities still alienate the Western audience (despite the flamboyant inclusion of some of these features in Baz Luhrmann's *Moulin Rouge,* 2001). Few critics attempt to enter into the spirit of the Indian film. It is not just the formal conventions of Indian cinemas that are said to pose an interpretative obstacle, but neo-colonialist viewpoints too continue to colour serious estimation. Reading or analysing the Indian Shakespeare film therefore becomes doubly problematic, especially when they are expected to live up to and conform to outmoded notions of the post-colonial by the Western reader.

This is evident from the critical reception of Vishal Bhardwaj's trilogy, *Maqbool/Macbeth* (2004), *Omkara/Othello* (2006) and *Haider/Hamlet* (2014), the first set of crossover Shakespeare films from India, which was received largely favourably in the Western media, but whose reviews afford revealing glimpses of observations emerging from pre-determined notions of Indian films. The songs, as expected, always an irritant to the Western ear, draw pejorative comments: 'It's a bit rum when Iago breaks into a song-and-dance number, when Desdemona's murder is followed by a trilling love song' wrote Matheou Demetrious in *The Independent* (30 July 2006) while reviewing *Omkara* (the film incidentally climbed into the top ten charts in the UK). Mike McCahill, in *The Guardian* (2 October 2014) found in *Haider* a 'surprising sense in staging the Mousetrap and gravediggers' scene as musical numbers'. Apart from the fact that Iago has a drinking song in the play which is often performed with stomping and swaying, that the gravediggers too have a song scripted by Shakespeare, and that Shakespeare's plays have a hallowed tradition of operatic redactions too, the mechanical dismissal of the multiple musics of a film which pick up the givens of the original and present them in their own way, smacks of prejudice and a refusal to parse other forms of creativity.

As has been noted before, songs in Indian films are not always a distraction; in Bhardwaj's films they are deeply integrated into the narrative, supplementing the words and articulating the ineffable.[2] The song on Dolly/Desdemona's death, '*Jaag jaa*' (wake up) harks back to the aubade in the play which Cassio organizes outside Othello's chamber with some musicians on the morning after the brawl at the beginning of act three. In the film, the song is initially sung by Omi/Othello to wake up Dolly/Desdemona from her post-coital slumber. Its recall at the end, as a voiceover, is a means to deepen the tragic irony of Omkara's devastation and regret when the truth about Dolly dawns on him and he realizes she will wake up no more, 'cold, cold, my girl' (5.2.276). The operatic staging of the Mousetrap with giant puppets, song and dance in *Haider*, on the other hand has been applauded by others: 'brilliant ... a highlight' said James Shapiro in an interview with Bhardwaj (*The Review Monk*, 17 May 2015), and went on to note that 'Music was essential to Shakespeare's culture ... [and] that was so exciting in your adaptation ... that you understood how to make the songs so central. That is another way in which you connect the live wires of Shakespeare's culture to contemporary Indian culture and practice, that makes the play live in ways that many American and British adaptations of Shakespeare on film just don't get.' Likewise, the gravedigger's song in the film, choric and sonorous, rewrites Shakespearean concerns to verbalize Bhardwaj's revisionist view of life, death and revenge in the film. In the play, the gravedigger sings of the pulse of life, of youth and love, while digging his pits of clay. In *Haider,* in contrast, the song: '*Aree aao na, ke jaan gayi, jahaan gaya, so jao . . . ke thak gayi hai zindagi, so jao*' (Come on now, life has gone, the world has gone, sleep. . . . life is now tired, sleep) welcomes death, its refrain, 'Come on now', accepting the restful sleep of death. But these fine-tuned shifts of meaning in *Haider* went virtually unnoticed by reviewers and the fact that Bhardwaj's adaptations modified Shakespearean tragic endings hardly drew any comments. In his trilogy both Hamlet and Claudius do not die; Iago has his neck slashed by Emilia; and Macbeth, in *Maqbool,* dies not fighting but resigned and accepting of his fate.

The more measured criticism emerging from academia too registers an unwritten assumption that, to succeed, a Shakespeare film must be inevitably targeted towards a European audience and conform to fixed ideological expectations. Sussane Gruss in a well-informed essay nevertheless points out what she sees as *Omkara*'s 'Western aesthetics' reminiscent of Hollywood 'spaghetti westerns', and thereby argues that the film was 'consciously created as a hybrid product meant to please several dramatically different audiences'. Thereby, according to her, it failed commercially, and also ideologically, by not being 'a subversive critic of a colonial "master-text"' (Gruss 2009, 234). Similarly, Florence Cabaret, in an otherwise resourceful reading, is surprised at 'the film's attachment to Hindu caste hierarchies (more than to race hierarchies)' and its targeted viewership: 'We may thus say that *Omkara* addresses first and foremost a coloured/Indian audience' (Cabaret 2015, 108, 110). Again, a reification of 'Bollywood' stereotypes and an inability to move beyond the parameters of a Hollywoodian aesthetic prompts such statements. The colour differentiations of black African versus white European have no salience in the Indian context as demographically Indians have evolved over millennia from the same two races – Aryan and Dravidian – exhibiting a spectrum of skin pigmentation. Caste, on the other hand, still deeply entrenched in democratic India, is the pernicious mode of discrimination in Indian society and forms an apt substitution for race which is primarily a Western preoccupation. As a matter of fact, colour semiotics in Indian culture do not demonize the colour black: traditionally it signifies the hue of divinity, valour, beauty and romance. Many Hindu gods, Shiva, Vishnu, Rama are envisaged with dark blue complexions, the goddess Kali is coloured black, Draupadi's dark complexion is held as a sign of beauty in the *Mahabharata*, and devotional songs in praise of the god Krishna express a yearning to don his dark colour. The colour consciousness of modern India, on the other hand, manifest in the marketing of 'Fair and Lovely' whitening creams, is a vestige of colonialism. It would be foolhardy for a film not to address the massive local audience. To impugn Indian *Othello* performances for erasing race is to impose a unitary inflexible model of the post-colonial emerging out of the Western academy which has at best a tenuous hold on the complexities of the living realities of the country. The balancing act between international approbation and local popularity with regard to the Shakespeare film in any context is a precarious one and parameters used for its evaluation neglect local audience reactions at their peril. Incidentally, Bhardwaj's trilogy did not set the box-office on fire at home, the films were not Bollywood enough.

In the context of globalizing Shakespeare, while it has become a cliché to say that others are appropriating Shakespeare to tell their own stories, it is more productive to investigate how and why departures from the original are introduced and what their impact is on the whole. This would show how other cultures are making meaning of the 400-year-old plays, how they keep them alive and what means they adopt to talk back to Shakespeare. A look at the rich legacy of *Romeo and Juliet* versions (which, not surprisingly, are the largest in number:

seventeen), among the various Indian cinemas, reveals the myriad turns and twists given to the local conversations with Shakespeare in Indian cinemas. The very first film in 1937, *Ambikapathy*, begins this interaction boldly for its time juxtaposing a well-known eleventh-century Tamil tale about the tragic love between a poet and a princess with Shakespeare's *Romeo and Juliet*, subversively equating the Tamil classic with the colonial icon. It worked in the balcony scene, dared to present a kiss between the lovers and incorporated lines of Shakespearean verse in Tamil translation, some of which found their way into a popular song of a later film, musically infusing Shakespeare's poetry into the subconscious of the Tamil people. Later versions of *Romeo and Juliet*, especially in Hindi, kept the feuding families, and the separated lovers, but succumbed to local taste and altered the Shakespearean tragedy into a reconciliation and happy ending. The tragic ending with the death of the young lovers became acceptable at the box-office only after the success of *Qayamat se Qayamat Tak* (1988), a trendsetting version of teenage angst, influenced by *West Side Story*, which went on to acquire a cult status. All Indian versions choose to add the rationale of class, caste or religious differentiation to root the ancient grudge between Shakespeare's 'two households both alike in dignity' and bring up Shakespeare to speak to the present. The latest version, *Sairat* (2016, Marathi) which features a doomed romance between a low caste boy and a brahmin girl, touched the chord of caste in such an empathetic manner that it has been remade in five other languages and three more are planned. Shakespeare speaks intimately to the concerns of Indian society and the cinemas endeavour to embed and home him in diverse local habitations and habiliments.

This wide-ranging dialoguing with Shakespeare in Indian films, unique in its variant moods, tones and inflexions, can be heard in films of as many as eighteen plays in thirteen languages. Here one may catch a veritable spectrum of voices and visuals: of homage through citation of *Hamlet* in *Rajapart Rangadurai* (1973, Tamil), through direct quotation in English of Sonnet 18

(*Eklavya*, 2007, Hindi, also with allusions to *Hamlet, Lear* and *Macbeth*) and by being blessed by the gods who descend to dignify the story of King Lear in *Gunasundari Katha* (1949, Telugu). We can find Shakespeare conversing with mythology and folklore which in turn supplement and add to *Hamlet* in *Karmayogi* (2012, Malayalam) and *Macbeth* in *Veeram* (2016, Malayalam). Action packed suspense is generated in *8×10 Tasveer (Hamlet*, 2009, Hindi) and unending laughter from the comic confusions between the two sets of twins of *The Comedy of Errors* in *Do Dooni Char* (1968, Hindi), *Angoor* (1982, Hindi), *Ulta Palta* (1997, Kannada, 1998, Telugu) and *Double di Trouble* (2014, Punjabi). Piquancy is added to family socials, e.g. *10ml Love* (*Midsummer Night's Dream*, 2010, Hindi and English) and *Life Goes On* (*King Lear*, 2009, English). Political angst and anger resonate in *Haider* (*Hamlet*, 2014, Hindi), *Othello-We Too Have Our Othellos* (2014, Assamese) and *Arshinagar* (*Romeo and Juliet*, 2015, Bengali) while cheeky tones of parody and satire are not missing in *Matru ki Bijli ka Mandola* (*Macbeth*, 2013, Hindi). To do justice to this vast and diverse cinematic interlocution with Shakespeare, which has only now begun to be established, is to read it as the evolving dynamic of the culture and entertainment industry through its history of colonial impositions, post-colonial resistances, and now post-independence freedoms of competing with and contesting the global. All Indian Shakespeare films embody differing degrees of transformation: acute acculturation, surprising relocation, often of opportunist and cavalier appropriation, and some even with a post-modernist sprinkling of citational fragments, reflecting what Homi Bhaba has termed 'hyphenated hybridity' which is an opening out and remaking of the boundaries and limits of culture (Bhabha 1994, 219). All of them constitute shades of post-colonial resistance, as argued by Bill Ashcroft with reference to Indian cinemas, of not rejection or opposition, but instead, of a transformation, which prioritizes the agency of the subjected and produces alternative modernities. He finds the appropriation of the technologies of cinema, emerging from the West, and their cultural remoulding in Bollywood, 'a form that has so exceeded its Western origins that it offers a stunning example of the possibilities of transformation' (Ashcroft 2012, 3). Heather Tyrrell points out that the increasing international success of Bollywood, the most prolific film industry in the world, is 'emblematic of resistance to the West', especially seen in Hollywood's attempt to dominate, and its limited success, in the domestic Indian market (Tyrrell 2004, 361).

The intercultural has largely been subsumed by the global and it is time that a level playing field is established for all intercultural Shakespeare films along with Europhone ones. Protocols of criticism need to evolve: parochialisms have to be shed and new sensibilities arrived at along with an openness to other forms of creativity and a receptivity to the nuances of other cultures. Interpretative communities have to walk that extra mile. Hope rises with some voices which have been raised in this direction: Mark Thornton Burnett in *Shakespeare and World Cinema* calls for 'an alteration in the canon of Shakespeare on film' which would necessitate a shift in the 'praxis of interpretation' (Burnett 2013, 3). Craig Dionne and Parmita Kapadia in *Bollywood Shakespeares* propose a process of 'dissensus' to better appreciate Bollywood and Shakespeare, which is a cracking opening from the 'inside' . . . 'regimes of perception' to 'sketch a new topography of the possible' (Dionne and Kapadia 2014, 6–7). Bridget Escolme, in response to the energizing intercultural impetus of the Globe to Globe festival (2012) hopes that it will lead to the 'beginning of a decentering of Shakespeare' in the English classroom, and to 'ways in which a Shakespeare beyond English might re-teach us Shakespeare' (Escolme 2013, 309, 311). Intercultural / non-Europhone Shakespeare films mark their difference by their embeddedness in specific local cultures; to work out their intricacies, there is urgent need for what one may term 'bi-focal' critical lenses: with one setting for close analysis, both textual and semiotic, and another for distant readings which estrange and re-centre. Better still, stretching the metaphor, 'progressive' critical lenses should be adopted which will incorporate the multi-foci in one and which may seamlessly enable us to read and make familiar the foreign. The intercultural globalizing Shakespeare film is always multi-focal and multi-vocal.

'Look what you have started!', was Deana Rankin's (Royal Holloway, University of London) remark referring to me as she opened up the discussion at the end of my plenary session at the 'Shakespeare in Bollywood' conference held in London in 2014. This was an initiatory event, which later flowered into the major 'Indian Shakespeares on Screen' three day conference (2016), with the participation of Bhardwaj and multiple screenings at the British Film Institute (BFI) the discussions from which form the kernel of this collection. While I cannot possibly in any manner claim a proprietorship over these monumental entities, Shakespeare and Indian cinemas, I am immensely gratified that a short podcast of mine on this subject for the BBC 3 radio essay (14 May 2012) fired the imaginations of younger researchers and academics whose energies are now bearing excellent fruit in ploughing this immensely rich field of the Indian Shakespeare film.

My recent co-edited collection of essays, *Shakespeare and Indian Cinemas: 'Local Habitations'* (2019) has extensively mapped this area for the first time, bringing into play the multiple contexts (local, regional, historical and cinematic) along with the literary, theatrical and theoretical parameters which embed Shakespeare in Indian culture. This new collection of essays builds on this ground to extend and re-focus the critical discourse to attend to the Europhone reception of the Indian Shakespeare film. It aims to provide the much needed 'multi-focal' lens to facilitate negotiations with Indian cinematic Shakespeare, particularly in the academy, through directly addressing their cultural and semiotic differences, thereby narrowing the gap and reformulating the modes of viewing. The contributors to this collection have been at the forefront of research and analysis of Indian Shakespeares, recouping, archiving, contextualizing and theorizing their knotted intricacies in informed ways. The provocations of their work will shift received opinions and, hopefully, draw many others into the fold of a growing field of intercultural and global Shakespeare.

Notes

1 See 'Filmography' and 'Introduction' in *Shakespeare and Indian Cinemas: 'Local Habitations'*, ed. Poonam Trivedi and Paromita Chakravarti (New York and London: Routledge, 2019), 319–32.
2 See Poonam Trivedi, 'Singing to Shakespeare in *Omkara*', *Renaissance Shakespeare: Shakespeare Renaissances*, Proceedings of the Ninth World Shakespeare Congress (Newark: University of Delaware Press, 2014).

References

Ashcroft, Bill. 'Bollywood, Postcolonial Transformation and Modernity', in *Travels of Bollywood Cinema: From Bombay to LA*, ed. Anjali Gera Roy and Chua Beng Huat. New Delhi: Oxford University Press, 2012.

Bhabha, Homi. *The Location of Culture*. London: Routledge, 1994.

Burnett, Mark Thornton. *Shakespeare and World Cinema*. Cambridge: Cambridge University Press, 2013.

Cabaret, Florence. 'Indianising *Othello*: Vishal Bhardwaj's *Omkara*', in *Shakespeare on Screen: Othello*, ed. Sarah Hatchuel and Natalie Vienne-Guerrin. Cambridge: Cambridge University Press, 2015.

Dionne, Craig and Parmita Kapadia. 'Introduction', in *Bollywood Shakespeares*, ed. Craig Dionne and Parmita Kapadia. New York: Palgrave Macmillan, 2014.

Escolme, Bridget. 'Decentring Shakespeare: A hope for future connections', in *Shakespeare Beyond English: A Global Experiment*, ed. Susan Bennett and Christie Carson. Cambridge: Cambridge University Press, 2013.

Gruss, Sussane. 'Shakespeare in Bollywood? Vishal Bhardwaj's *Omkara*', in *Semiotic Encounters: Text, Image and Trans-Nation*, ed. Sara Sackel, Walter Gobel and Noha Hamdy. Amsterdam and New York: Rodopi, 2009.

Tyrrell, Heather. 'Bollywood vs Hollywood: Battle of the Dream Factories', in *Film Theory: Critical Concepts in Media and Cultural Studies*, ed. Philip Simpson, Andrew Utterson and Karen J. Shepherdson. New York: Taylor and Francis, 2004.

INTRODUCTION
Indian Shakespeare Cinema in the West: Past, Present, and Future Directions
A Conversation between *Varsha Panjwani* and *Koel Chatterjee*

The following is a condensed and edited version of multiple conversations that took place over several months in 2021 and 2022 in the process of editing the collection. While the editors do discuss the chapters in relevant parts of the conversation, detailed descriptions of individual chapters follow this introduction.

Varsha Panjwani (VP) Let's begin by considering why and how we are recontextualizing Indian Shakespeare Cinema in the West.

Koel Chatterjee (KC) Before we even talk about that, I think it is vital to establish what research has already been done in this field and how we are at this juncture in scholarship. *India's Shakespeare: Translation, Interpretation, and Performance* was a pioneering collection which investigated the way in which Shakespeare's plays were taught, translated and adapted, as well as the literary, social and political implications of this absorption into the cultural fabric of India, though it only had one chapter on Indian Shakespeare films.[1] Much of our own research began with Sonia Massai's *World-Wide Shakespeares* which sought to explore global Shakespeares within local traditions and challenged notions of centre/periphery or big-time/small-time Shakespeare.[2] Further collections deepened the discussion around separate pockets of Indian Shakespeares mainly focusing on regional Indian theatres or Bollywood. *Bollywood Shakespeares* introduced the concept of 'crosshatched Shakespeare' where Bollywood Shakespeare adaptations are examined as both part of an elite Western tradition as well as an expression of a post-national Indian identity founded by a global consumer culture.[3] However, this collection served to highlight Hindi/Urdu Shakespeares from Bollywood at the expense of a rich archive of Shakespeares from the several other film industries in India which rarely reach Western film circuits or classrooms. The most recent collection, *Shakespeare and Indian Cinemas: 'Local Habitations'*, however, did explore this vast archive of Shakespeare in Indian cinemas, including less familiar, Indian language cinemas, to contribute to the assessment of the expanding repertoire of Shakespeare films worldwide.[4] This collection, consequently, tracks the intra-Indian flows and cross-currents between the approach that the various film industries in India take to Shakespeare.

However, these books tend to catalogue Shakespeare adaptations along geopolitical boundaries. This sometimes tends to continue the marginalisation of non-anglophone Shakespeares and limits the scope of what a truly global methodology for reading diverse Indian Shakespeare adaptations on film could offer to Shakespeare Studies.

VP I think it is important to establish that we do not wish to underplay the significance of all this essential ground-laying work which now enables us to steer the field into a different direction. Instead of continuing to note Shakespeare's travel to Indian screens, we track Indian Shakespeare cinema's arrival and survival in the West. As Sandra Young has reminded us, Global Shakespeare 'risks repeating earlier occlusions if it becomes simply an opportunity to affirm, uncritically, the extraordinary reach of Stratford's Shakespeare'.[5] So, in this collection we critically assess the reach and impact of Indian cinema's Shakespeare instead.

This move necessitated that we think about the voices that can comment on and read Indian Shakespeare cinema so that its transformative or at least potentially transformative effect on the field of Shakespeare Studies as a whole can be understood and realized. As Diana E. Henderson points out in her chapter in this collection, while it is crucial to 'value local expertise in contextualizing particular artworks, claiming linguistic and cultural embeddedness as critical prerequisites' has the counter-productive effect of providing 'an easy reason for novice outsiders not even to try to engage with this subfield and its artworks' and often this ends up giving the impression that Indian Shakespeare cinema has little to offer beyond information on its birthing milieu. To combat this notion, a range of scholars and practitioners with different levels of familiarity with Indian Shakespeare cinema have been assembled to examine the way in which their positionality refracts their experiences with these films and to reflect on how they have navigated or can negotiate their particular cultural knowledges and lacunae to learn from the rich archive of Indian cinematic Shakespeares on offer.

However, before going any further, it is crucial to acknowledge that not all Indian Shakespeare cinema travels. In Mark Thornton Burnett's words, 'whenever we are considering "Global Shakespeare" we are dealing with an inevitably skewed and partial sample. And what this means in turn is that generalizations become difficult and complex: we always have to be careful and contextual.'[6] Hindi/Urdu Bollywood Shakespeares continue to be the most easily accessible Indian adaptations available to audiences outside of local spaces, and thus the most circulated, talked about, and taught as attested by the choice of films that the contributors discuss in this collection. While Vishal Bhardwaj's Shakespeare trilogy – *Maqbool* (2004), *Omkara* (2006), *Haider* (2014) – has toured well, so many brilliant adaptations mentioned in *Shakespeare and Indian Cinemas: 'Local Habitations'* have not. Yet, it would also be inaccurate to claim that it is only Bollywood Shakespeare that has international visibility because films that I would characterize as Indian Independent Cinema such as Aparna Sen's *36 Chowringhee Lane* (1981) (discussed at length in Robert White's essay in this collection) and Vandana Kataria's *Noblemen* (2019) (which two of our contributors, Tula Goenka and Taarini Mookherjee, engage with) are fairly well-known globally through the film festival circuit and through streaming platforms such as Netflix and Amazon.[7] Sometimes, these might even be more well-known outside India than within it. This is why one of the aims of this collection has been to look at the ways in which the films circulate. For instance, in conversation with Helen de Witt, Anne Sophie Reskou's contribution to the volume discusses how Indian Shakespeare offerings sat within the British Film Institute's [BFI] 2016 programme dedicated to Shakespearean cinema; Goenka, in her interview piece, asks Indian Independent movie directors who have adapted Shakespeare about the reception of their films in India and beyond; and Jyotsna G. Singh talks about how the Indian Shakespeare film travels pedagogically.

KC Then we wanted to examine how these films are received after their travels and the ways in which Indian Shakespeare cinema can prove difficult to interpret in the West due to the narrative codes that may be unfamiliar to non-Indian audiences as demonstrated in Ana Weinberg's essay, or even subtle differences of meaning brought about by subtitles as you have highlighted in your chapter. Although Indian Shakespeares on screen have travelled to the West where they have made a space for themselves in film festivals, syllabi and critical discourse, they resist easy dialogue because their cultural codes, cinematic tropes and non-anglophone languages are not always familiar or at least considered unfamiliar. For instance, Amritesh Singh writes how '[i]rrespective of whether they are met with derision or fascination, Bollywood song-and-dance sequences are consistently characterized within the taxonomies of difference and, frequently, non-diegesis.'

VP So, let us make one thing clear that the agenda of the book is not to domesticate or insist on ways of assimilating these cinematic texts into the new habitat but to study this code-clashing or seeming code-clashing. Our contributors examine how context makes a difference in reception and interpretation and suggest how these encounters can open productive spaces for understanding Indian cinema and culture on the one hand but also Shakespeare on the other. They think through different strategies that might facilitate such an exchange of ideas. To take a few examples, Henderson urges collaborative work across continents, across different scholarly voices, across pedagogy, research and practice. Jyotsna G. Singh puts forward a 'pedagogy of cultural intelligibility' which 'eschews any "pure" identity, while recognizing the hybrid post-colonial world' to make fruitful use of Indian Shakespeare cinema in her American classroom. Amritesh Singh suggests that we concentrate on the contiguous histories of Shakespeare and Bollywood and contextualize the exotic-seeming Bollywood 'song-and-dance sequences as *a part of* than *apart from* a rich tradition of musical renderings of Shakespeare'. Shani Bans 'encourages Shakespearean adaptation studies to move beyond subtitles and commission more accurate and rigorous translations and, thereby, incite further dialogue and bolster the study of Indian film adaptations of Shakespeare in syllabi and critical discourse' whereas my essay argues for 'intercultural subtitles' which insist on exhibiting cultural difference that might incite curiosity in the viewers and make them want to work harder to understand the nuanced Indian and the Shakespearean text that they are watching.

KC Perhaps now we should explain how and why we found the 'familiar strangers' metaphor and framework useful.

VP Yes, it is interesting that we come to this framework from such different angles! To me, the word 'stranger' is important; today, we employ the word 'stranger' to describe someone whom we do not know. However, it is fascinating to me that in Shakespeare's time, the word legally referred to 'foreign-born national residents'.[7] So, strangers were born elsewhere, they were 'foreign' but were also familiar to a degree because they were already living amongst natives and were national residents. However, the usage was not restricted to the legal sphere but was also a religious, cultural, and socio-political category, and in all these realms, it was a slippery term. For example, during Shakespeare's lifetime, James VI's succession to the English throne was legally indefensible because according to the English Jesuit priest, Robert Persons, James VI was born in Scotland and 'excluded by the common lawes of Ingland from succession to the crowne' because the 'said lawes do bar al strangers borne out of the realme, to inherite', but for clergyman Andrew Willet, James's accession was right because he was 'no stranger' being 'a prince of the same language, of the Island, of the English royall blood'.[9] So here, enough familiarity in terms of language and religious affiliations outweighed the geography of birth and Willet was able to claim that James VI was 'no stranger' culturally even though he might be one legally. Similar debates and court cases complicated who could be considered a stranger and who could not even if they were born on foreign soil and the distinction between strangers and natives 'became increasingly troubled over the course of the sixteenth and seventeenth centuries'[10] because, as a result of living together, the natives began to register commonalities with the 'foreign-born' strangers or the strangers mastered the language and mannerisms of the host country, or England itself became more diverse and commodities and words considered 'strange' entered the English lexicon. Moreover, strangers in both worlds – the historical world that Shakespeare lived in and the world of his plays – received a mixed reception from native authorities and local communities. In the collaboratively written play, *The Book of Sir Thomas More*, censored during Shakespeare's lifetime, John Licoln, a carpenter remarks how 'it is hard when Englishmen's patience must be thus jetted on by strangers, and they not dare to revenge their own wrongs' (1.1.18-19) and Doll Williamson, a carpenter's wife, threatens that 'if men's milky hearts dare not strike a stranger', a woman will 'beat them down' (1.1.39-40). However, in the same play, in a speech that is attributed to Shakespeare, Thomas More urges the violent crowd to be humane to the strangers lest the tables turn one day and 'you must needs be strangers' (2.4.130) in another country.[11] In *Hamlet*, a short exchange sheds a different light on the stranger's case. In this play, Horatio remarks on the events of the fatal night on which the ghost of Hamlet's father orders Hamlet to execute his revenge by saying 'O day and night, but this is wondrous strange!' (1.5.163) and Hamlet urges him that 'therefore as a stranger give it welcome' (1.5.164) indicating that no matter how 'wild and whirling' (1.5.132) the encounters might be, strangers are to be welcomed – not only tolerated but welcomed – as they expand the frontiers of one's limited 'philosophy' (1.5.166).[12] In *Love's Labour's Lost* the 'stranger' (4.2.136) queen is admired and courted (even though she is not admitted into the King of Navarre's court) while the other stranger, a traveller from Spain, Don Adriano de Armado, is pronounced to be 'too picked, too spruce, too affected, too odd, as it were, too peregrinate' (5.1.12-14). He is found to be peculiar even when he is not only 'a most illustrious wight' (1.1.176) but also someone who knows all the 'fire-new words' (1.1.177) in the native language of Navarre.[13] Given the complicated definitions of strangers and the varied responses to strangers, I would like to suggest that Indian Shakespeare cinema is a stranger (in the Shakespearean sense) to Western audiences. Although born on Indian soil, its connection to Shakespeare also makes it kindred to the West where Shakespeare has immense cultural currency. While it speaks in different languages, it can also seem closer to English vernacular as it re-works Shakespeare. Besides Shakespeare, Indian cinema or at least Bollywood itself, is familiar to the West through film festivals, university courses, and regular screenings. At the same time, however, as you pointed out, Koel, the different or hybridized aesthetic codes of cinema employed by Bollywood particularly and Indian cinema generally continue to garner a disparate reaction from reviewers and audiences alike as many contributors in the collection attest. Thus, Indian Shakespeare cinema in the West is both strange and familiar, inside and outside the culture, to be admired or derided. This complexity of both its status and the response it garners demands critical frameworks and lenses that can sustain complexities and nuances. Thinking of this cinema within the framework provided by the discourse surrounding early modern understanding of a 'stranger' can thus be immensely useful.

KC Fascinating! However, I am using the 'familiar strangers' framework in the context of film adaptation inspired by two distinct theoretical approaches to adaptation by Linda Hutcheon and by Hans-Georg Gadamer. Hutcheon defines adaptation as 'repetition with variation' – a practice and experience where the comfort of ritual is combined with surprise, and the challenge of change is familiarized by acts of recollection and recognition.[14] However, as she emphasizes, the adapter's decoding and recoding of materials occurs in culturally specific contexts: 'Stories . . . do not consist only of the material means of their transmission (media) or the rules that structure them (genre). Those means and those rules permit and then channel narrative expectations and communicate narrative meaning *to someone* in *some context* and they are created *by someone* with that intent.'[15] So, according to her, '[t]here is a kind of dialogue between the society in which the works, both the adapted text and the adaptation, are produced and that in which they are received, and both are in dialogue with the works themselves'.[16] From my perspective, previous collections on Global and Indian Shakespeares have mapped and identified diverse Indian contexts and intents of the Indian Shakespeare adaptations and have concentrated on the relationship and long history between India and Shakespeare.

But the localized contexts and narrative traditions can prove challenging to an audience unfamiliar with Indian cultural contexts and film traditions. To directly address one of the anxieties that non-Indian scholars have of reading Indian Shakespeares, though, I would invoke Christina Della Coletta who proposes that 'understanding a different horizon does not involve crossing over into alien worlds unconnected in any way with our own but, rather, achieving that fusion of horizons that allows us to see the world from larger perspectives. A knowing audience enters the adaptive process with a varied set of experiences, memories, competencies, biases, emotional as well as conceptual presuppositions, namely with a "horizon of expectations".'[17] By entering into play with the adapting work, all these expectations undergo transformative changes while interpreting, and accordingly modifying both the adapting and adapted work. So, the horizon evolves and challenges fixed notions of priority, originality, univocity and stability of meaning.

Subsequently, as this collection seeks to understand what happens when we move away from the point of production and turn our lens to the point of reception and how Indian Shakespeare film affects and contributes to the broader landscape of Global Shakespeares in the West, I turn to the second theoretical approach to adaptation that was my inspiration for the 'Familiar Strangers' framework. Gadamer argues that the process of understanding is set in motion by the interaction between strangeness and familiarity, or put in another way, the complex dynamics that simultaneously make the familiar strange and the unfamiliar known produces understanding.[18] All dialogic encounters simultaneously inspire and challenge understanding: 'When one enters into dialogue with another person and then is carried along further by the dialogue, it is no longer the will of the individual person ... that is determinative, rather the law of the subject matter is at issue in the dialogue and elicits statements and counter statements and in the end plays them into each other.'[19] Thus, an encounter with an Indian Shakespeare film can test our preconceptions and prejudices and neutralize our stock responses and habitual interpretations, by inspiring a heightened non-jaded perspective – the complex dynamics, ultimately, which simultaneously make the familiar strange and the unfamiliar known which leads to understanding. Our contributors have taken myriad approaches to examine the code-clashing you have described and have used their positionalities to find the familiar within the strange and vice versa in their encounters with the Indian Shakespeare film. This is why we have divided the chapters and interviews in this book into two parts – 'Dismantling the Familiar' and 'Recontextualizing the Stranger' – to allow contributors to decide what is strange or indeed, what is familiar. As can be discerned by reading the chapter descriptions below, Part One concentrates on analysing and celebrating the strange within what might feel familiar while Part Two offers familiar frames through which what seems strange can be understood.

VP Exactly, and together these two parts establish that both these critical impulses are needed to analyse Indian Cinematic Shakespeares in Western contexts. So, now that we have established what we are doing, let us backtrack a bit and revisit how and why this collection germinated. I think that for the both of us, there is a broader desire to give sustained attention to the ramifications of border-crossing – an inclination that is both personal and therefore political. In weaving personal and political with the theoretical, I gain encouragement from feminists of colour who have long stressed how practical lived experiences can contribute to critical consciousness and draw us to certain subjects.[20] Pearl Cleage writes how 'racial analysis was presented to [her] as an integral part of [her] daily life, not a special ceremony during Black History Month' and Kim Hall notes that 'despite the bias against it in the academy, this type of everyday analysis of the workings of race has shaped [her] as a professional reader of literary texts as well'.[21] Similarly, living as a British-Asian (or my preferred term, Brasian) means being acutely attuned to the difficulty and joys of geographical, cultural, conceptual border crossings, and practical interculturalism becomes a life skill. Amongst other habits of mind, practical interculturalism includes the ability both to register contact points and common grounds between cultures and to accept (and cherish) difference and strangeness and the tendency to both unsettle the hegemonic/familiar way of looking at things in each culture as well as to allow the strange or unfamiliar to take root in new contexts. Hence, it is natural that we would be drawn to the study of texts not only in their originary contexts but also as they travel between cultures and it is pertinent that we would think about acknowledging commonalities and differences. However, as I was saying before, while there was already a growing body of work on Shakespeare travelling to India as cultural flows are usually charted from 'the "west" to the "rest"', work on journeys in the opposite direction is sparse.[22] So, how Indian Shakespeare films are changing or might revitalize the way in which Shakespeare is understood in the West remains under-theorized and under-explored.

This is why I was invested in mapping and studying this direction of travel during the 'Indian Shakespeares on Screen' – the international conference and film festival which we (along with Thea Buckley and Preti Taneja) convened in the UK amidst the 2016 Shakespeare celebrations during which we screened Vishal Bhardwaj's Bollywood Shakespeare trilogy followed by public conversations at the BFI Southbank. In the lead up to these events, I remember us becoming increasingly concerned with a number of practical, theoretical, and political questions regarding consuming Indian Shakespeare films globally: how much cultural acumen is required to profitably enjoy and appreciate these productions? How can we enhance the audience experience – would they welcome help from us while decoding some of the differences or would they rather enjoy seeing something unfamiliar and try to unlock it themselves? How much are the cultures already hybridized and therefore are people living in Britain familiar with the conventions and tropes of Indian films due to their own diasporic identities or consumption of Bollywood cinema?

How can we ensure that requisite information is available to people reviewing and critiquing these movies without patronizing them? Who has the right to interpret and analyse these films? Does Shakespeare act as a bridge or a stumbling block in intercultural encounters? Are people watching these films for insights into Shakespeare or for understanding Indian culture or both? At the conference and events, it was interesting to note that scholars, practitioners, and audiences were also considering some of the same questions in relation to practice, research, and pedagogy of these films. While both globalization and much foundational work had brought Indian Shakespeare cinema in all its variety to the attention of readers and practitioners, the questions about encounters had not yet been considered. This is when we decided that the book was needed.

KC Yes, for me too this book *is* the next step from all the logistical and curatorial issues we encountered while organizing the 2016 event. During the course of the 2016 conference, and subsequent events and essay collections which focused on Indian Shakespeares, such as *Shakespeare and Indian Cinemas: 'Local Habitations'*, the question of authority has begun to gain traction when discussing Indian Shakespeare films. Contributors in this book too have suggested that, as non-Indian scholars, they may not have the agency to explain or discuss Indian Shakespeares or include it in Western curriculum. However, exposure to Indian Shakespeare productions and discussions of Indian Shakespeares with its long history which has only recently been accepted into the realm of Global Shakespeares, can help us recognize and transcend what Alexa Huang describes as 'compulsory realpolitik' which is the conviction that the best way to understand non-Western works is by interpreting their engagement with practical politics.[23] This way of thinking has the disadvantage of implying that works from the global south or Asia are valuable only for their political messages rather than their aesthetic merits. Anglophone Shakespeares are assumed to have broad theoretical applicability and aesthetic merits whereas 'foreign' Shakespeares, even when they focus on artistic innovation on a personal rather than epic scale, are compelled to prove their political worth. Western (and westernized) critics single out adaptations for potentially subversive political messages in these works which are compulsorily characterized as allegories of geopolitical issues. This may be why *Haider* appears in so many Western Shakespeare courses for instance, or why the aesthetics of *Arshinagar* (2015) are ignored in favour of a discussion on how the director approaches Islamophobia in India. As a result, works by non-white authors are imagined to fix their intellectual content by way of a national ethnic or cultural location; Western white examples assume to be more effective in their exclamatory power while African, Asian and Latin American materials are recruited to serve as the exceptional particular. However, as this collection demonstrates, discussions on the ways in which Western students encounter Indian Shakespeares, or even which films they have access to, or the politics of subtitles, or how Indian women directors and actors approach Shakespeare, can promote self-reflexivity on social and personal levels which in turn promotes the awareness of, as Huang terms it, 'the theatricalization of difference'.

VP Precisely, one of the contributions of this edited collection, according to me at least, is that it expands the range of topics and methodologies that Global Shakespeares could and should consider. For instance, despite the fact that Shakespeares from around the world have made inroads into syllabi, the field has been slow to take stock of the pedagogy of worldwide Shakespeares. Recent work such as Eleine Ng-Gagneux's 'Reading Interculturality in Class: Contextualising and studying Global Shakespeares in and through A|S|I|A' takes a step in this direction and Jyotsna G. Singh's essay in this collection can be read as a companion piece to this.[24] I hope that this will inspire further forays into pedagogy of Global Shakespeares generally and Indian Shakespeares specifically. I am also inspired by Burnett's chapter in this volume which demonstrates how Indian cinematic Shakespeares can 'reverberate' and 'broker a partnership with' other global adaptations 'from Africa, Brazil, Canada, Denmark, Egypt and Greece'. He exemplifies how we can write rich global production histories that students and researchers of Shakespeare can draw from. This methodology rebels against the tendency of seeing non-anglophone Shakespeares as hermeneutically sealed off from anglophone Shakespeares originating in the UK/US. My own chapter on subtitles can be placed in productive dialogue with Robert Shaugnessey's study of subtitles in European stage adaptations of Shakespeare in order to focus on the language of global Shakespeares and the ways in which mediation can affect meaning.[25] Weinberg's contribution and Mookherjee's study of Kataria's film demonstrate the rich dividends gained from paying close attention to gender in the study of global Shakespeares and point towards other intersectionalities such as class and disability that the field must put greater pressure on as it researches global productions. Only by acknowledging how Shakespeare films from India are informing our thinking on every aspect of Shakespeare Studies such as Feminist Shakespeares, translation in Shakespeare, or the study of music in Shakespeare can the full potential of Global Shakespeare as a field be realized.

Chapter descriptions

Dismantling the Familiar

Re-generation: Remapping the Screenscape in Fractious Times

Diana E. Henderson
This chapter discusses the 'Indian Shakespeares on Screen' (2016) conference and film festival and its combination of professional practice and cultural context, close reading and performance awareness, and the leadership of the conference itself. It examines the new attention that Indian Shakespeare films have received in

the West and argues that part of the reason for this new, belated attention on Indian Shakespeare films lies in the increased mobility of people and media across the globe, both in evidence at the conference. The essay revisits the genealogy of and contrast between Poonam Trivedi's and the author's interpretations of the woman's part in *Omkara* as an exemplary location for moving Indian screen Shakespeares forward as a diverse community as well as a media subgenre and proposes that cross-generational international exchange and revitalized feminism are fundamental to such progress. The author recontextualizes biographical identities within cosmopolitan Shakespeare studies as multi-layered signifiers both visible and invisible and argues that through more explicit acknowledgement of the plurality of these layers within our scholarly analyses, we can better combine the virtues of analytic debate with those of artistic expression and more authentic civility.

Two Indian Film Offshoots of *Twelfth Night*

Robert White

Through an examination of two very different Indian film adaptations of *Twelfth Night*, this chapter underscores the critical benefits of putting cinematic adaptations from diverse geographies into conversation with each other and departs from the tradition of reading regionally-specific adaptations in isolation. There is substantial quotation and allusiveness to *Twelfth Night* in *36 Chowringhee Lane* whereas *Dil Bole Hadippa!* (2009) is based on and mediated through the American movie, *She's the Man* (2006), which is itself adapted more directly from *Twelfth Night* and targets an American college audience. Taken together, the different modes of adaptation in these movies 'raise methodological questions' about the intertextual nature of Shakespeare films and manifest the overlapping regional, linguistic, national and international concerns of each of these adaptations. They insist that we ask 'fresh questions' and come up with 'different paradigms of interpretation' to read these cinematic offerings.

'For never was a story of more woe': Dialogic Telling and Global Interchange in *Qayamat se Qayamat Tak*, a 'Bollywood' Film Adaptation of *Romeo and Juliet*

Mark Thornton Burnett
Ostensibly, *Qayamat se Qayamat Tak* (1988), a film adaptation of *Romeo and Juliet*, is an archetypal 'Bollywood' product. It displays typical features of the genre, including an epic structure, the ways in which narrative information is transmitted, the interlacing of several stories, distinctive characterization and intertextuality. In this chapter, however, Burnett concentrates not so much on the 'Indianness' of the film as with its points of global contact with other *Romeo and Juliet* film narratives. Drawing on contemporary theories about the haptic or mobile properties of cinema – namely, James Clifford's notion of art as travel, Dimitris Eleftheriotis' concept of movements of exploration enacted in cinema, and Giuliana Bruno's study of cinema as an inherently spatio-visual medium – he suggests that the film's mediation of Shakespearean language, the purposeful utilization of song and the representation of authority figures anticipate a distinctive grouping of contemporary adaptations of the play (most obviously, *Hobak Nair* (2004), *Amar Te Duele* (2002), *Maré, Nossa Historia de Amor* (2008) and *A Time to Love* (2005), from Egypt, Mexico, Brazil and China respectively). In terms of its modes of telling, *Qayamat se Qayamat Tak* repurposes issues of family fealty and honour for critical effect, responds to textual lacunae via narrative amplification, makes an interrogative intervention in generational debate, and references a mélange of cultural associations to reanimate Shakespeare's play for a popular audience; in so doing, it enters a dialogue with a host of related – world – *Romeo and Juliet* films in which a generation-specific deployment of Shakespeare serves particular cultural and ideological ends. 'Bollywood' is thus held up for scrutiny as an interpretive category, the emphasis falling instead on the ways in which the film enters a partnership with concerns and questions beyond its own ideological borders.

'Indian' Independent Cinema and Shakespeare

Sharat Katariya and *Vandana Kataria* in conversation with *Tula Goenka*

In this interview piece, the author of *Not Just Bollywood: Indian Directors Speak*, Tula Goenka talks to Indian independent filmmakers who have adapted Shakespeare's plays. Sharat Katariya's *10ml Love* (2010) is a reworking of *A Midsummer Night's Dream*, and Vandana Kataria's *Noblemen* is a take on *The Merchant of Venice*. The conversation reveals how hybrid these cinematic productions are as the directors are 'informed by the work of Indian masters such as Manmohan Desai, Shyam Bengal and Ritwik Ghatak' as well as 'well versed in world cinema, and inspired by techniques and aesthetics from Billy Wilder, Ernst Lubitsch, Kimberly Pierce, Stanley Kubrick, Alfred Hitchcock, Alfonso Cuaron and others'. They also use myriad modes of local and global performance styles in their films and their audiences, although not huge in number, are spread across the globe. The conversation problematizes the notion of 'Indian' Shakespeare film and demonstrates how it would be limiting to read these within strict geopolitical frames of reference.

Vandana Kataria's *Noblemen*: Global Frames of Interpretation

Taarini Mookherjee

Mookherjee's contribution can be read as a companion to Goenka's conversation piece as it zooms in on Vandana Kataria's *Noblemen* and shows how a film such as this can be productively analysed in multiple ways. Mookerjee situates the movie in diverse contexts ranging from the Indian indie milieu to the 'the play-within-the-film genre' (popular in both Bollywood and Hollywood Shakespeare films) to pedagogical Shakespeare cinema and to the role of women in Indian Shakespeare film directing. In providing these varied contexts she proves how Indian Shakespeare cinema need not be limited

Chutzpah: The Politics of Bollywood Shakespeare Subtitles

Varsha Panjwani

In this chapter, Panjwani focuses on English subtitles of Bollywood Shakespeare films as these are often overlooked in discussions of Shakespeare translation. Picking up on the tendency of subtitlers to provide what she refers to as 'assimilative' subtitles which prioritize the target culture, she argues instead for 'intercultural' subtitles which are more faithful to the local colouring or the originating cultural and linguistic milieu of the film. Analysing the subtitles of *Haider*, *Maqbool* and *Goliyon ki Rasleela: Ram-Leela* (2013), she teases out the political stakes of the decisions made by subtitlers when they concentrate on accommodating the English-speaking audiences to such an extent that it undoes the goal of Global Shakespeares to decenter anglophone Shakespeare and learn from world-wide Shakespeare adaptations. Her solution is to campaign for subtitles that maintain their distance from the anglophone audiences in order to make them work towards understanding Shakespeare afresh by hearing/seeing Shakespeare as refracted through Indian languages.

Recontextualizing the Stranger

Curating Indian Shakespeares at the BFI in 2016

Helen de Witt in conversation with *Anne Sophie Refskou*

When audiences in Britain think of Shakespeare cinema, the films that probably come most readily to mind for film lovers who frequently attend the BFI Southbank are Laurence Olivier's *Henry V* (1944), Peter Brooks' *King Lear* (1970) or perhaps Baz Luhrmann's *Romeo + Juliet* (1996). If asked about Indian

Shakespeare, perhaps only Merchant Ivory's *Shakespeare Wallah* (1965) might suggest itself. The Shakespeare 400 celebration in 2016 gave the British Film Institute (BFI) not only the opportunity to celebrate the Bard's influence on the cinema of his own land, but to demonstrate his global influence on the history of film. Specifically, India became a key focus for the BFI Southbank, the programme with Vishal Bhardwaj's trilogy (*Maqbool, Omkara, Haider*) screened in collaboration with the Indian Shakespeares on Screen team, twinned with a major conference on the subject at Asia House. With the director and several of his collaborators in attendance, the weekend of screenings accorded UK audiences the opportunity to experience Shakespeare's epic tragedies through different eyes. They found that the message and meanings of the plays were no less relevant for that. In many cases, as evidenced by audience feedback, they thought the meanings became more urgent. This conversation discusses the curation, delivery and impact of Indian Shakespeare on Screen at the BFI which led to policy and culture changes in programme delivery of the BFI as a whole.

'Travelling' with Shakespeare through Bhardwaj's *Haider*: From US Classrooms to the Global Shakespeare Movement

Jyotsna G. Singh

While the benefits of including Shakespeare adaptations from non-Western locations in the syllabus have been widely recognized by Global Shakespeare scholars such as Orkin, Huang, and Dionne, putting that into practice in the US classroom poses unique challenges. Singh's contribution takes us to her American classroom to think through productive pedagogical approaches for teaching global Shakespeare productions. Taking *Haider* as an example, she explores ways in which students can be trained to read global cultural difference through these films. She calls this approach a *'pedagogy of cultural intelligibility'* – which requires the students to read the

Shakespearean language and plot by refracting it through the tragic historical conflicts faced by Bhardwaj's protagonist in 1990s Kashmir. Thus, it unveils a complex two-way transaction showing us how Shakespeare goes 'native' as well as how the tragic, poetic language and representations in *Haider* give us a distinct emotional language to understand the disintegration of the characters caught up under the surveillance state of Denmark in *Hamlet*.

Understanding Nimmi: Tracing Interpretations of Vishal Bhardwaj's *Maqbool*

Ana Laura Magis Weinberg
This reflective chapter uses the writer's positionality as a scholar from a marginalized Western country, Mexico, to discuss her relationship with Vishal Bhardwaj's adaptation of Lady Macbeth in *Maqbool* over the length of a decade. In reading *Maqbool* as a tragedy of love, the writer examines the changed role of Shakespeare's women in Bhardwaj's films to 'rebalance Shakespeare' and scrutinizes her experiences in attempting to avoid misreadings and misinterpretations which may have arisen out of her own intersectionalities as a *videshi* [foreigner] in India.

'Nainā ṭhag: lemge': Visual Uncertainty in *Othello* and Vishal Bhardwaj's *Omkara*

Shani Bans
This contribution takes issue with Western critical assessments which see Shakespeare's language as becoming diluted in translation. Focusing on lyricist Gulzar's translation, interpretation and appropriation of Shakespeare's poetics in the song '*Nainā ṭhag lemge*' from Vishal Bhardwaj's *Omkara*, this chapter argues that it is only the English subtitles which lose much of the poetry and rhetoric that brings *Omkara* closer to Shakespeare's language in *Othello*. Through a translation and critical analysis of the song, the chapter demonstrates that

Gulzar's reading of vision in *Othello* emphasizes the unreliability of sight. By teasing out the imagery of visual uncertainty in Gulzar's poetics which foreshadow later motifs in the film and comparing them against the language of *Othello*, this chapter offers a close reading of *Omkara*'s language, especially Gulzar's lyrics to 'Nainā', alongside Shakespeare's language of visual uncertainty in *Othello*. It argues that more attention needs to be paid to the language of Shakespearean film adaption in order to facilitate cross-cultural engagement. By translating the language of *Omkara*, this chapter aims to eliminate the language barrier and, in doing so, not only offers a case study in how translating the language of Omkara can open up the film to further interpretation (for example, specific thematic issues such as visual uncertainty) but also demonstrates what is at stake if we ignore the word choices of such adaptations. More broadly, this chapter encourages Shakespearean adaptation studies to move beyond subtitles and commission more accurate and rigorous translations and, thereby, encourage further dialogue and bolster the study of Indian film adaptations of Shakespeare in syllabi and critical discourse.

A Pair of Homotextual Lovers: Bhansali's *Ram-Leela* and Shakespeare's *Romeo and Juliet*

Amritesh Singh

Singh's subject of study is the song-and-dance routines in Bollywood Shakespeare which, he contests, are met with both 'derision or fascination' in the West and either 'compel the critic to offer an apology or demand accommodation'. In either case, he argues that these are characterized as something 'strange' to Western sensibilities and Shakespeare. Rebelling against this approach, his chapter uses queer theory and the concept of 'homohistory' (as nurtured by Goldberg and Menon) to argue that these are not as far removed as critics would have us believe. Offering a close reading of the song-and-dance sequences in Sanjay Leela Bhansali's *Ram-Leela* along with Shakespeare's *Romeo and Juliet*, this chapter makes us see familiarity and sameness instead of strangeness and difference. In doing so, it asserts that we attune ourselves to the musicality of Bollywood Shakespeare and 'recognize Bollywood as a part of rather than apart from a long tradition of musical renderings of Shakespeare'.

'All the world's a stage': The Participatory Indian Cinema Audience and its Impact on Indian Shakespeare Films

Koel Chatterjee

The preoccupation with the Indian Shakespeare film and its sources and assimilation techniques within indigenous narrative practices has meant that current studies of film reception are hypothesized narrowly as how film audiences interpret or respond to Indianized Shakespeare films. Such understandings of reception, which neglect the group character of the audience and the social and interactive audience capable of collective action, are at odds with how audiences in India experience film. This chapter examines the spectatorshi culture in India which instead of conforming to the Western conventional view of the filmmaker as the 'giver' and the audience as the 'receiver', rather looks at how a shift in perspective to the filmmaker as 'receiver', and the consumer of films as the 'giver of audience' impacts our understanding of the collaborative work that goes into the making of the Indian Shakespeare film. Thus, instead of asking how Shakespeare films affect audiences, this chapter investigates how audiences shape Indian films – particularly Indian Shakespeare films.

Notes

1   Poonam Trivedi, and Dennis Bartholomeusz, eds., *India's Shakespeare: Translation, interpretation, and performance* (New York: University of Delaware Press, 2005).

2 Sonia Massai, ed., *World-wide Shakespeares: Local Appropriations in Film and Performance* (New York: Routledge, 2005).

3 Craig Dionne, and Parmita Kapadia, eds., *Bollywood Shakespeares* (New York: Palgrave Macmillan, 2014).

4 Poonam Trivedi, and Paromita Chakravarti, eds., *Shakespeare and Indian Cinemas: 'Local Habitations'* (New York and London: Routledge, 2019).

5 Sandra Young, *Shakespeare in the Global South: Stories of Oceans Crossed in Contemporary Adaptation* (London: Bloomsbury, 2019), 135.

6 Mark Thornton Burnett in conversation with Anne Sophie Refskou, 'Past and Present Trajectories for "Global Shakespeare"', in *Eating Shakespeare: Cultural Anthropophagy as Global Methodology*, ed. Anne Sophie Refskou, Marcel Alvaro de Amorim and Vinicius Mariano De Carvalho (London: Bloomsbury, 2019), 156.

7 For more on how I am defining Indian Independent Cinema, see Varsha Panjwani, 'Shakespeare and Indian Independent Cinema: *8×10 Tasveer* and *10ml Love*', in *Shakespeare and Indian Cinemas: 'Local Habitations'*, ed. Poonam Trivedi and Paromita Chakravarti (London: Routledge, 2019), 180–99.

8 Nandini Das, João Vicente Melo, Haig Smith and Lauren Working, *Keywords of Identity, Race, and Human Mobility in Early Modern England* (Amsterdam: Amsterdam University Press, 2021), 20.

9 Quoted in Nandini Das et al., *Keywords of Identity, Race, and Human Mobility in Early Modern England*, 24.

10 Nandini Das et al., *Keywords of Identity, Race, and Human Mobility in Early Modern England*, 20.

11 All in-text citations of *The Book of Sir Thomas More* are from Anthony Munday, Henry Chettle, Thomas Dekker, Thomas Heywood and William Shakespeare, *The Book of Sir Thomas More*, ed. Jonathan Bate and Eric Rasmussen with Jan Sewell and Will Sharpe (London: Palgrave, 2013).

12 All in-text citations of *Hamlet* are from William Shakespeare, *Hamlet*, ed. Ann Thompson and Neil Taylor (London: Bloomsbury, 2006).

13 All in-text citations of *Love's Labour's Lost* are from William Shakespeare, *Love's Labour's Lost*, ed. G. R. Hibbard (Oxford: Oxford University Press, 1990).

14 Linda Hutcheon, *A Theory of Adaptation*, (London: Routledge 2006), 4.

15 Ibid., p. 26.

16 Ibid., p. 149.

17 Cristina Della Coletta, *When Stories Travel: Cross-cultural Encounters between Fiction and Film* (Maryland: JHU Press, 2012), 14.

18 Hans-Georg Gadamer, *Philosophical Hermeneutics*. (California: University of California Press, 2008), 5.

19 Ibid., p. 66.

20 I am inspired by Sara Ahmed's assertion that 'the personal is theoretical'. Sara Ahmed, *Living a Feminist Life* (Croydon: Duke University Press, 2016), 10.

21 Pearl Cleage, *Deals with the Devil and Other Reasons to Riot* (New York: Ballantine Books, 1993), 30; Kim Hall, *Things of Darkness: Economies of Race and Gender in Early Modern England* (London: Cornell University Press, 1995), 257.

22 Inderpal Grewal and Caren Kaplan, 'Introduction: Transnational Feminist Practices and Questions of Postmodernity', in *Scattered Hegemonies: Postmodernity and Transnational Feminist Practices*, ed. Inderpal Grewal and Caren Kaplan (Minneapolis: University of Minnesota Press, 1994), 12.

23 As part of a lecture titled '*Asian Embodiment of a White Canon* organized by the Center for Global Asia: https://cga.shanghai.nyu.edu/asian-embodiment-of-a-white-canon-shakespeare-and-east-asia/

24 Eleine Ng-Gagneux, 'Reading Interculturality in Class: Contexualising Global Shakespeares in and through A|S|I|A', in *Shakespeare and Digital Pedagogy: Case Studies and Strategies*, ed. Diana E. Henderson and Kyle Sebastian Vitale (London: Bloomsbury, 2022).

25 See Robert Shaughnessy, *About Shakespeare: Bodies, Spaces and Texts* (Cambridge: Cambridge University Press, 2000), especially 35–60.

References

Ahmed, Sara. *Living a Feminist Life*. Croydon: Duke University Press, 2016.

Bate, Jonathan, and Eric Rasmussen with Jan Sewell and Will Sharpe, eds. *The Book of Sir Thomas More*, London: Palgrave, 2013.

Burnett, Mark. 'Past and Present Trajectories for "Global Shakespeare"'. In *Eating Shakespeare: Cultural Anthropophagy as Global Methodology*. London: Bloomsbury, 2019, 155–71.

Cleage, Pearl. *Deals With the Devil: And Other Reasons to Riot*. New York: Ballantine Books, 1993.

Das, Nandini, João Vicente Melo, Haig Smith and Lauren Working. *Keywords of Identity, Race, and Human Mobility in Early Modern England*. Amsterdam: Amsterdam University Press, 2021.

Della Coletta, Cristina. *When Stories Travel: Cross-cultural Encounters between Fiction and Film*. Maryland: JHU Press, 2012.

Dionne, Craig, and Parmita Kapadia, eds. *Bollywood Shakespeares*. New York: Palgrave Macmillan, 2014.

Gadamer, Hans-Georg. *Philosophical Hermeneutics*. California: University of California Press, 2008.

Grewal, Inderpal, and Caren Kaplan, eds. *Scattered Hegemonies: Postmodernity and Transnational Feminist Practices* Minneapolis: University of Minnesota Press, 1994.

Hall, Kim F. *Things of Darkness: Economies of race and Gender in Early Modern England*. London: Cornell University Press, 1995.

Hutcheon, Linda. *A Theory of Adaptation*. London: Routledge, 2006.

Massai, Sonia, ed. *World-wide Shakespeares: Local Appropriations in Film and Performance*. New York: Routledge, 2007.

Ng-Gagneux, Eleine. 'Reading Interculturality in Class: Contextualising Global Shakespeares in and through A|S|I|A.' In *Shakespeare and Digital Pedagogy: Case Studies and Strategies*, ed. Diana E. Henderson and Kyle Sebastian Vitale. London: Bloomsbury, 89–104.

Panjwani, Varsha. 'Shakespeare and Indian Independent Cinema: *8×10 Tasveer* and *10ml Love*.' in Trivedi and Chakravarti, eds., *Shakespeare and Indian Cinemas*. London: Routledge, 2019, 180–99.

Shakespeare, William. *Love's Labour's Lost*, ed. G. R. Hibbard. Oxford: Oxford University Press, 1990.

Shakespeare, William. *Hamlet*, ed. Ann Thompson and Neil Taylor. London: Bloomsbury, 2006.Shaughnessy, Robert. *About Shakespeare: Bodies, Spaces and Texts*. Cambridge: Cambridge University Press, 2020.

Trivedi, Poonam, and Dennis Bartholomeusz, eds. *India's Shakespeare: translation, Interpretation, and Performance*. Delaware: University of Delaware Press, 2005.

Trivedi, Poonam, and Paromita Chakravarti, eds. *Shakespeare and Indian Cinemas: 'Local Habitations'*. New York and London: Routledge, 2019.

Young, Sandra. *Shakespeare in the Global South: Stories of Oceans Crossed in Contemporary Adaptation*. London: Bloomsbury, 2019.

PART ONE

Dismantling the Familiar

1

Re-generation: Remapping the Screenscape in Fractious Times

Diana E. Henderson

When the editors asked me to contribute a personal reflection from the perspective of a later-career Shakespeare scholar who has spoken and written about particular Indian and Indian diaspora films, my response combined delight and trepidation: delight at the prospect of conveying what I saw as a new generation's enactment of long overdue attitudes and models, as embodied by the editors' own accomplishments; trepidation because I am not and can never be an expert specialist in Indian screen Shakespeares, as a number of others in this volume are. Moreover, multiple forms of societal privilege make my perspective even more suspect. Both those feelings amplified exponentially when 2020 brought the double-whammy of pandemic and yet more egregious cases of race-based social injustice, the violence and suffering from which persist as I write. Amidst the relational stresses and the distractedness that has come to be known as 'COVID brain'; the criminal negligence and state-sponsored censorship that is currently killing untold Indian and Kashmiri citizens during a government-abetted 'second wave' of coronavirus, compounding the outrage of ongoing territorial blackouts; and the chronic obviousness that Black Lives do not Matter to a sizeable proportion of the human population, I cannot take sprightly Boccaccio as a plague-surviving model, but instead turn to Montaigne. Essaying through somewhat humbler reflections in spacetime to gesture towards alternative futures, I not only celebrate the glimmers of hope as originally intended, but locate them amid a longer history and with some reference to the desperation that surrounds and precarity that threatens the institutional survival of our common interests. Tempered with skepticism, wishing but not presuming a sympathetic reader, perhaps these words will nonetheless furnish some instances of resemblance and productive change – yes, even in academia – that might suggest a path to reimagined community.

But the pathway has changed. Rather than begin with the professional punchline originally planned, I start at my national level, recalling an era when most of this readership had not yet been born, before proceeding as if time were primarily a calendrical vector. The first two years I highlight are 1957, when the United States enacted its first law opposing racial discrimination since the Reconstruction period in the aftermath of its Civil War and the abolition of race-based slavery, and 1965, when the 'Fabulous 89th Congress', having already passed the crucial Civil Rights Act of 1964, turned to the Immigration and Nationality Act of 1965 (first introduced as H. R. 2580, also known by the names of its sponsors as the Hart-Celler Act). This latter became law on 3 October – and with it came an unintended revolution in the place of many non-Europeans, including south Asians, in America.

Signed by President Lyndon B. Johnson at the foot of the Statue of Liberty, the Hart-Celler Act undid a system based on quotas tied with ethnicity, race and national origin that explicitly discriminated against non-Europeans – and indeed, any but those from a handful of northwestern European nations who at that time (though in the case of the Irish not always) were perceived as 'white'. This system, developed in the wake of the First World War and the influenza pandemic as well as resurgent white nationalism, was institutionalized for decades in the notorious 1924 Immigration Act. President Truman had attempted to overturn its 'isolationist limitations' in 1952 before leaving office, noting its 'absurdity' and 'cruelty' and adding – in what now echoes with ill-advised competition between injustices – 'In no other realm of our national life are we so hampered and stultified by the dead hand of the past, as we are in this field of immigration.'[1] But not until the precedent set by the 1964 Civil Rights Act did Congress finally make a change. Hart-Celler amended the 1924 statute to read that as of 30 June 1968, 'No person shall receive any preference of priority or be discriminated against in the issuance of an immigrant visa because of his race, sex, nationality, place of birth, or place of residence' – before proceeding to add substantial conditions and an overall cap of 290,000 visas annually.[2] It substituted rank-ordered categories of eligibility including 'immediate relatives' of US citizens, professional expertise and labour needs, as well as for the first time acknowledging refugee status beyond temporary asylum provisions.

Clearly Congress did not understand Asian families. Believing the law would not have an appreciable impact on the overall population, with some members more focused on their eastern European constituents and Cold War optics, neither the legislature nor the administration regarded the 1965 law as 'revolutionary'. But those 'immediate relatives' were not included in the East/West Hemisphere-based caps, and 'policymakers had vastly underestimated the number of immigrants who would take advantage of the family reunification clause'.[3] Of India in particular, Secretary of State Dean Rusk had estimated 'that there might be, say, 8,000 immigrants from India in the next five years ... I don't think we have a particular picture of a world situation where everybody is just straining to move to the United States'; in fact, more than three times his estimated number arrived, and by 1993 immigration from India totalled 558,980.[4]

I earlier mentioned 1957, the year of the first Civil Rights Act since 1875; it had been subjected (by segregationist Strom Thurmond) to the longest filibuster in history, and was considerably weakened in order to get through Congress at all, but it did pave the way for those more substantial laws to come. 1957 was also the year I was born, in Washington, D.C. By that second focal date of 1965, my father was working as a non-partisan staffer – the US once had them – for the Senate Foreign Relations Committee under its longest serving chairman, William J. Fulbright (he of the international fellowship programmes). But by the time of President Johnson's photo op signing the Immigration Bill, I was going to school in London, where my father was studying the possibility of Britain entering the Common Market; we had sailed out past the Statue of Liberty about the time Johnson signed the equally momentous Voting Rights Act of 1965, enforcing the 14th and 15th Amendments to the Constitution by prohibiting anti-Black racial discrimination at the ballot box.

It would be another ten years before the UK held its first-ever national referendum, on the very topic that allowed my childhood experience of England: the Common Market Referendum of 1975, handily ratifying its 1973 entrance into the EEC (European Economic Community) with a two-thirds majority. And it would be even longer before the consequences of the 1965 US immigration reform law would become visible to me and many others of my generation – or, more importantly for the central topic of this volume though aligned with that eventual visibility, would begin to affect the way in which Shakespeare was conceptualized and studied in my country.

Of course, those transformative laws and policies of the 'long 1960s' were not simply the product of top-down efforts in two national capitals, crucial though they were. In the US, a massive amount of grassroot work, involving protest movements and exceptional people taking personal risks, finally spurred their legislators and leaders to act. Chennai-born Shyamala Gopalan was among them, in 1958 at age 19 successfully applying (from the University of Delhi where she earned her Bachelor's degree in Home Science) to a Master's programme in nutrition and endocrinology at the University of California at Berkeley, going on to earn a doctorate in 1964 and subsequently becoming an important breast cancer researcher. Knowing the challenges women faced at that time in pursuing careers – and even more so doctorates in what we now call STEM areas – gives one pause, even before considering the activism and non-academic commitments she took on. While a graduate student Gopalan attended meetings of the Afro American Association, a formative group in creating Black Studies, the Black Panther Party and more, where she met Jamaican economics graduate student Donald Harris. She married him in 1963, giving birth to her doctorate and daughter Kamala (born 20 October) the following year. Immigrants, [they] get the job done, indeed.[5]

As I grew up on the other side of the North American continent, the activism that registered most personally involved the Vietnam War, feminism and Black/white integration. My siblings' college friends descended on DC to march (and be tear-gassed), and my brother's low draft lottery number had us worrying whether he would go to war or have to flee to Canada as others had (knowing each choice had ravaged close friends and families). Later, I would discover how many of the formative feminist scholars in my field had paid the price then: Annette Kolodny 'danced through the minefields' and became a leader in ecofeminist and indigenous studies only after giving up her Yale teaching position to accompany her husband (denied conscientious objector status) across the northern border; as a young nurse in the Pacific, Lynda Boose endured the trauma of filling bodybags far from where her husband was serving. She would much later turn from Shakespeare studies to address the ongoing atrocities she could not ignore in the Balkans and Middle East being abetted by 'technomasculinity' – a term she used to describe modern militarism long before video gamers and their critics popularized it differently. 'The personal is political' rang true during the 1970s far beyond its most overt use within the women's movement, and still does; nonetheless,

Gloria Steinem, Shirley Chisolm, Bella Abzug and Betty Friedan were the first 'characters' my pre-teen friends and I decided to enact for class projects (in my case, counter-balancing a stint as Titania). And finally, like the daughter of Shyamala Gopalan Harris, I was bussed to school, as the city of Alexandria, Virginia finally addressed its segregated history. I spent two years at what had formerly been a predominantly Black high school, before joining all the city's 11th and 12th graders at a single public [in UK terms, state] school; its integrated football team would later become famous when Denzel Washington played coach Herman Boone in *Remember the Titans*. That film, released in 2000 (seven years after Denzel's 'colourblind' casting as Don Pedro in Branagh's *Much Ado About Nothing* and nine years after his *Mississippi Masala* Romeo) heralded a new century's Hollywoodized reimagining of how we had moved on. It would take another two decades, however, before the school's being itself named for a segregationist would spark sufficient controversy for a name change effective July 2021 – and only then because of grassroots efforts once again led by the younger generation, in this instance the Black Student Union and its own President (Lorraine) Johnson.[6]

What has all this to do with Indian screen Shakespeares? First, it helps explain why many US academics of my generation seldom looked to Asia without seeing the damage of multiple wars (upon our parents and friends as well as the televized civilian populations) until we were adults, and also why those limitations of the local were sometimes not even visible. The influence of Gandhi's model of non-violence on Dr King was the revered exception, followed more lightheartedly by the Beatles' Indian sojourn and collaborations with Ravi Shankar (and I do have a cousin who has lived in an ashram ever since). While I knew well the entrenched racism and violence faced by those of us who crossed colour lines in our friendships, and became acutely aware of the class divisions that the dominant 'everyone is middle class' ideology tried so hard to ignore, my education remained primarily a study in Black and White. Similarly, Latinx experience was vastly under-represented in twenty-first-century terms: I knew more through my mother's support for the Cesar Chavez-led grape boycott on behalf of California's migrant workers (again modelled on Gandhian practices) than I did from interactions with my shockingly small number of Hispanic classmates. (Digging through old yearbooks to verify this, I discovered that only in the two years when all the city's students attended that one school in the mid-1970s did the percentage appear to rise even near the US Census figures of 4.5 percent [1970] to 6.4 percent [1980].) Again, as a reminder of the massive impact of crucial legislation spurred by grassroots action: not until 2000 did the Hispanic population officially reach double-digits at 12.5 percent.

Far more important than causing shifts in the perspective of people like me, these changes in immigration and demographics finally allowed those with different local knowledge to start reshaping first the general contours of US literary and cultural studies, then more specifically Shakespeare studies, and at last their intersection with film and media studies. For it was also in 1965 that Gayatri Chakravorty Spivak began her US professorial career, in Iowa. Given the dismissal of 'high theory' by many twenty-first-century scholars, it is worth recalling that both Edward Said and Spivak initially gained stature through their engagement with continental philosophy, through *Beginnings* (1974) and the translation and preface of Derrida's *Of Grammatology* (1976) respectively. Said's *Orientalism* appeared soon after (1978, the year before I arrived at Columbia for grad school and came to learn much from his students), but in the latter's case a decade passed before the appearance of *In Other Worlds* (1987) and 'Can the Subaltern Speak?' (1988).

My lengthy flashback I hope makes visible some of the differences collapsed when discussing the 'Anglo-American' academy, criticism, identity formation, and thus the conditions of possibility for various approaches to Indian Shakespeares on screen. This is true despite the transatlantic transits of key postcolonial scholars and a shared corpus of criticism and theory, and despite the far greater differences that Indian scholars and artists have negotiated to reach this moment in spacetime. It made, and makes, a difference that the post-Second World War immigration policy changes in the UK meant that many more Caribbean, African and Asian members of the Commonwealth nations arrived at about the same time to face common barriers and Othering. While much of what Delia Jarrett-Macauley sketches in *Shakespeare, Race and Performance: The Diverse Bard* as the UK culture faced by Black and Asian performers of the '1980s generation' likewise captures the academic world in which this contemporary US academic was trained, nevertheless core terms and assumptions about Blackness, BAME (Black, Asian and minority ethnic), under-represented minorities, quotas and the location of Indianness within the sociocultural landscape differed greatly – as much as did the common language George Bernard Shaw said divided those nations.[7] Whether in experiencing Macauley's notorious 1835 Minute Upon Indian Education with the eyeroll of overfamiliarity, the anger of enduring its living legacies, the laughter that a pioneer such as Tara Arts' founder Jatinder Verma could muster when faced with its absurdities, or the stunned shock of a US student hearing it as news, a variety of perspectives persists, consequentially. The class and regional associations outsiders presume regarding South Asian diasporic communities, and even basic familiarity with Indian history and culture, vary as well; the centuries intervening between Shakespeare's writing and our own moment continue to shape what audiences do and do not see on screens. For those who came of age in the last century, it makes a huge difference whether the first film that one saw associating Indian culture with Shakespearean themes was *Shakespeare Wallah* or *Mississippi Masala*. Most overtly in the different unravelling of race-based slavery, indentured servitude, colonial occupation, but less consciously (at least in the US) in the scale and opportunities shaped by the when and how of mass emigration – including the horrific incentive of Partition – these conditions help explain the time lag and the fragility of cross-race alliances even among the most progressive late twentieth-century thinkers in the US. And if true for them, how much more so within that cauldron of subgroups called Shakespeareans.

That said, the larger scale and decentralized diversity of US tertiary education, along with a more future-oriented, egalitarian national self-image (at least in theory) facilitated fairly swift incorporation of new scholarly approaches – once advocates gained entry into the halls of academe and conference circuits.[8] Whereas in 2017 Jarrett-Macauley still began by saying British 'scholars have been slow to include Black and Asian people in theatre histories in general and Shakespeare performance history in particular' as if 'Shakespeare belongs to an undifferentiated English society, pre-Windrush and suffering an amnesiac response to its imperial past' (1), US performance practices and scholarship have by contrast been areas of leadership in diversifying and relocating Shakespeare. The precedent of Joseph Papp's assertively democratic New York Shakespeare Festival, founded in 1954 and famous for its non-traditional casting from the 1960s onward, created an alternative performance history to the British, even as scholars like my graduate school mentor Bernard Beckerman bridged academic study and theatrical practice.

Even so, there have been other challenges bringing this diversity to bear upon Indian screen Shakespeares in the US. The 1960s/1970s avant-garde performance movement and subsequently founded performance studies programmes (led by the Richard Schechner/NYU School) moved away from focusing on, much less venerating, literary analysis of scripted drama, including Shakespeare, no matter how adapted or politicized. Alongside the continued dominance of text-based analysis in English departments (even or especially with the advent of post-modern theory), this helped perpetuate a 'text v. performance' debate that struck me as stale and exaggerated even during graduate school in the early 1980s. Performance interventions tended to focus on live theatre, often with the goal of better understanding Shakespeare's text or staging (an earlier era's version of practice-based research); screen media were seldom discussed. Furthermore, the advent of New Historicism in that same decade directed attention away from contemporary practice even as film and television studies were moving in new directions hospitable to more diverse forms of adaptation studies. Consider too that in the two decades between Zeffirelli's *Romeo and Juliet* (1968) and Branagh's *Henry V* (1989), there had been no Shakespeare film released in the West whose popular reach could be deemed to merit the new, more materialist cultural studies approach to the movie industry. It is perhaps not surprising then that among the first deeply analytic monographs moving beyond taxonomies or catalogues, Peter Donaldson's excellent *Shakespearean Films/Shakespearean Directors* (1990) gained scholarly respect by drawing on earlier film studies' auteurism, theorized close reading, and revised psychoanalytic models (the only Asian director included was, not atypically, Akira Kurosawa). Appearing at about the same time as the first generation of Indian applications of post-colonial theory to Shakespeare studies, these publications helped internationalize the field, albeit at some distance from the populist, reception-based and genre-focused impulses steadily gaining purchase in US media studies scholarship.

Thus, even when I arrived at MIT in the mid-1990s and taught a class interweaving popular narrative, film and gender (as well as a separate Shakespeare class) while another earlier career instructor was teaching Hong Kong and Bollywood cinema as action genres, I did not think to connect these topics. Nor in my archival primary research did I look much beyond European and silent films and US television spinoffs when cataloguing and critiquing the frequent reappearance of *The Taming of the Shrew* on screen. When working Indian material into a graduate comparative media studies seminar on 'Major Media Texts', I turned to Satyajit Ray's *Jalsaghar* (*The Music Room*, 1958) to exemplify an auteur's cross-medium adaptation rather than to Indian Shakespeares. Nor was I alone: when I led a seminar on 'Shakespeare and Film: Issues of Gender' at the 1998 annual meeting of the Shakespeare Association of America, the twelve papers (from pioneers in the area such as Barbara Hodgdon, Curtis Breight and Stephen Buhler, as well as emergent scholars) were focused primarily on Anglo-American examples, albeit addressing an expanding interest in popular culture and spinoffs; and although some directors studied did hail from other cultures and continents (e.g. Buchwetzki, Kozintsev, Polanski and Suzman), the only Asian named was again Kurosawa. Even a decade later, after the international release and circulation of both *Maqbool* (2004) and *Omkara* (2006), in Samuel Crowl's *Shakespeare and Film: A Norton Guide* that pattern persisted: Kurosawa yes, but no mention of South Asian cinema at all.[9] When Poonam Trivedi and Paromita Chakravarti stated in 2019 that 'until very recently' the world's 'largest corpus of Shakespeare films' had been unrecognized as such, and 'virtually invisible except to a few aficionados', they did not exaggerate.[10]

Nonetheless, with the approach of the new millennium, change was already on the way. An Indian-centred performance chapter or two featured in most post-colonial, 'world-wide' or screen-oriented scholarly collections during the 1990s and beyond, coinciding with the Branagh-initiated resurgence of more popular Shakespeare cinema. The shift in the representation of Indian cinema between *Shakespeare, The Movie* (1997) and *Shakespeare, The Movie 2* (2003) captures a paradigm shift in process, as well as reasons for trepidation among some who may have wished to join the conversation. In the 1997 volume, Valerie Wayne used recent post-colonial theorizing by Ania Loomba, Jyotsna G. Singh and Homi Bhabha to frame her analysis of Merchant–Ivory's *Shakespeare Wallah* (1965), emphasizing hybridity and the 'cultural friction' the film 'presents its viewers, Eastern and Western alike', providing 'opportunities to mimic, resist, or reject' Shakespeare's texts.[11] Six years later, the second collection replaced a majority of the essays with new contributions focused on the past decade's explosion of new screen Shakespeares, and further emphasized the role of new viewing technologies (then, the DVD) as transformative. Wayne's close analysis was replaced by Richard Burt's expansive survey of 'Asia in postdiasporic cinemas', invoking 'spin-offs and citations of the plays from Bollywood to Hollywood' as part of his theorization of a 'posthermeneutic' era.[12] Overstating (especially in retrospect) the claims that Bollywood in the US had 'failed' and of a possible 'end of postcolonial Shakespeare criticism' on the basis of technology's ability to have 'undone the diaspora', and likewise underestimating the enduring appeal of individual creativity – be it a director's or a playwright's – Burt's essay nonetheless helped rethink Indian cinema as dynamic and relocatable in ways that cannot be controlled (Burt 2003, 276, 297).

In so doing, the essay resisted the less helpful consequences of identity- and location-based authority at a time when its assertion served as a powerful form of gate-keeping. While obviously valid to demand accuracy in scholarly judgements and to value local expertise in contextualizing particular artworks, claiming linguistic and cultural embeddedness as critical prerequisites provided an easy reason for novice outsiders not even to try to engage with this subfield and its artworks. Within Wayne's earlier essay, a footnote signals that she was carefully negotiating that landscape: herself located at the University of Hawaii, she states that she is responding to 'implied critique' by Lubna Chaudhry and Saba Kattak, two of her initial talk's audience, who said it had 'partly triggered' their own article on 'Images of White Women and Indian Nationalism' (which they find less hybrid and more imperialistically nostalgic) in *Shakespeare Wallah* and *Junoon* (Wayne 1997, 102). By moving away from individual close readings as the dominant methodology, Burt's essay also makes space for wider discussion of Bollywood films among other genres and in dialogue with other regions. Three years later when editing *A Concise Companion to Shakespeare on Screen*, I included Anthony Dawson's different tack on the common endeavour of making more room for cross-cultural interpretation through overtly self-conscious discussion of his methodology in 'Reading Kurosawa [yes, again!] Reading Shakespeare'. I placed it right before Douglas Lanier's chapter on 'Recent Shakespeare Film Parody and the Politics of Popularization' and right after Mark

Thornton Burnett's comparisons of varied Anglo-American films 'Figuring the Global/Historical' – that is, resisting the orientalizing temptation to locate any cinematic domain as prior to or outside globalization's diverse transformations and transits.[13]

Nonetheless, in the early years of the twenty-first century, the application of theoretical models often remained more judgemental than expansive – leading to some familiar ruts in both global and post-colonial studies (as Ania Loomba presciently recognized some years before) as well as in Anglo-American Shakespeare performance and analysis.[14] It was thus with some fear as well as excitement that I presented my own first work on Indian screen Shakespeares at an international conference in Taipei in 2012. The curse of all multi-media presentations did not help: presenting the beedi number from *Omkara* without the sound projecting effectively was, to put it mildly, a challenge.[15] What truly surprised me, however, was the generosity with which my analysis was received, including from an attendee from New Delhi who subsequently became a valued friend and who without doubt knows more about Indian films generally and what Vishal Bhardwaj was rendering audibly than did I. (Perhaps in retrospect the absence of sound was a blessing?) In part this reception might be attributable to its being a primarily pan-Asian gathering at a time before Bhardwaj was as widely known as he became internationally post-*Haider* – although *Maqbool* was already being studied in Shakespeare on Film classes in the US, including at MIT. But I believe some of the good will also derived from my having adopted a more overtly collaborative methodology and discursive mode than that which dominated my training and which still persists in much academic discourse (in which the implicit goal is to be deemed the smartest person in the room). I had the help of my friend Tara Raman in understanding where the English subtitles departed from the Hindi, Urdu and Uttar Pradesh dialect, and an illuminating correspondence with Poonam Trivedi that helped me localize my feminist assumptions.

Acknowledging these collaborative efforts does not in any way diminish the value of scholarly debate or rigorous critique of either the artwork or my own positionality; indeed, Poonam and I continue to interpret *Omkara*'s conclusion through different lenses, and have said so in print. But by bringing a similar skepticism about positivist/empirical models of knowledge to bear upon the film artefact and contemporary local identification that I do (and perforce must) when studying early modern spacetime, and mixing in a good measure of humility as an overly entitled outsider, a space emerges for other kinds of interpretive work, potentially enlivening Indian Shakespeares for new and even more diverse audiences. Conversely, such methods and dialogues can help refocus Anglo-American Shakespeare studies away from micro-attention, judgemental performance criticism, and overly familiar author-focused debates – or at least can supplement and refresh them.

All of which leads me to the event which motivated this essay's reflections from the start. In April 2016, something happened that gave me reinvigorated hope for the future of Shakespeare studies. It was not the staggering array of events commemorating the 400th anniversary of the death of William Shakespeare, as valuable as many of those were. Indeed, I myself spent that 23 April at a delightful conference held within Kronberg Castle at Helsingor, Denmark, and with strange appropriateness dined (thanks to Anthony Guneratne) at a *Hamlet*-themed banquet during which only one woman in period clothes collapsed – no accidental slaughter ensued, and the conference Ronan Paterson organized was forward-looking to 'the next 400 years' of a globally connected, creative and critical dialogue. Within that context, both the potential and limitations of international interactions were made vivid by the fact that, while North American student performers had managed to join the mostly European delegation, the student group from a Kolkata college could not, and we saw them only on screen. Now that a pandemic has made virtual conferencing a necessity and prompted more extensive reconsideration of the inequities and privileges all types of gatherings convey, the enthusiasm expressed then by the on-screen participants may strike some readers as troublingly partial, and rightly so; still, like all our Zoom talks during lockdown, screen contact can be much better than nothing. Yet even while gratefully acknowledging the dedicated labour and good intentions of organizing this and other virtual forms of contact – including a multicontinental birth/death-day toast – we were still in 'Hamlet's castle' and the stylish graphics on the obligatory conference tote bag featured a deathly skull on Kronberg's black background: the very weight of the architecture recalled things dying, whereas my theme here lies with things new-born.

For that, I had to leave Elsinore (amidst sleet) and fly to London, to a conference whose ivory and gold tote bag saluted Mother India in its craftsmanship and its branding; the conference was 'Indian Shakespeares on Screen'. Granted, my description is in one sense as fanciful as was Virginia Woolf's in opening *A Room of One's Own* by juxtaposing luncheon at an Oxbridge men's college (in autumn) followed by dinner at a women's (in spring). But this is how the latter conference felt to me at the time: a breath of springtime and pastures new, with new paradigms to match. And that feeling's primary source was a generational change in leadership.

First and foremost, this was a conference (and more) organized by four early career female scholars, Asian British and/or from the subcontinent. I do not think I have ever attended a more future-oriented conference, even giving due credit to both the Shakespeare Association of America's (SAA) structural innovations and the early years of the conference of the Group for Early Modern Cultural Studies (which was constructed primarily by friends in eighteenth-century studies at a time when their leading society was still lightyears more traditional). Although mentors with the institutional clout to help make 'Indian Shakespeares on Screen' possible were in attendance, for the most part they remained supportively in the background, and allowed these early career women – Thea Buckley, Koel Chatterjee, Varsha Panjwani and Preti Taneja –

to construct an adventurous programme emphasizing creative alliances.

And creative it was, most notably including not only scholars but directors, screenwriters and actors from different regions of the subcontinent and the diaspora. Moreover, we convened in Marylebone at Asia House for the day's presentations, and at the BFI Southbank for three special screenings – indicative of the public-facing spirit with which the presenters introduced as well as analysed a wide array of screen Shakespeares in many languages of the subcontinent and diaspora. The programme mixed historical classics with the very new, and works by major directorial names with indie and unduly obscure films; I recall talks ranging from Shani Bans on 'Gulzar's Ocular Poetics' to Kinga Földváry comparing Indian and Western generic conceptions of melodrama, from Paramita Dutta on Shakespeare's comedy transformed in *Bharantibilas* (1963) and *Angoor* (1982) to Parthajit Baruah on 'Shakespeare and Assamese Parallel Cinema: Politics of Identity and Political Realism'. I heard Felicity Kendall thinking back to the era with which I began this essay, when she was growing up as a teenager in India and played Lizzie Buckingham in *Shakespeare Wallah*; she also made insightful observations about inverted emphases in performing Shakespeare within Indian culture versus Indian culture within Britain – though alas, the pandemic's combination of restricting access to my office files and addling my memory means they are currently beyond recall. In retrospect, the sheer number of productions and topics to which I was introduced, which in the subsequent five years have become deeply familiar, makes it hard for me to distinguish new and old – a sign of how swiftly this dynamic group of specialists has helped reorient and transform the Global Shakespeares canon. The screenings at Asia House included Jayaraj's *Kaliyattam* (with anticipation for his forthcoming *Veeram*, 2016), Sharat Katariya's *10ml Love* (2010), Bhansali's *Ram-Leela* (2013), Aparna Sen's *Arshinagar* (2015), and even a 'workshop' advance screening of Bonila Chatterjee's *The Hungry* (2017) ... dare I say it, a virtual feast of consumption.

Yet the conference's value lay just as much in its thinking beyond its participants alone to its larger pedagogical mission, hoping to enlarge these works' impact. As I regularly offer a seminar featuring Tom Stoppard's plays where we study roles originally created for Kendall (including the lead in *Indian Ink* as well as *Hapgood*), in listening to her I already felt keenly the expanding list of intersections between 'Indian Shakespeares on Screen' and my 'other' teaching. Furthermore, learning about Sangeeta Das's *Life Goes On* (2009) from the director herself helped me solidify an interest in romance *Lear*s that would feed back into both my classroom and scholarship; although the article I published subsequently emphasizes the film's generic departure in allowing renewal, my thinking about it in dialogue with David Lean's *Hobson's Choice* (1952, based on the 1915 Brighouse play whose 2016 revival I likewise saw in London) led me to see them as additionally linked in rethinking British family relations across generations, from heritage to modernity – and in that sense allowing a different sort of 'mainstreaming' of Indian identities within the UK 'local'.[16] Its very locality had been a reason *Life Goes On* was new to me in 2016 as a US visitor, and why I had not come to it presuming a link instead with *Second Generation* (2003) – which I suspect was productive ignorance. Again, complicating notions of location while also expanding interpretive opportunities and associations can help our geographical and cultural diversity create new perspectives, new possibilities – just as that film both does and represents.

Because my MIT students had already studied Bhardwaj's works that spring, I came primed with questions they hoped this featured director would answer. For one more remarkable feat the organizers managed, with the kind of entrepreneurial boldness my home institution so values, was the redoubled appearance of Vishal Bhardwaj along with two of his screenwriting collaborators, Abbas Tyrewala (*Maqbool*) and Robin Bhatt (*Omkara*) – both at Asia House where my students' questions could be asked informally, and also on stage at the BFI Southbank where they engaged in public post-screening

Q&A sessions about Bhardwaj's three major remediations of the tragedies. In advance, Koel Chatterjee and Preti Taneja had helped lay the groundwork by previewing and contextualizing the conference's featured films in *Sight and Sound*, and the popularity of the Southbank screenings had a significant effect on the BFI's subsequent programming. It seemed an act of cosmic justice that Bhardwaj more than lived up to the occasion, showing great generosity of attention and openness to all questioners, including sharing his deep investment in his musical scores as a motivation for becoming a director (and even singing a bit of 'O saati re' at the *Omkara* screening). Moreover, in having invited and arranged the trans-hemispheric travel arrangements for Bhardwaj's off-screen co-creators, the organizers prioritized the collaborative processes too often forgotten – whether due to celebrity culture, auteurism, intellectual abstraction or simply unfamiliarity with the pragmatics of production. In this reorientation lies a new path forward, suggesting ways for humanities pedagogy and scholarship to rethink individualistic standards of evaluation and modes of work, which lag so far behind both our theorizing and life experiences.

And in this regard, thinking back to my pre-teen feminist icons, it strikes me as far from incidental that all the organizers were women, and that women's voices framed the events at Asia House. I was honoured to help in 'Setting the Scene' alongside Deana Rankin and Poonam Trivedi the first morning, and to participate in making more overt the productive resemblances between the collective work of artistic creation and the half-century's work in gender studies initiated by women. Further connecting the analysis of artistic process and gender with the conference's particular topic, as I had argued in my essay on *Omkara*, has the potential to make an important intervention in contemporary media studies and in the emergent subfield of Global Shakespeares.[17] In a *Shakespeare Studies* Forum article and a reflective piece published that same year, I tried to make the urgency of this wider project in the academic humanities clear: public skepticism, institutional reprioritization, systemic inequities and the growing precarity of the next generation of scholars had and have been obvious since (at least) the global financial crisis of 2007–8.[18] Retreating into the British Library or the Folger Shakespeare Library, the minutiae of marginalia, or the delights of new interpretations – no matter how salutary, illuminating, and indeed necessary for us as a personal balance to daily professional pressures – is insufficient to the day. When I was preparing my Forum essay, a respected male colleague told me he agreed fully but felt it unlikely we could alter the culture of academic selfishness: here, in as unexpected a location as Marylebone, I found not only reasons to hope but the beginning of alternate career visions and public-facing social activism effectively producing change. While we three senior scholars from three continents could set the stage that had been hard-fought to attain – a space in which women had the institutional authority to have their voices heard, travel across oceans to think together and challenge the exclusionary models that had disciplined us – it was that next generation speaking from places of precarity but with utter conviction and generosity who were leading forward not only the conference but the project that, in its multi-medial adventurousness and boundary-crossing, could save us all. And thus, it was entirely fitting, and inspirational, that the closing plenary session was led by our early career leaders, standing next to a projected image that melded Shakespeare differently even from the marvellous conference poster's cross-cultural fantasia. Shakeshifting that authorial figure into a gender-blended doubled human image, its voice had been transferred to and transformed by those Asian British women at the microphone, the playwright hailed from history into the land of the living.

A half year after 'Indian Shakespeares on Screen', my nation took a frightening turn with the poll-defying election of Donald Trump as President: an actively racist, misogynist, financially and ethically corrupt demagogue triumphed over what would have been the first female leader of the United States. The years since have reminded many that this was not an historical aberration or fluke, although its rendering was more shamelessly selfish and destructively consequential than even some students of government history imagined. Republican legislators have let lapse or are actively undoing provisions of the Civil Rights legislation with which I began. Most recently, as if returning to the years before the 1965 turning point for Asians in America, a surge of anti-Asian violence necessitated the creation of the COVID-19 Hate Crimes Bill, which President Joe Biden signed into law on 20 May 2021.

The impact of newly emboldened anti-democratic forces tapping familiar patterns of bigotry will not quickly disappear. Much of the hardest work in addressing the thorniest problems is (all too unsurprisingly) falling on the shoulders of Shyamila Gopalan's daughter, addressing border regulation and immigration reform, systemic racism and gendered workplace inequities that have shaped her own life. Yet another woman of colour is tasked with realizing the next steps her mother helped advocate for and model in the 1960s. But even so, the ripple effects of those decades and the intercultural connections they abetted expand. A murder in Minneapolis has sparked marches around the globe while, in a much humbler key, films from the Indian subcontinent such as *Haider* now resonate vividly for incarcerated white women in my US online classroom – to such an extent that some choose to watch without subtitles. Across the Atlantic, and despite the current UK government's attempts to undo the more decisive 1970s referendum that led to European federation as well as the cultural transformations that embrace – but far exceed – the particular branding of Shakespeare, the demographics of age and ethnicity continue to bend the arc of history towards justice.

As many forms of assumed civility and alliance collapsed both in the wider world and within academia, and even amidst the hatred and ugliness social media encourage and spread, I have repeatedly taken heart in the resourceful creativity of the next generation, including those scholars making grassroots changes to our pedagogical and research practices through digital collaborations and one-on-one personal dedication. That includes the fine DH wizards with whom I have been pleased to create Global Shakespeares curricular modules and open-access edX courses, among whom Sarah Connell, Michael Lutz, Cathleen Nalezyty, Meghan Perdue and Mary Erica Zimmer all demand naming. Most of us, including all those with a university affiliation, still work in hierarchical institutions and it would be delusional to deny it – and thus I am officially 'Principal Investigator'; my responsibility is to use that clout I have earned to advance the real leaders of disciplinary innovation, those named above. I likewise have found myself repeatedly involved in the whirlwind of activity that continues to swirl around the four organizers of 'Indian Shakespeares on Screen': as an editor, editee, co-author, workshop co-leader, embedded voice in a collective essay, podcast interviewee, social media correspondent and friend.[19] Each of our interactions has reinforced my sense of renewal and hope . . . if we who are *not* young (thank you, Preti) – nor as creatively open to the future – will more intentionally try to share with the emergent generation only what might be useful from our longer pasts, and then step back to listen, learn, and try to keep growing, alongside them.

Notes

1 Harry S. Truman, *Public Papers of the Presidents of the United States* (U.S. Government Printing Office: Washington, D.C., 1961), 443–4. Presidents Eisenhower and Kennedy likewise opposed the quotas before Lyndon Johnson finally signed the 1965 act into law (see same source, 1961: 308–10 and 1964: 594–7 respectively). My citations draw heavily on material from the Center for Immigration Studies, in part because its stated 'Low-immigration, Pro-immigrant' bias differs from my own; see https://cis.org/Report/Legacy-1965-Immigration-Act. I am also indebted to historian Emma Teng for materials on early twentieth-century anti-Hindu cartoons and anti-Asian laws.

2 Section 2(a), see https://www.saada.org/item/20140421-3552. Legislators connected the two laws directly. Rep. Robert Sweeney (D-OH): 'I would consider the amendments to the Immigration

and Nationality Act to be as important as the landmark legislation of this Congress relating to the Civil Rights Act. The central purpose of the administration's immigration bill is to once again undo discrimination and to revise the standards by which we choose potential Americans in order to be fairer to them and which will certainly be more beneficial to us'; Rep. Philip Burton (D-CA): 'Just as we sought to eliminate discrimination in our land through the Civil Rights Act, today we seek by phasing out the national origins quota system to eliminate discrimination in immigration to this nation composed of the descendants of immigrants' (*Congressional Record*, 25 August 1965; 21765, 21783). For a 2020 reminder of the connection and the need for its reassertion aimed at Asian Americans, see comedian Hassan Minhaj's impassioned Netflix episode 'We cannot stay silent in the wake of George Floyd': https://www.youtube.com/watch?v=i_FE78X-qdY&feature=youtu.be.

3 https://history.house.gov/Historical-Highlights/1951-2000/Immigration-and-Nationality-Act-of-1965/.

4 Proceedings of the U.S. Senate, Subcommittee on Immigration and Naturalization of the Committee on the Judiciary (Washington, D.C., 10 February 1965), 65, cited from *cis.org*. As a reminder that not only the Johnson administration had trouble predicting the future, historian Josh Zeitz's 'The 1965 Law that gave the Republican Party its Race Problem', written less than three months before the 2016 election, presumed that Donald Trump would lose to Hilary Clinton: https://www.politico.com/magazine/story/2016/08/immigration-1965-law-donald-trump-gop-214179.

5 To offset my upbeat citation, see this reuse of the musical documenting the ongoing horrors faced by would-be immigrants: https://www.youtube.com/watch?v=6_35a7sn6ds (2017: song by K'naan, Snow Tha Product, Riz MC, and Residente, *The Hamilton Mixtape*, 2016). In another telling convergence, President Biden has assigned the work of addressing the Mexican border situation to Kamala Harris. For more biographical facts, see https://www.whitehouse.gov/administration/vice-president-harris/.

6 See Rachel Weiner, 'Graduates celebrate new beginning for T. C. Williams High School', *The Washington Post*, 12 June 2021.

7 Delia Jarrett-Macauley, *Shakespeare, Race and Performance: The Diverse Bard* (London: Routledge, 2017), 1–19. This volume also includes Jatinder Verma, 'Classical Binglish in the twenty-first century', 30–42, which comments on his embedded 1996 address, itself given two decades after he founded the UK's first Asian-British theatre company, Tara Arts; he shares his ability to laugh at Macauley's Minute, as cited below.

8 Throughout my career, scholarly conferences have played a huge role in determining what gets read and studied – if anything, now more than ever. This has held true even during a pandemic and as economic and climate crises raised major objections to their being convened in person; simultaneously, new online formats such as podcasts, twitter amplification and video interviews are gaining traction.

9 Samuel Crowl, *Shakespeare and Film: A Norton Guide*, New York and London: WW Norton & Company, 2008.

10 Poonam Trivedi and Paromita Chakravarti, *Shakespeare and Indian Cinemas: 'Local Habitations'* (New York and London: Routledge, 2019), 1–2.

11 Valerie Wayne, '*Shakespeare Wallah* and Colonial Specularity', in Lynda E. Boose and Richard Burt, *Shakespeare the Movie: Popularizing the plays on film, TV, and video* (London and New York: Routledge, 1997), 95–102, esp. 101.

12 Richard Burt, 'Shakespeare and Asia in Postdiasporic Cinemas: Spin-offs and citations of the plays from Bollywood to Hollywood', in Lynda E. Boose and Richard Burt, *Shakespeare, the Movie, II: Popularizing the plays on film, TV, video, and DVD* (London and New York: Routledge, 2003), 265–303.

13 Anthony Dawson, 'Cross-Cultural Interpretation: Reading Kurosawa Reading Shakespeare' 155–75; Douglas Lanier, 'Popular Culture: Will of the People: Recent Shakespeare Film Parody and the Politics of Popularization' 176–96; Mark Thornton Burnett, 'Globalization: Figuring the Global/Historical in Filmic Shakespearean Tragedy', 133–54; in *A Concise Companion to Shakespeare on Screen*, ed. Diana E. Henderson (Oxford: Blackwell, 2006).

14 Ania Loomba, 'Shakespearean Transformations', *Shakespeare and national culture*, ed. John J. Joughin (Manchester: Manchester University Press, 1997), 109–41.

15 The technological challenges of different computer systems and insufficient software interoperability remain a hurdle; my problem on this occasion was in no way the responsibility of the most generous and capable of conference hosts, Bi-qi (Beatrice) Li.

16 Diana E. Henderson, 'Romancing *King Lear*: Hobson's Choice, Life Goes On, and Beyond', *Shakespeare on Screen: King Lear*, ed. Victoria Bladen, Sarah Hatchuel and Nathalie Vienne-Guerin (Cambridge: Cambridge University Press, 2019), 125–39.

17 Diana E. Henderson, 'Magic in the Chains: *Othello, Omkara*, and the materiality of gender across time and media', *The Oxford Handbook of Shakespeare and Embodiment*, ed. Valerie Traub (Oxford: Oxford University Press, 2016), 673–93.

18 Diana E. Henderson, 'Star Wars and Shakespearean SpaceTime: On Mentors and Our Collective Future', *Shakespeare Studies* 44 (2016): 137–48; and 'Tempestuous Transitions and Double Vision: from early to late modern gendered performances on stage, film, and in higher education', in *Rethinking Feminism in Early Modern Studies: Gender, Race, and Sexuality*, ed. Ania Loomba and Melissa Sanchez (New York: Routledge, 2016), 59–71.

19 To cite only a few of the accessible results, see 'De-centring Shakespeare, Incorporating Otherness: Diana E. Henderson in conversation with Koel Chatterjee', in *Eating Shakespeare: Cultural Anthropophagy as Global Methodology*, ed. Anne-Sophie Reskou, Marcel Alvaro de Amorim and Vinicius Mariano de Carvalho (London: Bloomsbury, 2019), 121–35; Preti Taneja, 'American Fall', *Five Dials*, published 31 January 2019 online: https://fivedials.com/reportage/american-fall-preti-taneja-jennifer-croft-chika-unigwe-sarah-weinman-shobha-rao-sharmila-sen-danielle-evans-diana-henderson-jeanne-mcculloch/; Varsha Panjwani, 'Women and Shakespeare' podcasts season 2, episode 1 recorded 24 January 2020; 23 January 23 2021 release: https://podcasts.apple.com/ca/podcast/s2-e1-professor-diana-henderson-on-virginia-woolf-shakespeare/id1501971708?i=1000506252998; and I thank Thea Buckley for sharing her Queen's University, Belfast research cohort's Indian Shakespeares screen inventory: https://www.qub.ac.uk/schools/ael/Research/ResearchinEnglish/ResearchProjectsinEnglish/INDIANSHAKESPEARES/

shakespeare%20and%20indian%20cinematic%20
traditions%20qub/.

References

Burnett, Mark Thornton. 'Globalization: Figuring the Global/Historical in Filmic Shakespearean Tragedy', in *A Concise Companion to Shakespeare on Screen*, ed. Diana E. Henderson. Oxford: Blackwell, 2006, 133–54.

Burt, Richard. 'Shakespeare and Asia in Postdiasporic Cinema: spin-offs and citations of the plays from Bollywood to Hollywood', in *Shakespeare, The Movie, II: popularizing the plays on film, TV, video, and DVD*, eds. Lynda E. Boose and Richard Burt. London and New York: Routledge, 2003, 265–303.

Crowl, Samuel. *Shakespeare and Film: A Norton Guide*. New York and London: WW Norton, 2008.

Dawson, Anthony. 'Cross-Cultural Interpretation: Reading Kurosawa Reading Shakespeare', in *A Concise Companion to Shakespeare on Screen*, 2006, 155–75.

Henderson, Diana E. 'Romancing *King Lear*: *Hobson's Choice*, *Life Goes On*, and Beyond', in *Shakespeare on Screen: King Lear*, eds. Victoria Bladen, Sara Hatchuel and Nathalie Vienne-Guerin. Oxford: Oxford University Press, 2019, 125–39.

Henderson, Diana E. 'Star Wars and Shakespearean Spacetime: On Mentors and Our Collective Future', *Shakespeare Studies* 44 (2016): 137.

Henderson, Diana E. 'Tempestuous Transitions and Double Vision: From Early to Late Modern Gendered Performances on Stage, Film and in Higher Education', in *Rethinking Feminism in Early Modern Studies: Gender, Race, and Sexuality*, ed. Ania Loomba and Melissa Sanchez. New York: Routledge, 2016, 59–71.

Jarrett-Macauley, Delia. *Shakespeare, Race and Performance: The Diverse Bard*. London and New York: Routledge, 2017.

Lanier, Douglas. 'Popular Culture: Will of the People: Recent Shakespeare Film Parody and the Politics of Popularization', in *A Concise Companion to Shakespeare on Screen* 2006, 176–96.

Loomba, Ania. 'Shakespearean transformations', in *Shakespeare and National Culture* ed. John J. Joughin, Manchester: Manchester University Press, 1997, 109–41.

Trivedi, Poonam, and Paromita Chakravarti, eds. *Shakespeare and Indian Cinemas: 'Local Habitations'*. New York and London: Routledge, 2019.

Truman, Harry S. *Public Papers of the Presidents of the United States*. U.S. Government Printing Office, Washington, D.C., 1961.

Wayne, Valerie. '*Shakespeare Wallah* and Colonial Specularity', in *Shakespeare, the Movie: popularizing the plays on film, TV, and video*. London and New York: Routledge, 1997, 95–102.

2

Two Indian Film Offshoots of *Twelfth Night*

Robert White

This chapter deals with two films which directly or indirectly reference *Twelfth Night*, revealing different kinds of Shakespearean adaptation in India. First, extensive Shakespearean quotation and allusiveness in an Indian educational setting infuse the Anglo-Indian *36 Chowringhee Lane* (1981). Secondly, *Dil Bole Hadippa!* (2009) is an offshoot of both *Twelfth Night* and the Hollywood movie, *She's the Man* (2006). The latter was itself based on *Twelfth Night* and targeted in particular an American college audience. Taken together, the different modes of adaptation raise methodological questions about the intertextual nature of transmission of the Shakespearean text through films, and capture the range of negotiations between regional, linguistic, political, national and international aspects of appropriations of Shakespeare in India which form the substance of this edited collection. They take us well beyond the surely exhausted debate about 'fidelity to the text' in Shakespearean movies, asking fresh questions and requiring different paradigms of interpretation focusing on recontextualizing the source.

There seems no reason to doubt that *Twelfth Night* is any less popular in India than other plays by Shakespeare, on the stage and in educational practice. However, in terms of the Indian cinematic repertoire it is not prominent, lagging behind even the other play based on twins, *The Comedy of Errors*, which is usually regarded as a less rich play but has generated at least eight movie versions in India.[1] There were two early movies where *Twelfth Night* seems to have been spliced with elements of *Errors*, *Bhul Bhulaiya*, ('Maze' in Hindi, silent, 1929) and *Bhul Bhulaiyan* (presumably a remake, 1933). Two other early movies perhaps illustrate the introductory comments in this book describing the alienation of resisting 'easy dialogue because their cultural codes, cinematic tropes, and non-anglophone languages are strange for their [Western] audiences and users'. *Twelfth Night* was the primary source in the Tamil-language *Kanniyin Kaadhali* (or *Kathali*) or 'The Maiden's Lover' (1949) produced in Madras / Chennai and directed by K. Ramnoth who also adapted *Hamlet* as *Marmayogi*. Now almost inaccessible, it features some very melodic and catchy songs by the later famous composer Kannadasan in his first movie, one of which is preserved on You Tube and suggests the unifying force of love as the central motif:

Mekala: [Heroine]
King of the Earth – Beloved Light of my Life
Without separation, in our lives of love, may we – forever
Like the wave joining the sea, be in pleasure.
We, upon this earth, are lovers without compare.[2]

Musicality is not just a quirky convention of Indian films but true to Shakespeare as well, since *Twelfth Night* is a play with several songs and musical interludes from its opening moments onwards, whose presence shapes and enhances its lyrical atmosphere. There is no Malvolio subplot in the film, but the reviewer Randor Guy wrote in the *Hindu Times* of a comic palace watchman played by 'lean and lanky, Sayeeram, a talented but sadly underrated comedian', whose physique perhaps makes him an equivalent of Andrew Aguecheek.[3] The English-language poster describes the movie as 'A comedy of errors with a romantic background perfectly paced to the heart-beat of human desire'.[4] Secondly, *Uran Khatola* or 'Flying Cart' (1955) is a Hindi movie which can be viewed on You Tube, though without English subtitles.[5] Illyria becomes a make-believe, all female society into which is pitched a male, Kashi, who combines aspects of the roles of shipwrecked Viola and Feste as singer. He becomes love object to both the Olivia figure, the ruling female aristocrat who travels in the titular 'flying cart', and a humble-born young woman, Soni, who disguises as a man to meet Kashi surreptitiously. Elements of *Twelfth Night* can be glimpsed, 'like a tangled chain, nothing impaired but all disordered' (*A Midsummer Night's Dream*, 4.1), in joyously Bollywood fashion of romantic musical comedy and wish-fulfilment. These two movies are used by Jonathan Gil Harris to argue that '*Twelfth Night*'s gender fluidity proved a vibrant resource for Indian filmmakers', in what he calls generically 'Masala Shakespeare'.[6] This term has been challenged as contentious and 'idiosyncratic' by some scholarly reviewers, by over-simplifying the complexities and pluralities of Indian culture (and cooking).[7] Moreover, in all cultures in earlier times, films had to be careful in presenting the disguise of Viola as a mere theatrical convention rather than providing analogies for same-sex relationships as overtly as Trevor Nunn's 1996 British movie. However, my quarry here is not these two early versions of *Twelfth Night*, but rather two more recent offshoots, which were intended for a wider international distribution and reception.

36 Chowringhee Lane (1981)

This movie is a neglected, poignant gem, and historically significant as a pioneering Indian feature film directed by a woman, Aparna Sen. It is available on DVD (2006) and can also be watched (in a lower quality reproduction) on You Tube.[8] It brings back to the screen Geoffrey Kendal of *Shakespeare Wallah* fame (1965), significantly here playing an elderly brother of the central figure, confined in a nursing home and living in the past. The two movies raise comparable but different aspects of the love-hate relationship India has had with Shakespeare in times of national change, reflecting his ambiguous status. By some, he is revered as bard, by others, hated as a reminder of British imperialism, both parties reacting to an educational system prioritizing a figure who could be seen as personifying British colonization yet who has broken the shackles since the plays have taken root in Indian popular culture. Aparna Sen was asked in a recorded interview whether in Bengali culture Shakespeare 'is seen as an imperial icon but at the same time indigenised in different ways?', and significantly she answered, 'I think he is seen as more than an imperial icon. I think he has grown above that ... Shakespeare lives on among the people who love literature ... what one can do is keep reinventing him and I think his greatness lies in the fact that his texts allow themselves to be reinterpreted in so many times and so many ways'.[9]

The action concerns not the stage competing with the movie industry, an issue which runs through *Shakespeare Wallah*, but the place of Shakespeare in pedagogy in Indian schools. The setting of 36 Chowringhee Lane in old Calcutta (now Kolkata) carries the central ambiguities. The *locus* is memorably described by Paromita Chakravarti as redolent with nostalgic associations, for example embodied in the final shot of the Victoria Memorial as 'the legacy of Calcutta's imperial past':

> The image, the lines and the scattered Shakespeare allusions provide an idiom of a lost past for the city – its colonial and cosmopolitan history, which lingers in nostalgia. The film's name describes more than Miss Stoneham's address – it evokes the '*Saheb paara*', the 'white city' where the British lived and where the colonial architectural past of the city still exists in old offices, clubs, museums, markets and particularly the crumbling apartment houses where the dwindling Anglo-Indian community still lives. The Chowringhee Road, Calcutta's iconic artery and its

neighbouring streets also housed many theatres, including the fashionable Chowringhee Theatre (1813–1839) and *Sans Souci* (1839) which staged Shakespeare plays. It was Chowringhee Theatre which gave Theatre Road its name, which is now renamed as Shakespeare Sarani.[10]

As Chakravarti points out, the director of *The Last Lear* also set his film in the same Kolkata region, as a gesture to Bengali love of Shakespeare and a superseded world of the heyday of English theatre in India.

Jennifer Kendal (Kapoor married name), Geoffrey Kendal's daughter who was herself born in India, performs brilliantly the role of Violet Stoneham, an ageing, Anglo-Indian schoolteacher undergoing the humiliating experience of 'demotion' from teaching Shakespeare to later classes, to preliminary grammar in the junior year. Her place teaching Shakespeare is taken by a young Indian woman. Facing domestic as well as professional loneliness, Miss Stoneham readily agrees to allow her tiny apartment in Kolkata to be used in the daytime by a previous student, Nandita (Debashree Roy) and her boyfriend Samaresh (Dhritiman Chaterjee). Their plan is to use the rooms ostensibly for him to write, but in truth as venue for their lovers' trysts. This is one of the first Indian films to openly raise the issue of pre-marital sex, and in this sense, it was more innovatory and provocative than its rather modest subject and gentle style would suggest. Although the arrangement is mutually agreeable, since it provides Violet with congenial company and friendship (superficial, but nonetheless an emotional lifeline), yet she is finally exploited by the well-meaning but thoughtless young characters who outgrow her hospitality. Her real passion, however, is teaching, and especially Shakespeare, a spiritual vocation which is slipping away from her grasp as even her students lose interest. In this sense, the film has no sentimental 'Goodbye Mr Chips' undercurrent that she will be missed.

The film is awash with lines from *Twelfth Night* and the tone resembles that of the play which is often described as 'autumnal'. After the camera hovers over a grave, a church bell and then a school bell chime, and we enter the classroom where Miss Stoneham reads Orsino's opening speech to her students:

> If music be the food of love, play on;
> Give me excess of it, that, surfeiting,
> The appetite may sicken, and so die.
> That strain again! it had a dying fall:
> O, it came o'er my ear like the sweet sound,
> That breathes upon a bank of violets,
> Stealing and giving odour! Enough; no more:
> 'Tis not so sweet now as it was before.
> O spirit of love! how quick and fresh art thou,
>   [fade out]
>
>   (1.1.1–9)

Subliminally this immediately connects her name, Violet, with the play and its heroine (Viola), and more important, the passage helps establish a tone and atmosphere which will run through the film. *Twelfth Night*, as Shakespeare's last romantic comedy, has a distinctive mood created through its poetry, of languor and nostalgia, communicating (in Barbara Everett's words) 'the fusion of joy and sadness', and like a tuning fork Orsino's words adjust a tone at the outset of play and film alike.[11] The pupils, however, are distracted and not on the same reverential wavelength as their teacher, some surreptitiously reading a mildly erotic comic book. As in her attitude towards the lovers in her flat, Miss Stoneham is oblivious to – or overlooking – the fact that the young are more interested in sex than fine writing.

We then move to Violet's apartment, filled with Victorian furniture, old photographs and culturally miscellaneous bric-a-brac, as though, like Illyria, it is a place where time has stopped long ago, at least for the shrinking Anglo-Indian social class to which Violet belongs, an issue in the film described by an unnamed reviewer in this way:

The difficult position of the Anglo-Indians is a central discourse in the film. I've seen some references to Anglo-Indians as simply British people living in India, but the term properly refers to mixed race families who under the Raj were given access to professional jobs in the railways, customs etc., which Indians found difficult to enter before 1947. After independence the Anglo-Indians were caught between two national cultures, neither of which wanted to claim them. Jennifer Kendal uses an accent and general way of speaking that corresponds to an Anglo-Indian type. Her eventual fate is as much connected to racial identity as it is to age and spinsterhood.[12]

She has only her cat, 'Sir Toby Belch', for companionship. In the play the 'fly caught in amber' impression is intensified by Olivia's vow to remain veiled for seven years in mourning, 'to season / A brother's dead love, which she would keep fresh / And lasting, in her sad remembrance' (1.2.32–3);[13] and in the movie we learn through flashbacks and a dream that the grave Violet was visiting held her husband-to-be, who had died young in action during the war, perhaps forty odd years ago, and for whom she still grieves. Loss permeates her life as it does both Olivia's and Viola's grief for their brothers, since her wedded niece (Soni Razdan) has just emigrated to Australia. Her brother (played by Geoffrey Kendal) is in a nursing home in a state of advanced senility and 'stuck in the time-warp of the Raj'.[14] Violet in her solitude is reminiscent of Viola's fictional 'sister' who 'never told her love': she 'Sat like Patience on a monument,/ Smiling at grief' (2.4.105–10 *passim*). The oblique cultural references to *Twelfth Night* act here not with much discernible narrative application but creating a set of strong emotional reverberations. The young Indian lovers erupt into Violet's life with refreshing vitality, and despite their shallowness and casual selfishness they make her laugh and hold at bay the increasing social isolation and pathos of her situation. Like Feste she views them indulgently but with mature hindsight:

> What is love? 'Tis not hereafter;
> Present mirth hath present laughter;
> What's to come is still unsure.
> In delay there lies no plenty,
> Then come kiss me, sweet and twenty;
> Youth's a stuff will not endure.
>
> (2.3.41-5)

This refrain is not quoted in the movie but relevant to its perspective framed through Violet's eyes. In her life, youth has not endured.

Shakespeare, and in particular his play *Twelfth Night*, advert to a situation analogous to Mis Stoneham's own, a relic of a past age but still holding a respected but tenuous cultural position in modern Indian pedagogy. The change of teaching arrangements in the English-speaking school (nonetheless with Indian students and staff) comes as a brutal blow to many. The school principal, showing 'consideration for her advancing years and failing health', replaces Miss Stoneham with a new young teacher, 'the only one with a special degree in teaching English literature class', who is promoted above more senior teachers to head the department of English, and delegated the plum job of teaching Shakespeare to the senior years. Her colleagues are shocked by the unprecedented 'drastic changes' in the school, and one teacher who is young enough to have career prospects decides to emigrate to Canada. Miss Stoneham is the main casualty of the teaching restructuring in the new 'big brother is watching you' environment where it is said 'walls have ears'. At the same time, no matter how sorry we may feel for her shattered dreams, a similar culturally significant point is being made here to the one in *Shakespeare Wallah*. Although Shakespeare may still 'live on', his works need to be recontextualized, since India has moved on. The director of the film herself asserts that she wanted to show Violet teaching 'very badly... and nobody is interested'.[15] Her teaching through self-absorbed concentration on the poetic, English-language text alone is seen as anachronistic, while the new teacher's emphasis on performance and collaborative involvement by the Indian students, on their feet and active, brings the play alive in a new place and new time for a new generation. She encourages the students to take possession of the play in their own voices and distinctive rhythms and patterns, in ways which Miss Stoneham did not.

The next quotation from *Twelfth Night* holds both comic and tragic effects, as Miss Stoneham passes the schoolroom in which the new teacher is rehearsing the girls in the scene of Malvolio's humiliation: 'OLIVIA: Why, how dost thou, man? what is the matter with thee? / MALVOLIO: Not black in my mind, though yellow in my legs' (3.4.23-4). First, there is a contrast in teaching styles between the valuing of lyrical love poetry which Miss Stoneham had foregrounded (to the manifest boredom of her students), and the comic scene in which the girls perform the Malvolio scene with hilarity. However, we see in Miss Stoneham's face complex emotions as she stops by the open door, registering acute alienation as she stands in an empty corridor, effectively locked outside the room now filled with laughter. She reflects a Malvolio-like pang of humiliation, as if she too has been ridiculed and laughed at. But with diligent professionalism and stoicism, she enters her own new room to teach elementary grammar, admitting 'that grammar is not a very interesting subject, but has to be learned to master the language properly'.

Just as *Twelfth Night* teeters on the edge of comedy shading into tragedy, so too does the film. Painful scenes follow upon each other, with Violet's child-like, institutionalized brother, followed by an equally disconcerting one where Violet witnesses the lovers kissing in her room, yet another death-conscious scene in the old people's home followed by her brother's funeral, and the hurtful betrayal by Nandita and Samaresh, who knowingly keep her away from celebrating their marriage, casually unaware of how much emotional attachment she has invested in them. All that is left to Violet is Sir Toby and her memories, as she hums 'auld lang syne' to herself in her apartment in the semi-darkness.

Another different Shakespearean quotation ends the film, anticipating the very similar end of *Withnail and I* (1987) in which the protagonist in a rain-sodden zoo quotes at length to an indifferent wolf from *Hamlet*'s dispirited 'What a piece of work is a man' speech. Violet walks disconsolately at night through a deserted, windswept road in front of the Victoria Memorial, with the company of only a stray dog trying to scavenge her food parcel. She recites this time from *King Lear* in its conflated textual version, a play which has several clear references to the earlier *Twelfth Night* (reproduced as she speaks the lines):

> Pray, do not mock me:
> I am a very foolish, fond old man,
> Fourscore and upward,
> Not an hour more nor less; and to deal plainly,
> I fear I am not in my perfect mind.
> ...
> Come let's away to prison.
> We two will sing like birds in the cage.
> When thou dost ask me blessing
> I'll kneel down and ask of thee forgiveness,
> So, we'll live, pray, sing, and tell old tales.
> At gilded butterflies, and hear poor rogues
> Talk of court news; and we'll talk with them too,
> Who loses and who wins; who's in, who's out;
> And take upon's the mystery of things,
> As if we were God's spies: and we'll wear out,
> In a wall'd prison, packs and sects of great ones,
> That ebb and flow by the moon.

Even this quotation provides another allusive glance at *Twelfth Night*, drawing attention to an intriguing relationship between the two plays in the second of which Shakespeare quotes himself. In each the fool in motley sings in a spirit of resignation and acceptance: 'For the rain it raineth every day' (5.1.Epilogue refrain). This line is not used in the film, but its spirit poignantly permeates throughout, and especially in the ending to this touching movie. Shakespearean allusion functions unobtrusively but strongly in establishing its overall, emotional ambience which documents the waning of an almost forgotten Anglo-Indian past in the face of a new future.

Symptomatically, although the film is almost entirely in English, the lovers when alone with each other speak Bengali, while outside the apartment, and outside the schoolrooms Hindi masses chant and demonstrate with political slogans. The emotionally liminal and elegiac atmosphere of *Twelfth Night* hints at inevitable transition and change in the whole country, just as the Shakespearean performance context had implied in *Shakespeare Wallah*. Shakespeare can and must adapt or be consigned to the oblivion of history as surely as was the British hegemony in India.

Dil Bole Hadippa!

In *Dil Bole Hadippa!*, roughly translated as *The Heart Says Hurray!*, we see realized an example of the necessary recontextualization of *Twelfth Night* to intervene in political issues facing the subcontinent today. It is a Hindi movie set in the Punjab and made in 2009, directed by Anurag Singh.[16] It is an adaptation of *Twelfth Night* at one remove, mediated through the Hollywood *She's the Man* (2006) directed by Andy Fickman and starring Amanda Bynes, and the official website for the Indian film punningly indicates this, using the catch-phrase 'She's the 11th Man'.[17] Both films were commercially successful at the box office, though less appealing to critical reviewers. The Indian version might be described as displaying second order reception, adapting an adaptation without the audience necessarily knowing of the Shakespearean original. However, in some respects it is arguably closer to Shakespeare's play at points where it parts ways with *She's the Man*, so it looks likely that the makers did consult the play as well. Both are predicated on cross-dressing, and in each a young woman with the skill and desire to play a traditionally male sport disguises as a man in order to participate at the highest level. In *She's the Man* the sport is football (soccer). In *Dil Bole Hadippa!* it could have been one of two national sports, and since women's hockey, this time without the need for disguise, had already offered the vehicle for the inspiring *Chak De! India* (2007), which had covered some of the same issues of sexism and ethnic divisions, then it had to be cricket instead. There are dozens of Indian films set on the cricket field, pre-eminently the incomparable, post-colonially inflected political allegory *Lagaan: Once Upon a Time in India* (2001), and even more movies based on Shakespeare, but this is the only one I know which links the two national obsessions as conflicted legacies of English rule. The settings for the cricket matches alternate between Amritsar in the state of Punjab, a highly significant city in terms of the legacy of the Partition of India, and thirty miles away in Lahore, capital of the Pakistani Punjab, both states in which Hindus and Sikh Muslims continue to live in a state of potentially explosive tension.

The American off-shoot adaptation of *Twelfth Night* is not unprecedented in the teen high school genre, since it was preceded by a cult-status movie, *Just One of the Guys* (1985). The heroine (Terri), using her lookalike brother's clothes, impersonates a man (Terry), in order to get her journalism writing exercises more fairly marked. If this sounds like a call for feminism and equality, it is not entirely so, since the cross-dressing becomes mainly a vehicle for soft porn, locker-room suggestiveness. Furthermore, it turns out that Terri was not unfairly marked because she was a woman but for the quality of her work. *She's the Man* signals much more clearly its indebtedness to Shakespeare's *Twelfth Night*, explicitly in the opening credits and also through the names chosen. Viola switches to Illyria College where her twin brother Sebastian is nominally a student, while he absconds to London with his band. Viola impersonates him in male disguise in order to join the men's soccer team, her room-mate being the predictably desirable Duke Orsino who is captain of the team. Meanwhile, her lab partner, Olivia, becomes infatuated with 'Sebastian', who has been charged by Duke to be a go-between, as in the play. Viola does eventually make the team, much to the chagrin of the killjoy coach Dinklage, who finds 'him' effeminate. Your guess is as good as mine why he is called that, but his role may mirror Malvolio's with his hatred of others enjoying themselves. In *She's the Man* Malvolio appears also as a pet tarantula, and his most famous pronouncement finds its way into the movie but without irony: 'Some are born great'. Due to a prior, complicated family arrangement, Viola is forced to impersonate both Sebastian and his twin sister Viola almost simultaneously at a school fair, so that their mother will not know of her children's aberrant life-choices. At a kissing booth Duke Orsino is impressed by the twin sister of his apparently male room-mate, and meanwhile Olivia is seen by the jealous Duke kissing the 'real Sebastian', who has turned up unexpectedly. The resulting mistaken identities leading to violence and jealousy resemble those in *The Comedy of Errors*, showing indirectly that Shakespeare often borrows from himself. All is eventually sorted out on the soccer field by the dramatic revelation that one Sebastian has a penis and the other has breasts. An onlooker comments on the surprising amount of 'nudity' in the game. Since Illyria College officially does not discriminate on grounds of gender, Viola is allowed to finish the game, no longer needing to conceal her gender, and of course kicks the winning goal. They all end up with what – or who – they want, although as in *Twelfth Night* with its multiple ironies, all is not quite as it seems. Olivia ends up with Sebastian even though she fancied 'Sebastian' (Cesario), and Duke Orsino with only a future simulacrum than a present reality:

> Cesario, come –
> For so you shall be while you are a man,
> But when in other habits you are seen,
> Orsino's mistress, and his fancy's queen.
>
> (5.1.359–65)

In the movie, Viola becomes his 'fancy's queen' in a splendid dress at the ball, much to her mother's relief. As an adaptation of *Twelfth Night*, *She's the Man* no doubt was intended primarily to exploit the play's popularity in American college syllabuses and to lure students to the movie. Attention to the play-source is fixed on the level of plot, names and roles of characters, and on the titillation of handling gender differences in normally single-sex environments such as the male dressing room. Only a mild social critique based on equal rights emerges in favour of non-discriminatory sports policies. As a recontextualization, *She's the Man* is entertaining but hardly a vehicle for challenging attitudes, since the central issue of sexual attraction unreservedly reinforces Hollywood stereotypes of gender roles and consolidates the normativeness of heterosexual relationships. Almost absent are Shakespeare's elegiac tones struck by Feste, and his edgier questioning of the boundaries between sex as biological fact and gender as social construction: 'What I am, and what I would, are as secret as maidenhead' (1.5.176).

In *Dil Bole Hadippa!*, the plot of *Twelfth Night* is once again played out on the sporting field, but here the issues are much weightier. For the heroine, these include a place in an all-male, representative Indian cricketing team playing an 'Aman (Peace) Cup' match against traditional rivals Pakistan, alternating between grounds in Amritsar and Lahore. For the viewer, the movie deals with a set of very ambitious themes, encompassing women's rights, gender stereotypes, equality, ethnicity, nationalism, and even freedom of religion. I will not take time summarizing the complicated plot, since anybody who knows either *She's the Man* or *Twelfth Night*, will find it perfectly predictable. But the crucial change here, from both Shakespeare's play and *She's the Man*, is that there is no convenient twin brother, and Veera must present herself as a man, Veer Pratap Singh, in order to be chosen for an Indian cricket team. This may reveal another point at which the Indian film is closer to the spirit of Shakespeare than the Hollywood product, since Viola believes her brother to be dead and presents herself as a different character, Cesario – 'I am all the daughters of my father's house, /And all the brothers too – and yet I know not' (2.4.116–17) – unlike in *She's the Man* when she knows her brother Sebastian is alive.

In this deliberately inclusive movie, Veera Kaur (Rani Mukerji) embodies multiple personae even before she disguises as a man. She works as a professional dancer in a *nautanki*, a travelling folk dance theatre company,[18] which supplies a theatrical context in which nothing is as it seems and where disguising, role-playing, singing, dancing and overt fictiveness rule, as in the kind of *theatrum mundi* to follow. The musicality and romantic tones of Bollywood movies are established primarily in this part of the plot. She is also 'Buffalo Girl' who, despite her aggressively tomboy 'clumsy and unkempt behaviour', assertively personifies a rural, agricultural and proudly traditional Indian way of life based on local village community. On the cattle-drawn theatre truck, she first meets, inauspiciously, her Orsino equivalent, Rohan Singh (Shahid Kapoor), who turns out to be a professional cricketer playing for a county in England and living in London with his divorced mother. His initial love-interest, the Olivia equivalent, is a vain and shallow westernized woman, Soniya the glamorous Miss Chandigarh 2008 (Sherlyn Chopra), who doesn't really love Rohan but sees him, as he does her, as a status symbol. He is lured back to India after being emotionally blackmailed and manipulated by his father who tells one of the film's various 'lies' and is persuaded to captain the perennially losing 'Indian Tigers' cricket team.

Veera's second persona is as an emergency stand-in dancer in the company, for which she must appear either in a woman's role or a man's, depending on staging necessity in emergencies. This androgynous, theatrical role-playing gives her the idea about how to pursue her real passion as a 'left-hand, right-hand batsman'. Driven by her skill as a cricketer but disallowed to play because of her gender in an openly sexist society, Veera disguises herself with turban, moustache and beard as a Sikh, Veer Pratat Singh. Looking in the mirror s/he observes, 'Now it's my game, and your face'. Harris, in concentrating on the 'gender mingling' in the movie, puckishly suggests that the accoutrement of a bat acts as a phallic symbol denoting the exclusively sexist world against which the transgressing, transvestite actress is rebelling.[19] Thus disguised, and acting with an infectious, liberated vivacity, Veera as Veer finally breaks into the Tigers team on sheer merit and, of course, even with a broken arm and batting left-handed, she wins not only the crucial game played in the Ghadaffi Stadium in Lahore against the all-conquering Pakistan Champs with her extraordinary and significantly ambidextrous batting and bowling, but also the love of her grumpy captain, Rohan Singh.

There are complications, of course, since the course of true love never runs smooth in a Shakespearean romantic comedy. As in *She's the Man*, comic moments are caused by her gender difference in a male dressing room, and by having to learn 'man to man talk' with the man she loves, as does Cesario with Orsino, and to tolerate male camaraderie in the team. There are one or two exchanges that indirectly invoke *Twelfth Night*: for example, drawing attention to her moustache and beard she muses, 'Between me and a cricketer this is the only difference', comparable with the banter about Viola's beardlessness in Feste's sarcastic comment, 'Now Jove, in his next commodity of hair, send thee a beard!' (3.1.38). Veera is entrapped by circumstances as surely is Viola, finding herself accidentally accused of sexual harassment by Soniya. She is then compromised when Rohan sees her *in propria persona* as a woman in the shower, upon which she must 'impersonate' herself as Veer's sister, with whom Rohan promptly falls in love. From then on, she feels the kind of sexual frisson but inability to express her love that confronts Viola in *Twelfth Night*, forced to speak of herself as the woman who 'never told her love'. The burgeoning love is one aspect of the film's larger theme of unification, since it represents a breaking down of barriers between the humble Hindu nationalist and the privileged, London-based expatriate. As one of the film's songs declares, 'in this land love is the only god'.

The big match is in Lahore, announcements are made in Urdu, another unifying factor since, derived from Hindustani and Arabic, it is also the national language of Pakistan. By now, Rohan's mother has come from London to join her son, and a reconciliation with his father looms. On the field in the middle of the game, Veera inadvertently reveals her deception through the tiniest revelation, as Rohan finds her tinted contact lens which had changed the colour of her eyes as part of her disguise. Creaky as this device seems, the emphasis on the eyes and 'seeing' constitutes the *anagnorisis* or recognition scene in *Twelfth Night*, 'A natural perspective, that is and is not!' (5.1.201). The immediate result is not yet a resolution but a darker complication, as Rohan's extreme anger that follows the revelation is based on a sense of 'betrayal'. He accuses Veer/Veera of tricking him through a lie, and refuses to let her take her place as opening batsman. His violent words recall Orsino's excessively bitter invective against Cesario when he discovers that Olivia seems sexually involved with his own, apparently male messenger:

> Why should I not—had I the heart to do it—
> Like to th'Egyptian thief at point of death,
> Kill what I love—a savage jealousy
> That sometimes savours nobly?
>
> (5.1.106–9)

Since the Olivia figure has by now been discarded by Rohan, his Orsino-like rage is directed solely at Veera's lying about her identity. However, this aspersion on her duplicity is conveniently parried with the adage that 'A lie is wiped out by the truth', and after his team loses nine wickets for few runs, he allows her to resume her role. Rohan literally unmasks Veer to the onlookers in a very public way, but eventually, forgiveness and reconciliation predictably make all well and bring on a hard-won happy ending through the agency of Veera. Initially the spectators are not happy to find they have been 'duped' by a disguised woman, but Veera silences their hostility with a heartfelt speech advocating equality and condemning injustice. In a stirring speech she points out that there is no girls' team in her village, and that her inability to play cricket is the result of discrimination and patriarchalism, a set of social problems which have denied fulfillment to most women apart from some role models she mentions, such as Indira Gandhi. She points out that it is society which has forced her to disguise, as the only way to realize her legitimate dreams.

Some of the larger significances of the fable are clear even from this brief description. Fulfilling dreams is a running theme, as is the use of disguise and role-playing to achieve the desired end, and so is the consistent advocacy for equality based on talent and skills between men and women, while denying opportunity to women, which has made Veera's position as frustrating as Viola's, 'like patience on a monument' (2.4.110), unable to reveal her secret even while living out her dream.

These associations acquire not only personal but much more ambitious international and religious associations towards the end. The game between the Indian Tigers and Pakistan Champs signifies a final reconciliation to conflicts and tensions relating to the enemy nation-states. Cricket is presented as a unifying force, regularly bringing together Rohan's father and his Pakistani equivalent, as longstanding friends for whom mutual interest in the game is explicitly designed to erase differences: 'the idea is to wipe out differences, whether it is across borders or across chairs' as one of them puts it. The final scene shows Indian and Pakistani cricketers happily fraternising and mingling their respective flags. It also reconciles Rohan's estranged mother and father into a reunited family unit, in the spirit of Shakespeare's early *The Comedy of Errors* and his late romances like *The Winter's Tale* and *Pericles*. Indian nationalism itself is played out in the triangle of Rohan's family representing paternal tradition in the face of the maternal need to change. Indian nationalistic chants are repeated several times and as 'Buffalo Girl' Veera has derided the Anglo-Indian Rohan as living his own kind of lie. However, set against uncompromising traditionalism, also repeated is the phrase 'Times must change', and Veera's actions and final speech provide a catalyst for more fundamental social and political changes towards gender and class equality. Even a plea for religious tolerance is repeatedly invoked in the refrain, 'There is only one god. His name is truth'. In a metatextual sense, the relationship between the Indian film's Hollywood analogue, *She's the Man*, provides a cameo meeting place of the two major international movie traditions. Drawing together all the different threads and representing diversity and potential conflict, is a vision of unifying multiple differences and divisions between ancient and unresolved tensions. Even the ambidexterity of Veer, able to bowl and bat with left and right hand, is as meaningful as her disguise, while her capacity to imagine life from different points of view, depending on her different assumed identities, gives a direction for others to accept change. This is one of the deeper lessons taught by Shakespearean drama. Veera's inspirational speech is directed at the film's audience as much as the assembled populace, arguing passionately for equal rights for men and women even beyond the cricket field in modern India, since otherwise women's talents are wasted. This message carries the day with acclamation, Miss Chandigarh falls by the wayside as an outdated stereotype, Veer and Veera are elided as equal in gender terms and she may now live with a unitary, integrated personhood, and Rohan and Veera can be married on the woman's terms.

Differences may lie in English and Indian cultures; gender prejudices between men and women in an unequal society; between personal identities that may drive an individual towards different destinies, represented in the different personae adopted by Veera; in national rivalries on the sporting field; between Pakistan and India; and between different religious beliefs even if under all there can be conceded to be one 'truth'. At a metaphorical level, there is reference to uniting even day and night as part of the same natural cycle.

Dil Bole Hadippa! makes *Twelfth Night* do a lot of work to achieve these ambitious ends. If not dismissed as light entertainment or as merely derivative from *She's the Man*, the film can be claimed to offer a more general reading of the play. The predicaments faced by both Viola and Veera are created not by the disguise, but by a world in which, so long as conflicts, prejudices and unnecessary animosities prevail, prevent the disguise and false expectations to be shed, and for people simply to be themselves. In this sense Veera's disguise is a symptom of the multiple ways in which society splits people into different identities in order to cope, as in Brecht's use of the same device in *The Good Person of Szechwan*. Once the external divisions are removed, prejudices discarded, and interpersonal problems resolved, then individuals may be liberated from their constrictions within conventions of gender, class, nation-states, and religion, and can fulfil their personal destinies in 'Aman'.

It is partly in the very act of translation, adaptation, and recontextualization that the cycle depicted in Shakespeare's play of disguise, difference, love and reconciliation can be allowed repeatedly to play itself out for different age-range audiences, in contexts as diverse as an ageing English teacher in Calcutta facing a bleakly lonely future in modern India, soccer in an American college in *She's the Man*, and Indian and Pakistani cricketing fervour in *Dil Bole Hadippa!*. Especially significant is the fact that *Twelfth Night* has led to such wildly different movies as the ones analysed here, surely giving proof to the play's subtitle, *Or What You Will*. Like Whitman, *Twelfth Night* contains multitudes, which is surely one of the many reasons Shakespeare is still being performed around the world in multiple adaptations, both direct and allusive, over 400 years after his death.

Notes

1 As recorded by Koel Chatterjee and Thea Buckley, 'Shakespeare Films in Indian Cinemas: An Annotated Filmography', in *Shakespeare and Indian Cinemas: 'Local Habitations'*, ed. Poonam Trivedi and Paromita Chakravarti (New York and

London: Routledge, 2019), pp. 319–32. In the same volume, see Amrita Sen, 'Indianising *The Comedy of Errors*: *Bhranti Bilash* and its Aftermath', pp. 251–67.

2 Accessed 14 March 2019: https://www.youtube.com/watch?v=B3G9gfeaccY and https://www.youtube.com/watch?v=okJTPVr3bUI. For the translation from Tamil I am grateful to Arani Ilankuberan (through Thea Buckley), who suggests it is related to a traditional folk song.

3 Accessed 14 March 2019: https://www.thehindu.com/todays-paper/tp-features/tp-cinemaplus/kanniyin-kaadhali-1949/article3021024.ece.

4 From *The Indian Express*, 6 August 1949.

5 https://www.youtube.com/watch?v=Vy61PAn4uhk.

6 Jonathan Gil Harris, *Masala Shakespeare: How a Firangi Writer Became Indian* (New Delhi: Aleph, 2018), p. 133.

7 For example, reviews by Harish Trivedi, *LSE*, South Asian Centre, 18 October 2019, and Poonam Trivedi in *The Book Review Literary Trust*, 14 June 2020.

8 Accessed February, 2019: https://www.youtube.com/watch?v=HJ5J2q0FcS0.

9 'Interview with Aparna Sen by Paromita Chakravarti', in *Shakespeare and Indian Cinemas* (above), p. 306.

10 Paromita Chakravarti, 'Cinematic *Lear*s and Bengaliness: Locus, Identity, Language', in Trivedi and Chakravarti, *Shakespeare and Indian Cinemas* (above), p. 164.

11 Barbara Everett, 'Or What You Will', *Essays in Criticism* 35 (1985), 294–314, at 297.

12 'The Case for Global Film', 27 August 2008, accessed 15 March 2019: https://itpworld.wordpress.com/2008/08/27/36-chowringhee-lane-india-1981/.

13 References are to the New Cambridge Shakespeare edition of *Twelfth Night*, ed. Elizabeth Story Donno (Cambridge: Cambridge University Press, 1985). However, where the quotation is in a movie, it is transcribed verbatim.

14 Movie review by Ushasri for *Incredible Women of India* at https://incrediblewomenofindia.wordpress.com/2017/05/12/movie-review-36-chowringhee-lane/.

15 'Interview with Aparna Sen' (above), p. 306.
16 Another Hindi film, *Veer-Zaara* had appeared in 2004 and there seem to be links of personnel (Aditya Chopra, Producer) and some curious details which seem to be deliberate quotes in *Dil Bole Hadippa!*, as well as the same name for the central character and a love that transcends the war between India and Pakistan. However, it is far more tragic in tone and in some ways is more indebted to *Romeo and Juliet*.
17 'Yash Raj Films', https://www.yashrajfilms.com/movies/dil-bole-hadippa, accessed 17 October 2018.
18 Harris, 'Masala Shakespeare', pp. 138–9, points out that in this form men often play women and women men.
19 Harris, 'Masala Shakespeare', pp. 136–7.

Films Cited

36 Chowringhee Lane (1981). Dir. Aparna Sen, perf. Jennifer Kendal. Film-Valas.

Chak De! India (2007). Dir. Shimit Amin, perf. Shah Ruk Khan. Yash Raj Films.

Dil Bole Hadippa! (2009). Dir. Anurag Singh, perf. Shahid Kapoor, Rani Mukerji. Yash Raj Films.

Just One of the Guys (1985). Dir. Lisa Gottlieb, perf. Joyce Hyser. Sony Movie Channel.

Kanniyin Kaadhali ('The Maiden's Lover') (1949). Dir. K. Ramnoth, perf. Anjali Devi, Madhuri Devi. Jupiter Films.

Lagaan: Once Upon a Time in India (2001). Dir. Ashutosh Gowariker, perf. Aamir Khan, Paul Blackthorne. Aamir Khan Productions.

Shakespeare Wallah (1965). Dir. James Ivory, perf. Shashi Kapoor, Felicity Kendal, Geoffrey Kendal. Merchant Ivory Productions.

She's the Man (2006). Dir. Andy Fickman, perf. Amanda Bynes. Dreamworks.

Veer-Zaara (2004). Dir. Yash Chopra, perf. Shah Rukh Khan, Preity Zinta. Yash Raj Films.

References

Chatterjee, Koel, and Thea Buckley. 'Shakespeare Films in Indian Cinemas: An Annotated Filmography', in *Shakespeare and Indian Cinemas*, ed. Poonam Trivedi and Paromita Chakravarti. New York and London: Routledge, 2019, 319–32.

Dionne, Craig, and Parmita Kapadia (eds.). *Bollywood Shakespeares* New York: Palgrave Macmillan, 2014.

Everett, Barbara. 'Or What You Will', *Essays in Criticism* 35 (1985), 294–314.

Harris, Jonathan Gil. *Masala Shakespeare: How a Firangi Writer Became Indian*. New Delhi: Aleph, 2018.

Leonard, Kendra Preston. 'The Sounds of India in Supple's *Twelfth Night*', in Dionne and Kapadia, *Bollywood Shakespeares*, 147–64, 148.

Piallai, Swarnavel Eswaran. *Madras Studios: Narrative, Genre, and Ideology*. New Delhi: Sage Publications, 2015.

Sen, Amrita. 'Indianising *The Comedy of Errors*: *Bhranti Bilash* and its Aftermath', in Trivedi and Chakravarti, *Shakespeare and Indian Cinemas*, pp. 251–67.

Shakespeare, William. *Twelfth Night*, ed. Elizabeth Story Donno. Cambridge: Cambridge University Press, 1985.

Trivedi, Poonam. and Paromita Chakravarti (eds.). *Shakespeare and Indian Cinemas: 'Local Habitations'*. New York and London: Routledge, 2019.

Yadav, Dr Mukesh. 'Domesticating Shakespeare: A Study of Indian Adaptation of Shakespeare in Popular Culture', *European Journal of English Language and Literature* 2 (2014), 48–58.

3

'For never was a story of more woe': Dialogic Telling and Global Interchange in *Qayamat se Qayamat Tak*, a 'Bollywood' Film Adaptation of *Romeo and Juliet*

Mark Thornton Burnett

To all intents and purposes, *Qayamat se Qayamat Tak* (dir. Mansoor Khan, 1988), a film adaptation of *Romeo and Juliet*, is an archetypal 'Bollywood' product. It displays many of the hallmarks of the genre, which, according to Claus Tieber, extend to an epic structure, the ways in which narrative information is transmitted, the interlacing of several stories, distinctive characterization and intertextuality (Tieber 2012, 11–24). In this discussion, however, I concentrate not so much on the 'Indianness' of the film as its points of global contact with other *Romeo and Juliet* film narratives. In particular, I suggest that the film's mediation of Shakespearean language, the purposeful utilization of song and the representation of character types reverberate with a related grouping of contemporary adaptations of the play (from Africa, Brazil, Canada, Denmark, Egypt and Greece respectively). In terms of its modes of telling, *Qayamat se Qayamat Tak* repurposes issues of location for critical effect, responds to textual lacunae via narrative amplification, makes an interrogative intervention in generational debate, and references a mélange of associations to energize Shakespeare's play for a popular audience. In so doing, it enters a dialogue with a host of affined – world – *Romeo and Juliet* films in which a generation-specific deployment of Shakespeare serves cultural and ideological ends. 'Bollywood' is thus held up for scrutiny as an interpretive category, the emphasis falling instead on *Qayamat se Qayamat Tak*'s strikingly contiguous acts of imagining and the ways in which it brokers a partnership with concerns and questions beyond its own borders.

In a classic study of travel, James Clifford observes that 'centres ... regions and territories ... are sustained through ... contacts' and that 'practices of crossing and interaction' trouble 'the localism of many common assumptions about culture' (Clifford 1997, 3). His comments prompt us to think about cultural texts and products not so much at the level of their local frames of reference but, rather, their participation in global interchange. Adaptation is particularly pertinent here. According to Cristina Della Coletta, adaptation 'points in multiple directions and engages different voices in synergistic and transformative tension' (Della Coletta 2012, 5). Or, to put the point another way, in the work of adaptation there is invariably movement that foregrounds a range of registers, ideologies and geographies. Cinema, *par excellence*, brings these practices and characteristics into play. For, as mobility theorist Giuliana Bruno reminds us, 'motion pictures', by definition and method, constitute a 'moving, haptic space'

(Bruno 2007, 172). 'Bollywood' cinema can be said precisely to occupy such a 'space'. Far from presenting itself as a hermetically sealed category, 'Bollywood' cinema is abundantly alive to interconnections. Rajinder Dudrah sees 'Bollywood' as a 'blend and polygot of a number of other cultural sources', so much so that it is continually 'in dialogue with processes of globalisation' (Dudrah 2012. 3). In fact, as part of a recent discussion about how the work of Shakespearean adaptation might be newly theorized, Douglas Lanier introduces a not dissimilar dialogic concept – what he terms 'the Shakespearean rhizome'. By attending to rhizomatic relations, he suggests, we can the better understand the 'mutability . . . between otherwise unconnected elements' and appreciate links 'between "Shakespeare" and realms of culture hitherto distinct from it' such as 'Shakespeare in other languages' (Lanier 2014, 28, 35). This chapter pursues the 'Shakespearean rhizome' and reads *Qayamat se Qayamat Tak* both as an adaptation that is fundamentally dialogic in nature and as a cinematic statement that encourages reflection on 'global' Shakespeare – its features, applications and possibilities.

Romeo and Juliet, of course, centres on an 'ancient grudge' (Prologue, 3) with seemingly no cause. The 'grudge' is just that, no explanation for its origin being provided. Claus Tieber notes that Hindi cinema invariably tells 'the whole backstory of the protagonists', a filmic 'convention' (Tieber 2012, 15), and his observation holds true for *Qayamat se Qayamat Tak* in which, at the start, two families are presented as locked in irresolvable conflict. Ratan Singh, son of a wealthy landowner, is engaged to be married, but the abandoned Madhu Singh, from another wealthy family with the same name, is pregnant with his child. At the wedding, after Madhu has taken her own life in desperation, Ratan is shot dead by Madhu's enraged brother, Dhanraj, who takes upon himself the revenger role. The opening excursus thus introduces many of the film's priorities – the place of *dharma* or duty, the pressures of social convention, the effects of gendered marginalization, and the doubling of the *Romeo and Juliet* narrative (Madhu's suicide recapitulates the ending of Shakespeare's play in miniature). The feud, in addition, impels subsequent action. Dhanraj/Old Montague experiences flashbacks to the fatal day, while his son, Raj/Romeo, exclaims, '[we] are not prepared to become the heirs of ... hatred', his insistence on a new dispensation setting him apart from the continuation of animosity. Its deployment of markers of 'Bollywood' notwithstanding, *Qayamat se Qayamat Tak* operates here in concert with related filmic adaptations of Shakespeare's play which show a predilection for rooting – and thus hypothesizing – the infamous conflict in a carefully rendered set of circumstances. World cinema adaptations of *Romeo and Juliet* make a virtue of and, indeed, owe their impetus to a lack in the Shakespearean source. Hence, the Egyptian adaptation, *Hobak Nair/Loving You is Hard* (dir. Ihab Radhi, 2004), set in contemporary Alexandria, includes, well into the story proper, a flashback in which an angry knifing during a card game precipitates a breakdown in relations between the Assas/Capulet and Zainaty/Montague families. It is this seminal episode, the film suggests, that moulds Assas/Capulet and Zainaty/Montague as particularly inflexible species of patriarch. Similarly, the Burkinabé Shakespearean adaptation, *Julie et Roméo* (dir. Boubakar Diallo, 2011), reveals how, years previous to the main action, the theft of some eggs followed by an accidental killing places the families of the lovers, Julie/Juliet and Roméo/Romeo, at odds in such a way that, should further fraternization take place, ancestral retribution will ensue. All three films, then, find in *Romeo and Juliet* excuses for extension. They commence by looking not so much forwards as backwards, embedding stories-within-stories, and mixing and matching concepts of lineal time, in a fashion that bespeaks interconnected interpretive strategies.

To reimagine the play's ancient grudge is also to reimagine its central players. A recurring identifier of *Romeo and Juliet* in the global imaginary is a norm-breaking Juliet, an agitator for self-assertion and self-expression. Exemplary in this respect is *Hobak Nair* in which Salma/Juliet, in a play with gendered expectation, and echoing the conventions of the all-male Shakespearean stage, first appears in a crash-helmet and full motorbike leathers. It is only when she takes off her helmet that her identity as a woman is clarified. Playing with ideas of empowerment, the scene discovers Salma/Juliet as the superior 'engineer' (she is able to fix Karim/Romeo's rickety car) and as possessed of the greater mobility (she zooms off on her motorbike once the job is done). Mobile in a different way is Julie/Juliet in *Julie et Roméo*. Having been magically transported back in time to avert the death of her fiancé, Julie arrives precisely at the inception of the 'ancient grudge'. Intervening so as to prevent the incident that catalyses the family quarrel and Roméo's death, Julie is imagined not only as conflating gendered binaries (the villagers' 'Amazone' designation is indicative) but also as assuming the abilities and powers of a 'witch' (she embodies and internalizes thereby crucial aspects of her African heritage). Indeed, inversion is pointed up in the very title of the film; Shakespeare's romantic hero is placed second in the title order, with Julie first, the primary position suggesting both a gendered reorientation and the character's intervention in the workings of time.

In an insightful discussion of *Qayamat se Qayamat Tak*, Koel Chatterjee rightly points out that Rashmi/Juliet 'actively pursues ... forthright behaviour' (Chatterjee 2019, 98): to this one might add that the character's youthful impulses and energies are of a piece with a broader, and more global, cinematic figuration of Shakespeare's heroine. Crucially, Rashmi/Juliet is glimpsed, first, from Raj/Romeo's point of view riding a horse, but the camera's more general panning over her yellow, red and green patterned (modern) dress declares her an icon of independence. Although she claims she is prevented from occupying a speaking position – 'I can't open my mouth in front of my father' – she makes up for any vocal inhibition in her representational expressiveness. At the Mount Abu hill-station/resort, Rashmi/Juliet photographs her natural environment, including the figure of Raj/Romeo against the setting sun, functioning as a producer of her own space, an artist creating images according to her own purposes. At once, Rashmi's artistry indexes Juliet's line about cutting Romeo 'out in little stars' to 'make the face of heaven so fine' (3.2.22–3), a process akin to immortalization. In another way, Rashmi/Juliet as photographer upsets the gendered norms which define her in a familial setting. Outside the restaurant, she creeps up unawares on Raj/Romeo, photographing him when he turns around. The resulting image both reveals his shocked expression and, because he has thrown a blanket around his head to disguise his identity, suggests his transformation into a shawl-wearing woman: through her craft, Rashmi/Juliet exercises agency. As creator and transformer, Rashmi/Juliet is discursively akin to a host of later cinematic counterparts.

As a film directed at a youth audience, *Qayamat se Qayamat Tak* is distinctive for realizing Rashmi/Juliet and Raj/Romeo in terms of a college setting. Both are discovered as, in complementary ways, wedded to education, to the efficacy of learning and hard work as routes to personal/professional success. As indicator of his subscription to his college's values, Raj/Romeo mounts a 'musical programme' in his final year: the episode both recasts the poetic bent of Shakespeare's Romeo and signals Raj's winning credentials (the walls of the hall are decorated with plaques and medals). Later in the play, when Raj/Romeo and Rashmi/Juliet attempt to escape from an angry Randhir/Old Capulet, they take refuge in the college library. This episode serves to distinguish the moral compass of the two generations via their relation to art and the book: Rashmi/Juliet and Raj/Romeo are empathetically at home among the library's galleries and shelves, while Randhir/Old Capulet is lost in an environment that suggests his philistinism. In such a setting, Randhir/Old Capulet can be quickly outwitted.

Discovering Romeo and Juliet characters through a relation to the book – or the arts more generally – is a recurring trope in world cinema adaptations. In *Era Uma Vez/Once Upon a Time* (dir. Breno Silveira, 2008), a Brazilian adaptation, Dé/Romeo and Nina/Juliet both possess a copy of Zuenir Ventura's 1994 volume, *Cidade Partida*, a classic journalistic study of

Rio de Janeiro as a divided society; indeed, the two bond over their admiration for the work. Cinema is the common denominator binding Salma/Juliet and Karim/Romeo in *Hobak Nair* as when they are represented watching the US-Argentine arthouse film, *Naked Tango* (dir. Leonard Schrader, 1991), together: the film's theme of attempting to escape social and cultural restrictions by assuming a new identity reflects back on the couple's predicament. Word and image combine in several adaptations to illustrate a shared mindset. The South African film, *uGugu no Andile/Gugu and Andile* (dir. Minky Schlesinger, 2008), shows Gugu/Juliet as a high school student being introduced, in class, to Shakespeare's *Romeo and Juliet*. In interrelated scenes, she both answers precisely a question about the 'pilgrims' hands' (1.5.99) exchange and sheds a tear at her teacher's delivery of Escalus' 'Some shall be pardon'd, and some punished' address (5.3.308): such moments establish her sensitivity and receptivity, her capability for seeing Shakespearean relevancies in her own situation (a divided township and conflict zone).

Similarly engaged with his environment in this film is photojournalist Andile/Romeo; for him, the camera (bringing Rashmi/Juliet and *Qayamat se Qayamat Tak* to mind) serves as an instrument with which he records political violence, and, at the end of the film, his incriminating photographs, it is suggested, clear the way for accountability and exposure: art meets a reparative agenda. Whether as students studying culture, or protagonists who are culturally attuned, *Romeo and Juliet* adaptations in world cinema imagine the young lovers as responsive and reformative at one and the same time, invested in social agendas and ready to subject them to critique.

The classroom episode in *uGugu no Andile* also illuminates the extent to which cinematic adaptations of the play self-consciously meditate on their Shakespearean inspiration. More specifically, a shared tendency is to indicate an alliance with *Romeo and Juliet* via quotation. Several adaptations cite, either as part of the dialogue or as on-screen announcements, Juliet's 'What's in a name' address (2.2.43), the effect of which is to bring into the open issues around marginalization, debates about ethnic difference and lost opportunities.¹ Extended speeches are also instanced. Hence, in the Montreal-set adaptation, *Roméo et Juliette* (dir. Yves Desgagnés, 2006), Laurence/Friar Laurence states in voiceover, 'For never was a story of more woe / Than this of Juliet and her Romeo' (5.3.309-10). As the camera tracks her figure to the end of a jetty, we realize that the scenic emphasis is on private consolation rather than public grief. Escalus' address is referenced in a more directly visible fashion in the Danish adaptation, *Rami og Julie* (dir. Eric Klausen, 1988), which centres on the relationship between Julie/Juliet, a young Danish woman, and Rami/Romeo, a Palestinian *émigré*. At the close, a juxtaposed Danish-Arabic translation of Escalus' speech is superimposed on a backlit image of Julie/Juliet contemplating her lover's demise, with the columns of different national languages pointing up the impossibility of movement across cultural divides. Or adaptations might simply gesture to notions of Shakespeare's language, utilising quasi-Shakespearean speech in echoing conjurations. Before the exile sequence, Salma in *Hobak Nair* reflects, 'Which Karim would I stand by? My love whom I have chosen amongst all people, or my enemy who killed my cousin?', her retrospective dilemma suggesting Juliet's observation, 'My only love sprung from my only hate! . . . I must love a loathed enemy' (1.5.138, 141), but only in a suggestively allusive way. Across the range of *Romeo and Juliet* adaptations, there is a multiplicity of strategies for indicating a Shakespearean (linguistic) connection.

These adaptations lead back to *Qayamat se Qayamat Tak*. Douglas Lanier reminds us that adaptation is as much about the relation between the text and a particular film (for example) as it is about engaging with a 'more inchoate and complex web of intervening adaptations [and] . . . protocols', a 'web' of 'forces and productions that . . . lay claim to the label "Shakespearean" but that has long exceeded the canon of plays and poems' (Lanier 2014, 23, 27). While clearly in dialogue with other global film adaptations of *Romeo and*

Juliet, *Qayamat se Qayamat Tak* would seem to fit this description. The film was not billed as an adaptation of the play *per se* (the connection emerges in part in the sphere of its reception) and approximates rather than translates Shakespearean language; in this sense, it caters to a category of the 'Shakespearean' and aims at expressions that consort with, but do not reproduce, the play's formality and rhetoric. Hence, Rashmi's portentous line, 'Fate has put us together in this way', may recall Juliet's similarly imagined sentiment, 'I have an ill-divining soul' (3.5.54), while Raj/Romeo's conviction, 'the setting sun will one day make us meet together', could summon Juliet's injunction that 'fiery-footed steeds' gallop towards 'Phoebus' lodging' (3.2.1-2).[2] And, even if the language is not approximated, the infamous line, 'What's in a name?' (2.2.43), may lurk behind the play with names in the scene where Raj/Romeo is confused with the suitor, Roop Singh/Paris, because of the 'R' emblazoned on his fashionable college jumper (a filmic rehearsal of the perils of identity). Koel Chatterjee astutely recognizes that, in referencing destiny, chance and the stars, and in deploying the 'setting sun' motif, *Qayamat se Qayamat Tak* fraternises with and is informed by other intertexts, films such as *Ek Duuje Ke Liye* (dir. K. Balachander, 1981), theatrical productions such as Utpal Dutt's *Bhuli Nai Priya* (1970) and the 'codified vocabulary and imagery of Bollywood' more generally (Chatterjee 2019, 95, 100, 101, 103). Here, I think, is a polyvalent example of Lanier's rhizome thesis, a 'web' that makes visible not only tendencies in adaptation but also past histories, present genres and future interpretive directions. *Qayamat se Qayamat Tak*'s take on Shakespearean language is symptomatic of the ways in which the film is richly traversed by its rhizomatic interface.

'Bollywood' is perhaps most popularly known for its song-and-dance sequences, and *Qayamat se Qayamat Tak* is no exception. One of the film's signature episodes is the musical number, 'Ae Mere Hamsafar'. The whole, with its prelude included, amounts to a meditation on waiting, as indicated in a shot of Raj/Romeo in the office next to his calendar and the ticking on the soundtrack of a clock, its rhythms lending the overlaid song its distinctive beat. Looking forward to the birthday of one of Raj/Romeo's friends, the lovers meet in a department store; properties and location here serve thematic ends, the pots and pans suggesting an idyllic domesticity far from the lovers' experience and the transactions of commerce pointing up the more important business of amatory exchange. Once the song proper commences, fantasy and real-life scenarios blend and blur. On the one hand, at the birthday party, Raj/Romeo and Rashmi/Juliet are prevented from closer communication, the garden's bushes functioning as barriers to contact. On the other hand, in an imagined universe, the lovers, either spectating on each other in the fields or enjoying a romantic dinner, are able to come together, their intimacy being indicated in Rashmi/Juliet's reading of Raj/Romeo's poem and a cross-cut montage that reveals both in rooftop settings. An additional scene that discovers Raj/Romeo looking longingly upwards at Rashmi/Juliet in her bedroom recalls the 'balcony' meeting in the play and firmly entrenches the lovers as Shakespearean archetypes. The accompanying lyrics – 'O my dearest, this is a short period of waiting ... now there is a period of separation: it will only last for a moment' – confirm the number's preoccupation with time's operations, the sequence ending with Rashmi/Juliet ticking off dates on her calendar on her bedroom wall. 'Ae Mere Hamsafar' is thus neatly framed by the place of work and the *domus* and by complementary realizations of the lovers' projections and anticipations.

Gregory Booth notes that music numbers in Hindi films 'provide commentary on the story and regularly contribute plot development' (Booth 2000, 126). He is joined by Lalitha Gopalan who coins the phrase 'cinema of interruption' to capture the ways in which Indian cinemas enlist music and dance in extensions to, and enhancements of, the narrative (Gopalan 2002, 16). Yet, where world *Romeo and Juliet* film adaptations are concerned, song and dance numbers are often a constituent part of the exegesis: 'Bollywood' does not have the musical monopoly. Arguably, the legitimizing imprint of *West Side Story* (dir. Robert Wise and Jerome Robbins, 1961), which carved out a popular cinematic niche for *Romeo and Juliet* as a musical, is a factor here, but so too is the extent to which the dramatic intensity of the play's set-pieces is readily accommodated in other idioms. The generational conflicts animating *Romeo and Juliet* can be reimagined as class antagonisms via song and dance numbers as a Brazilian adaptation such as *Maré, Nossa Historia de Amor/Maré, Another Love Story* (dir. Lúcia Murat, 2008) demonstrates. In an emblematic scene, Jonata/Romeo and Analídia/Juliet and their friends leave their Rio de Janeiro favela for a day by the sea only to find that the more privileged – and bourgeois – holidaymakers abandon the beach in disgust. The episode is the prompt for the film to showcase the rousing pop anthem, 'Minha Alma' ('My Soul') in which the lovers and the company join in a musical arraignment of middle-class blindness; as the lyrics state, 'the condo is for your protection . . . but maybe it's just you in prison'. Particularly forceful are the ways in which the dancers' bodies, draped around the stationary cars or prostrated on the tarmac, connote vitalities ignored and a form of protest. Other adaptations marshal the song insert more radically, using musical numbers to populate and propel a narrative that is almost entirely dialogue-free. Allowing them a handful of lines only, the Canadian film, *Roméo et Juliette*, contrasts the tongue-tied condition of the lovers with expressive songs about the first flush of love. Typical are such lyrics as 'No one's there to save you . . . Welcome to my life', and 'I came to say that I love you', which canvass familiar tropes of inarticulacy, self-absorption and abandonment. Both films intersect with each other in meditating upon Shakespearean preoccupations and conditions, with song and dance extending outwards to bring to the forefront debates around self-expression and social justice. Music is integrally related to the act of Shakespearean reinvention.

Even as we need to recognize the distinctiveness of 'Bollywood' tropes and conventions, therefore, it is also helpful to approach song and dance in a film such as *Qayamat se Qayamat Tak* as dynamically related to a broader network of *Romeo and Juliet* adaptations. More specifically, music and, crucially, movement and song in the film surrogate for what is otherwise missing, making up for moments that the adaptive process elects to leave out or cannot easily translate. It is in such a light that we can read the final song sequence in *Qayamat se Qayamat Tak*, 'Akele Hain To Kya', in which Raj/Romeo and Rashmi/Juliet enjoy a brief respite from the feuding frenzy of their families in an abandoned Shiva temple. As substitute for the lovers' morning greeting (after-consummation) scene, which presents particularized adaptation challenges, the film includes the extended domestic bliss episode of Raj/Romeo and Rashmi/Juliet at home in their mountain retreat. An emphasis on *gestus*, and a pronounced kinetic energy, combine to suggest a space and experience of idyllic togetherness. The upward lift of the flutes and violins acoustically registers the buoyancy and affirmation of the moment, while the marking out of rooms reinforces a sense of joyous reconstruction. In addition, the sacralizing implications of Raj/Romeo's reflection, 'This is really heaven', is then taken up in the *puja* that the lovers inaugurate (complete with gifts of garlands) in order to bless their temple residence. If some elements of the song sequence suggest gendered hierarchies (Rashmi/Juliet unsuccessfully tries to cook, while Raj/Romeo, appropriately shot against the characteristic Shiva trident that adorns the temple, performs manly lifting tasks), other dimensions communicate a jointly shared industrial-recuperative endeavour. For example, Rashmi/Juliet and Raj/Romeo share the burden of carrying poles, join forces to repair the roof, mirror each other in their flying movements and stand together on a dam: such is their combined strength, it is suggested, they can hold the forces of the world at bay. In these sunny, mountain environs, as Raj/Romeo and Rashmi/Juliet sing in harmony of 'desire ... within our grasp', of a 'world' now realized, one finds a rhizomatic development of the play's representation of 'jocund day' (3.5.9), of 'misty mountain tops' (3.5.10) and of the pleasures of 'sweet discourses' (3.5.53). Here, then, and in concert with global adaptive trends, is a multi-layered expression of mutuality and reciprocity, a meditation on Shakespeare that, even if it eschews the implications of a morning greeting, is nevertheless erotically freighted: 'Akele Hain To Kya' includes a controversial kiss.

Yet, if Shakespeare exerts pressure in this scene, so too do a host of other intertexts, contributions to the rhizomatic chain. Earlier in the film, when Rashmi/Juliet and Raj/Romeo find themselves lost in a forest, 'wandering' in the wilderness, the Indian epic, *The Ramayana*, is indexed, not least the wanderings of Rama and his consort, Sita, in exile. The connection with the epics is confirmed both in the 'Ae Mere Hamsafar' sequence in the department store in which Raj/Romeo is shot against a figurine of Arjun in his chariot (in *The Mahabharata*, this warring brother similarly wrestles with questions of *dharma*) and in the topographical reference, later, to the 'hillock of Hanuman' (Hanuman being the monkey-god in *The Ramayana* blessed with magical strength and transformative powers). Particularly at the close, when the lovers enjoy their sojourn in the mountains, the delights, and sacrificial asceticism, of the epics are abundantly in evidence. The rocky location, complete with verdant greenery and a lake, recalls Rama's discovery of a wonderful place to recuperate in *The Ramayana*, a 'perfect spot ... a pond close by ... fragrant lotuses ... [a] river ... [and] mountains', while the temple itself resembles the same epic's description of a 'spacious ... hut ... with a thatched roof supported by pillars, rafters of bamboo and a level floor' (Valmiki 1996, 240, 241). In such a setting, there are also counter-romantic tendencies, interludes of difficulty and deprivation. *The Ramayana* specifically references how Sita has 'given up [her] family and friends, splendour, wealth and adoration' to live in the 'forest' (Valmiki 1996, 225), and the equivalent scene in *Qayamat se Qayamat Tak* occurs when Rashmi/Juliet is represented, unsuccessfully, attempting to cook *rotis* and *brinjal* curry on a primitive stove. Her resplendent red sari, with white stripes and floral detailing, makes for a sharp contrast with her begrimed and dirtied appearance as she tries with comic results to play the domestic goddess, the implication being that Rashmi/Juliet, like Sita, while brought low in her circumstances, is to be applauded in her virtue and devotion to duty. What these modes of dialogic telling (Shakespeare is apprehended through the epics and the epics are apprehended through Shakespeare) suggest is the easy interchange between different cultural registers, the fact that *Romeo and Juliet* can be felicitously merged with, and mediated through, other narratives and mythologies. Enmeshing various sources and traditions, the film agitates to establish how Shakespeare sits happily alongside Indian representations and forms.

While *Romeo and Juliet* speaks here through the voices of the indigene, the play is no less powerfully animated in *Qayamat se Qayamat Tak* via its association with comparable trajectories of interpretation running across Shakespearean adaptations on the global cinematic scene. Aligning Shakespeare and an epic narrative is not a unique manoeuvre. The conceptually arresting Greek film, *Kanenas/Nobody* (dir. Christos Nikoleris, 2010), converts the Capulets and the Montagues into displaced Albanian and Russian youth. Not only is their illegal street racing in downtown Athens an indication of their contention; it also serves to underscore a pervasive condition of mobility. Hence, neither Russian ex-law student, Goran/Romeo, nor Albanian schoolgirl, Julia/Juliet, feel at home in Greece, to the extent that the former reflects, 'Have you ever felt like the wrong person, in the wrong place, at the wrong time?' Discovering Goran/Romeo as ill-at-ease in clearly identifying himself ('I'm nobody', he claims, 'nobody' being a dominant motif in the dialogue), *Kanenas/Nobody* announces its association both with Shakespeare and with Homer's epic, *The Odyssey*. And, when Julia/Juliet reads aloud from *The Odyssey* and sees, in her lover's experience, a modern-day version of Odysseus' trick to outwit the Cyclopes (the Homeric hero claims his name is 'nobody'), the parallel is made explicit.[3] A copy of *The Odyssey* is cradled by Goran/Romeo throughout, functioning as a talismanic object and a signifier of the film's epic subtexts. Both Shakespeare and Homer come together at the close. On the ferry taking them away from Greece, Julia/Juliet again reads aloud from the epic (this time the passage about the wandering heroes pleading for succour and hospitality in their homeward journey), the recourse to Homer suggesting the lovers' predicament as themselves wanderers looking for a 'homeland'.[4] By the same token, both the new name he has acquired (Goran/Romeo is identified as Roman Montegu in his fake passport), and the route the lovers take westwards across the Ionian Sea, suggest that Italy is their destination point, a 'homeland' that holds out the prospect of a European welcome and the appropriately 'original' location for the Shakespearean story.

Placing *Kanenas* and *Qayamat se Qayamat Tak* in juxtaposition helps to contextualize the ways in which adaptations of *Romeo and Juliet* draw upon localized narrative traditions to add lustre and gravitas to individual interpretive decisions. Paramount here is a perceived need to imbue the arc the narrative traces with the appropriate authority. In the Brazilian and favela-set adaptation of *Romeo and Juliet*, *Maré, Nossa História de Amor*, for example, the chorus/prologue is lent credibility and granted pro-active involvement. The 'Nação Maré' rap group substitutes for the Shakespearean choric voice and, interrupting the action at regular intervals, affirms an authenticated perspective on events (the group originates in the *Maré* favela) and, combining an African-American style with Rio de Janeiro slang, asserts the valences of multi-culturalism. *Qayamat se Qayamat Tak* is comparatively invested in honouring the choric function. After the credits, a voiceover informs us of the fate of the families in the wake of murder and suicide (appropriately gravelly tones lend a heightened seriousness), while, at the start, a rhyming Urdu-language poem is delivered again in voiceover. Ananya Jahanara Kabir writes that Urdu is 'the language of North Indian Muslim high culture, revolution, glamour and romance' (Kabir 2009, 140), and all of these associations are held in play as the film commences: the accompanying logo of the production company, Nasir Hussain Films (letters on a plinth, with stormy skies and lighting bolts in the background), confirms the adaptation as an august undertaking, a work in which turmoil and destruction are dominant features. These additional stories-within-stories, or metanarratives that comment on the narrative proper, are in keeping with each adaptation's mode of telling, but they also participate in the interchange that defines how *Romeo and Juliet*, in particular, is brought to the global screen.

In keeping with its subscription to the arc of the Shakespearean story, *Qayamat se Qayamat Tak* ends with the deaths of the 'star-crossed lovers' (Prologue, 6). Echoing the destructive, rather than creative, aspects of Shiva, the final stages discover a fake family reunion in the lovers' rocky hideaway and the accompanying mayhem precipitated by the thugs who have been hired to prise Rashmi/Juliet and Raj/Romeo apart. In an extended sequence, Raj/Romeo and Rashmi/Juliet are shot, the dying Raj/Romeo killing himself with an ornamental dagger, with the final image of the setting sun serving to illustrate the fatal costs of the family feud and the impossibility of reconciliation. The closing exchange reinforces the idea of a union that is prohibited in the mortal world ('Now no one can separate you from me', the dying Rashmi/Juliet states), while the soundtrack and *mise-en-scène* are equally communicative of youthful passions crushed by parental opposition: the rocks serve as a type of crypt, and the slow reprise of 'Papa Kehte' recalls a happier moment of the college romance. The Brazilian adaptation, *Maré, Nossa História de Amor*, also ends with the lovers' deaths (Jonata/Romeo and Analída/Juliet are accidentally killed by a brother and cousin respectively); similarly, in a South African adaptation such as *uGugu no Andile/Gugu and Andile*, Gugu/Juliet and Andile/Romeo are killed by parties from both sides of the conflict. To honour the doom-laden trajectory of *Romeo and Juliet* is, in the global adaptive process, a recurring manoeuvre. Yet not quite. As the example of *Kanenas* suggests, a no less insistent priority is to alter the expected end or to find in it meaning and value. Countering the pull of pessimism are further adaptations (for example, *Hobak Nair* and *Julie et Roméo*) in which the lovers survive and in such a way as to emphasize recuperative instincts, spectacles of mended community and an overcoming of conflicted local contests. Via the discovery of regeneration and purpose in the midst of acrimony and waste, such adaptations shift the linear orientation of the play, take to task the 'ancient grudge' and make visible an alternative course of events.

Interestingly, *Qayamat se Qayamat Tak* is congruent with this interpretive reversal. Koel Chatterjee notes that the film 'was scripted with a happy ending by the screenplay writer Nasir Hussein, Mansoor Khan's father; in fact the formulaic happy ending had been shot when Khan decided to rescript it ... he ... ended up rewriting the entire scene on set' (Chatterjee 2019, 95). One can read the decision in several ways – as a will to seek legitimacy via a Shakespearean connection or as an expression of filial independence from paternal control. In a broader context, however, the two endings of *Qayamat se Qayamat Tak* – one archived, the other in public circulation – make sense inside a theory of adaptation that stresses, as does Douglas Lanier, an idea of 'becoming' rather than 'being', of 'the flux of becoming-different' and of 'the fluidity of ceaseless change' (Lanier 2014, 29). If, according to Lanier, reality is what an adaptation might become, and if, as he argues, a rhizomatic notion of adaptation entails a 'double process' of de-territorialization and re-territorialization (Lanier 2014, 28), then *Qayamat se Qayamat Tak* presents itself as a wonderfully multivalent example. It involves itself in a number of tendencies in terms of how to decipher Shakespearean endings; it gestures to, and moves away from, an ameliorative construction of tragedy; it indexes its own location of production at the same time as it reaches outside of itself to currents in global Shakespearean filmmaking. In this sense, *Qayamat se Qayamat Tak* is perhaps *par excellence* an adaptation of becoming, and that becoming is immersed in, and inseparable from, the film's global interchange and modes of dialogic telling. This is not to suggest that *Qayamat se Qayamat Tak* is somehow or other uncannily prescient; nor is it to imply that it is conscious of its intersections and interconnections. Rather, we might substitute for both Dimitris Eleftheriotis' concept of 'travelling': 'the process of knowledge itself is perceived as a journey, as a gradual progression of a subject towards every increasing knowledge' (Eleftheriotis 2012, 12). *Qayamat se Qayamat Tak* operates in these capacities. Even as it increases knowledge of global Shakespeare, the film progresses onwards to new manifestations of itself and is animated and reconfigured by conversations with adaptations that take us on a journey beyond its immediate horizons.

Notes

1 See, for example, the adaptations, *Go!* (dir. Yukisada Isao, 2001), *Sud Side Stori* (dir. Roberta Torre, 2000) and *A Time to Love* (dir. Jianqi Huo, 2005), from Japan, Italy and China respectively.
2 The film's portentous subtexts are also apprehended in the film's title which translates as 'From the End of the World to the Day of Judgement'.
3 For the relevant passage, see Homer 1995: I, 343, 345, 346, 349.
4 See Homer 1995: I, 335.

References

Booth, G. 'Religion, Gossip, Narrative Conventions and the Construction of Meaning in Hindi Film Songs', *Popular Music* 19.2 (2000): 125–45.

Bruno, G. *Atlas of Emotion: Journeys in Art, Architecture and Film*. New York: Verso, 2007.

Chatterjee, K. '"Where wert thou Muse that thou forget'st so long, / To speak of that which gives thee all thy might?": *Qayamat se Qayamat Tak* (1988) – A Neglected Shakespearean Film', in P. Trivedi ,and P. Chakravarti (eds.), *Shakespeare and Indian*

Cinemas: 'Local Habitations'. London and New York: Routledge, 2019, 93–110.
Clifford, J. *Routes: Travel and Translation in the Late Twentieth Century*. Cambridge, MA and London: Harvard University Press, 1997.
Della Coletta, C. *When Stories Travel: Cross-Cultural Encounters between Fiction and Film*. Baltimore: Johns Hopkins University Press, 2012.
Dudrah, R. *Bollywood Travels: Culture, Diaspora and Border Crossings in Popular Hindi Cinema*. London and New York: Routledge, 2012.
Eleftheriotis, Dimitris. *Cinematic Journeys: Film and Movement*. Edinburgh: Edinburgh University Press, 2012.
Gopalan, L. *Cinema of Interruptions: Action Genres in Contemporary Indian Cinema*. London: BFI, 2002.
Homer. *The Odyssey*, tr. A. T. Murray, rev. G. E. Dimock, 2 vols. Cambridge, MA and London: Harvard University Press, 1995.
Kabir, A. J. *Territory of Desire: Representing the Valley of Kashmir*. Minneapolis and London: University of Minnesota Press, 2009.
Lanier, D. 'Shakespearean Rhizomatics: Adaptation, Ethics, Value', in A. Huang, and E. Rivlin, eds., *Shakespeare and the Ethics of Appropriation*. Basingstoke: Palgrave, 2014, 21–40.
Shakespeare, W. *The Arden Shakespeare Complete Works*, ed. Richard Proudfoot, Ann Thompson and David Scott Kastan. London: Methuen/A & C Black, 1998.
Tieber, C. 'Aristotle did not make it to India: Narrative modes in Hindi Cinema', in L. Khatib, ed., *Storytelling in World Cinemas*. Chichester: Wallflower, 2012, 11–24.
Valmiki. *The Ramayana*, ed. A. Sattar. New York: Penguin, 1996.

4

'Indian' Independent Cinema and Shakespeare

Sharat Katariya and *Vandana Kataria* in conversation with *Tula Goenka*

The construction of modern upscale shopping malls with multiplex theatres in metropolitan Indian cities in the early 2000s, changed the landscape of cinema. It allowed filmmakers to break away from the dichotomy of the traditional pan-Indian *masala* or popular movies and the smaller neo-realistic art or parallel films, and create hip, contemporary stories for a niche and more Westernized urban audience. Indian independent cinema's style and aesthetics of storytelling are similar to indie cinema worldwide which are created outside the studio system. They are original, diverse, concise, usually made quickly on a low budget with non-movie stars, and do not feature the regular song and dance sequences of the mainstream three-hour feature blockbuster. Indian indies have grown in popularity and attention over the years and are more likely to be India's official selection for the Oscars or screened at the proliferating South Asia themed film festivals both nationally and internationally. The advent of over-the-top [OTT] streaming platforms such as Disney+, Hotstar, Netflix and Amazon Prime have also increased their audience, especially among the South Asian diaspora. The scholarship on indie cinema has also developed steadily. Although there were scattered studies and articles earlier, I was one of the first to look beyond Bollywood and provide comprehensive interviews with filmmakers across the Indian spectrum in my 2014 book *Not Just Bollywood: Indian Directors Speak*.[1] Ashvin Immanuel Devasundaram published *India's New Independent Cinema: Rise of the Hybrid*[2] in 2016 and introduced the term 'glocal' – global and local in sensibility and content – to describe the hybridity of Indian indies. Is it just a coincidence that most of the scholars studying indies live abroad, and can perhaps fully appreciate the glocal? The two directors interviewed for this chapter definitely demonstrate the glocal or transnational way of storytelling by melding Indian issues and stories with Shakespeare. Sharat Katariya's *10ml Love* [2010] is an adaptation of *A Midsummer Night's Dream*,[3] and Vandana Kataria's *Noblemen* [2019] is an adaptation of *The Merchant of Venice*.[4]

There are striking similarities between Sharat Katariya and Vandana Kataria, apart from the fact that their debut features are adaptations of classic Shakespeare plays. Both received rigorous filmmaking education and training at prestigious institutions and are informed by the work of Indian masters such as Manmohan Desai, Shyam Bengal and Ritwik Ghatak. They are both well versed in world cinema, and inspired by techniques and aesthetics from Billy Wilder, Ernst Lubitsch, Kimberly Pierce, Stanley Kubrick, Alfred Hitchcock, Alfonso Cuaron and others. They effectively use other modes of performance in their storytelling – Katariya uses Indian folk theatre in *10ml Love* and Kataria uses Shakespeare theatre in *Noblemen*. Both moved from Delhi to Bombay [Mumbai] and gained entrance and honed their craft in the Hindi film industry under the mentorship of an established indie filmmaker –

Katariya with Rajat Kapoor and Kataria with Dibakar Banerjee. Their audiences are equally transnational and varied, and their films have screened at international film festivals and online, although Sharat Katariya's *10ml Love* was released before worldwide web streaming was the norm.

Looking at Indian indie Shakespeare gives us a new lens and expands the definition of what 'Indian film' generally and what 'Indian Shakespeare film' specifically can mean. The 2019 essay collection *Shakespeare and Indian Cinemas: 'Local Habitations'*[5] enlarges the understanding of Indian Shakespeare cinema beyond Bollywood and discusses regional Shakespeare films in India, but I believe that these films need to be situated both locally and globally. In the case of these indies, Indian Shakespeare cinema has not only arrived in the West at the point of consumption, but it has already been to the West and back by digesting a range of world cinema to mix it with its own diverse hybridity. Not only do they reflect Shakespeare's own hybridity where characters from three different worlds are already mixed up in *A Midsummer Night's Dream*, and cultures clash in *The Merchant of Venice*, but they also make us question who 'owns' Shakespeare since both directors mention his works casually as part of their childhood legacy rather than as a foreign influence. Ultimately, both *10ml Love* and *Noblemen* give us a chance to change the way in which we study Global Shakespeare so that instead of dividing the films along national lines – Indian Shakespeare, African Shakespeare – we start to adopt a more networked approach that studies the interstices, the cross-influences between different cinemas and different Shakespeares.

Sharat Katariya, writer and director of *10ml Love* in conversation with Tula Goenka, 20 May 2020

Tula Goenka (TG) Was *10ml Love* always a Shakespeare adaptation or was that something that happened later?

Sharat Katariya (SK)   I had written a couple of scripts but there were no takers. In those days, I used to sit alone in cafes and listen to the chit chat of all the lovers at tables around me. I started thinking about doing a farcical film on love – what if there was a magic potion, and you give the potion to someone to convince them to love you. A friend then suggested I read *A Midsummer Night's Dream*. The characters that I had been toying with fit in exactly with the story, and it became a simple process.

TG   Did you study Shakespeare growing up?

SK   I know the plays that you read in school, and also some simplified versions which were 25-30 pages with photographs. Some of them were interesting, and some were not. I still don't understand *The Two Gentlemen of Verona*!

TG   What's so interesting about your adaptation is that you cover the different classes and the different religions in India. It reminded me of the 1997 Manmohan Desai film, *Amar Akbar Anthony* in which three brothers get separated and grow up in Hindu, Muslim and Christian households.[6]

SK   A friend of mine said the same thing after he read the script! I just found it cool to have a Catholic character, Peter Pereira [Lysander played by Neil Bhoopalan], and there is Ghalib [Oberon played by Rajat Kapoor] and his Muslim family, and then all the Hindu characters. Their lives are completely different, and they all come together in a wedding, with their own agendas. I think it is pure comedy when people with different mindsets and different notions clash.

Then there is the *Ramlila* [an Indian folk dramatic tradition in which scenes from the epic *Ramayana* are performed] group which is about class difference. They are the workers [mechanicals] who have been hired to set up the wedding and cook the feast. The idea of *Ramlila* in *10ml Love* came after reading *Midsummer Night's Dream*. I thought it would be funny to have the character of Chand [Bottom played by Manu Rishi Chadha] who is fed up of playing the monkey-god Hanuman, and he wants to try other parts but he's not allowed to. He ends up falling in love with Roshni [Titania played by Tisca Chopra] for one night, and his life changes, especially because Hanuman is supposed to be a *brahmacharya* [celibate], and this iconic mythological figure has a romantic entanglement in the jungle with a Muslim woman. I don't know if I could make a film like that now. Things have become so politicized.

TG   Has the Hindu fundamentalism sweeping India really affected storytelling and filmmakers?

SK   Yes, it has affected some of us, and it hasn't affected others. One thing that I always remember about writing a script is something that Billy Wilder said in an old interview. He said that your writing should be so smart that it doesn't need curse words. You don't need to say a spade is a spade, but you still make a point, and nobody can censor your stuff. He also made *Kiss Me, Stupid* [1964] and *The Apartment* [1960] which were about wife swapping and infidelity. But he got away with these 'immoral' stories because they were so smart and cleverly done.

There is also this film by [Ernst] Lubitsch, *To Be or Not to Be* from '42. There are two actors doing a Shakespeare play in Poland, and they talk about anti-Semitism, Nazis, what's going on in the world, cultural commentary, a lot of political things. It is indirect and clever, and in the garb of humour.

TG   *10ml Love* ended up getting an 'A' rating, which really affects the audience size. Did you think about cutting out some things?

SK   The day we went to the censors, they told me right away that they're giving me an adult certificate because Ghalib is 'selling those medicines for sex'. I said, 'But there is no curse word or anything in even one scene.' He said, 'You're clever but your theme is adult because it's dealing with infidelity. If you want a UA certificate you have to do a lot of cuts.' But I didn't have the money to go back to the editing table because the negative had already been cut. It was all shot on film and we did not have digital those days. Anyway, the film was released only on twenty screens, so it didn't matter what certificate it had. It was not going to reach many people.

TG But you got your first film made and released, and it is truly funny and entertaining. How did you become a filmmaker?

SK I remember watching a series on Doordarshan [public service broadcaster funded by the Government of India] called *Portrait of the Director* by Ramesh Sharma. There were episodes on senior directors like [Shyam] Bengal, Manmohan Desai, [Ritwik] Ghatak, and I knew that's the job I wanted to be a part of. After studying at Jamia [Milla Islamia], it was pretty clear that I couldn't make films in Delhi in 2000–2001. It was not the digital era like now where you can actually make a film anywhere. So, I came to Bombay, and I met Rajat Kapoor right away.

TG That's lucky!

SK Yes, I was very lucky. He was making *Raghu Romeo* [2003], and that was my first job on a film set. I worked as an assistant director on the film, and that's where I picked up my writing skills. I used to watch the director and the writer working together closely during the writing sessions. Sometimes I would give them some lousy ideas, and I would be always asked to shut up! [Laughter]

Rajat told me later that I don't have the skills to be an assistant director because I was really bad at clerical stuff. I just couldn't remember anything – what I'm supposed to do after the day is over, who all do I need to call, what is a call sheet? So, he suggested that I should stick to writing because that's what I was most excited about in the whole process.

TG   Your dialogue is so clever, and your characters are so real.

SK   Yes, I enjoy comedy. *10ml Love* is not the first script I wrote but it was the first film I directed. Rajat was the first person who read it, and the first thing he said was, 'Is there a role for me in it?' He wanted to play Ghalib from the start. He also said to me, 'Your dialogue is so nice, will you write some dialogues for us for a new movie?' So, I wrote for *Bheja Fry* [2007], and it was a super-duper hit.

Then Sunil Doshi, the producer of *Bheja Fry* said to me, 'This is the amount of money I can offer you. Can you do a film with this much money?' I accepted right away.

TG   *10ml Love* was a very low budget film. In fact, you have a company called Dirt Cheap Pictures. So, does it become a self-fulfilling prophecy that the films continue to be low-budget?

SK   I am facing the brunt of it because nobody is offering me good money now. Someone once said to me, 'Why did you call it *10ml Love*. Why not 20ml, 30ml or 50ml?' And I said, 'Look it's Dirt Cheap Pictures presenting a Handmade Films production. How can it be anything more than 10ml?'

TG   As a filmmaker I could tell the forest scene was day-for-night. Then the carwash stands in for the rain machine. Does making a really low-budget indie film, affect your production aesthetics?[7]

SK   It was my DOP's [Director of Photography's] idea because when he read the script he said there's 15–20 minutes of the film which is in the woods. He said we should do day-for-night because we don't have the money to light up the whole jungle. So we did some small camera tests, and he also showed me some old clips that used the technique. I thought overall it's pretty cool and decided that even if we have the money we should still do day-for-night.

TG It definitely enhances the surreal mindset of the people. They are all drugged out, and you viscerally feel that.

SK We also used contact lenses for the actors that were different from their natural eye colour. If you noticed, Koel's [Helena played by Minnie Mehta] saree border had lots of glittery stuff so we could tell her form in the dark, and it caught the light and sparkled. We also put charcoal on the teeth so that they would not be too bright. This is a film which was shot on celluloid and was not graded on computers. It was colour corrected the old-fashioned way in the lab.

TG Do you think if the movie was made today on digital, it would have a very different aesthetic?

SK Probably not. If you noticed in both my recent film, *Dum Laga Ke Haisha* [2015] and *10ml Love*, the shooting style is not very different. The effort was always to have long takes and shots that hold. We did multiple rehearsals and then four takes, and then we moved on. I still follow the same discipline, and I don't shoot too much, even with the advent of digital technology. I take more time in creating the shot, experimenting with complicated camera movements instead of just shooting and covering the story.

TG The interaction between the actors seems spontaneous. Did you rehearse a lot or was there some improvisation also?

SK There is one scene between Rajat [Ghalib/Oberon] and Neil's [Peter/Lysander] characters. They meet for the first time at the wedding, and they pretend to know about each other, but they both know the other person is lying. We were doing the rehearsal, and they started improvising and then Neil banged into one of the props by accident, and Rajat says 'Shhh...', and then Neil bangs into it again. We ended up shooting exactly that.

There's improvisation in another scene among the wedding workers. Brijendra Kalra who plays Ghanshubhai [Peter Quince], the director of the *Ramlila*, kept coming to me when we were about to start shooting, 'Why am I not giving Chand a role?'. I said, 'Because it's funny. You are going by the market driven strategy that he's popular at this so that's all he can do.' During one of the rehearsals he just added all those improvisations about Chand's father. It was hilarious, and I said, 'Yes, let's keep all of it.' Their chemistry is outstanding in those scenes.

TG Definitely! The sub-plot about Chand being an orphan was interesting considering that the play, *A Midsummer Night's Dream*, is about an orphan Indian boy that Oberon and Titania battle over. The dynamic of the wedding workers reminded me of *Monsoon Wedding* [Mira Nair, 2001].

SK When I saw the rehearsals of that scene, I realized I should make *Dum Laga ke Haisha*. I really enjoyed this semi-urban or you could say semi-rural banter between these people, and how they think. It's very funny and very modern at the same time. The [*Ramlila*] rehearsal scenes and the beginning of the film are my favorite parts of *10ml Love*.

TG When you are writing your script, do you write it all in English and then translate the dialogue or do you write English directions and Hindi dialogue? Your use of Hindi is so particular and specific.

SK English directions and Hindi dialogue. But I use Roman Hindi, not Devanagri. I can't type in Hindi. The software is available, but I'm used to writing in Roman, and most of the actors prefer reading that in their scripts. When I'm on set and I'm making changes in dialogue, I write it by hand in Hindi on my script. Then one of the assistant directors takes it and types it in Roman so that others can understand it. We now have laptops and printers on set, so it's done quickly. Earlier, all the actors could read Hindi but not now.

TG Who is the audience for the movie?

SK I don't know. I have never thought of that for any of the three films I've made so far. After I finished *10ml Love*, I was standing in line for a movie and I remember saying to my wife, 'Are these people going to come and see my film?' You can't tell who's going to watch your film, so why bother about people who you don't know. No filmmaker will tell you that I know my audience, or I am sure of what the audience wants.

TG It's completely the opposite of what I teach my students! You don't know exactly who is going to watch your movie, but you have some sense. For instance, I would classify *10ml Love* as indie cinema, which is made possible because of multiplexes. In fact, it was chosen as a PVR Director's Cut release.

SK Yes.

TG You can make a small niche film now, and it doesn't have to be the big masala film with all the different things in it. So, do you set out with a certain sensibility? Is it for an urban audience or for smaller towns or for rural India?

SK You know when it was made and or even when *Dum Laga ke Haisha* was made, there was no big audience for films about smaller towns. They were considered indie films or Doordarshan kind of films, and not seen as mainstream theatrical releases. That only came much later.

So, I couldn't decide who was going to see what. The joy was purely that I wrote something, and people got excited to work on it, and there was someone who was excited to produce it. I can only hope that people will like it. This is a question that is asked to me every time I make a film, or I pitch a film. 'Who is going to watch it?' You then say, 'Whoever gets to know about it.' So, you put it back to the producers that the more they tell people about it, more people are going to come and watch it.

TG Do you think a film based on Shakespeare is relevant and important in India even if it doesn't reach a Western audience?

SK Indian film audiences want to go and see a great story and big movie stars. Or a concept that catches the audience's fascination or fancy. Shakespeare is not a crowd pulling name for our movie audiences. Actually, I don't think there is any writer or novelist whose name you put on the movie or poster that's going to get people to flock to the theatres to watch it, especially in India. People don't care.

TG Have you thought about releasing it on a platform like Netflix or Amazon so more people could see it?

SK The film was sold to 21st Century Fox so it was shown on Star Movies, which ended up being bought by Disney+ and so it's now on Hotstar.

TG But it would do so well with the diaspora audience, people like me that are in the West and don't have access to Hotstar.

SK That is the producer's call finally. Rights are sold worldwide, and sometimes you cannot sell different countries separately. It was screened at the New York Indian Film Festival many years back.

Vandana Kataria, writer and director of *Noblemen* in conversation with Tula Goenka, 23 May 2020

Tula Goenka (TG) You adapted a Shakespeare play for your feature directorial debut, *Noblemen*. How did that happen?

Vandana Kataria (VK) I had been doing art direction and making music videos and ad films for several years, and I finally took a year off to study scriptwriting. I wrote my first feature which I am actually filming right now, and while I was pitching that script, I signed up with a talent agency. They were the ones who told me about this new venture by Saregama's Yoodlee Films to pick up literature in the public domain and adapt it to a feature film for Indian audiences. It had to be made in one year for a minimal budget, and I decided I have nothing to lose and I should just jump into the experiment.

TG Did you think of setting your *The Merchant of Venice* version in a boy's boarding school in India from the start?

VK I picked [*The*] *Merchant of Venice* from the start, but I wrote a completely different ten-pager for them. It was set in a Bombay slum with petty thieves, chain snatchers, bar dancers, eunuchs, brothel workers as characters. But then I realized that I need at least six months to research because I don't know their lives.
 That's when Siddharth [Anand Kumar, Vice President] of Yoodlee Films who had also studied in boarding school suggested that I think of a story set in a school with a gay boy or something like that. I thought, 'Good idea – *ek school ki kahani* [a school's story]. Having studied in a boarding school, I know this world, I'm halfway there already so my research will be much shorter.' It's a project that took one-and-a-half years to finish, from blank page to final delivery.

TG How did you start working with indie director, Dibakar Banerjee?

VK I just walked up to him, and said, 'Hey, I'm from NID [National Institute of Design], and I know you're from NID. I would love to assist you.' And sure enough, I got a call to work on an ad, and I started regularly with his production company. When *Oye Lucky! Lucky Oye!* [2008] happened, he offered me production design and I was hesitant at first, but I figured it out. Between the three feature films with him including *Shanghai* [2012], and [*Detective*] *Byomkesh Bakshy!* [2015], I've directed commercials, music videos, et cetera.

TG What are your memories of Shakespeare?

VK I used to read a lot as a child because my father has a crazy amount of books. I remember reading these paperbacks of Shakespeare's plays when I was younger. I also studied *Julius Caesar* and *Macbeth* in school, and I watched Shakespeare on stage, on TV and in movies.

TG Why did you pick *The Merchant of Venice*?

VK Even when I read it the first time, I thought of Shylock as the hero. Not Antonio and Bassanio. It is a Shakespearean tragedy in which Shylock is the tragic hero, the guy who decides to rise up against his oppressors but gets so caught up in his desire for revenge that he makes the wrong choices, and that becomes the reason for his downfall.

It's maybe Shakespeare's only underdog or commoner story. Every other story is about a king, princess, children or relatives of monarchs, whereas Shylock is just a common man. I am so perplexed that it has always been marketed as a comedy. Whatever little comedy there is, it's slapstick.

TG *Noblemen* is not a literal adaptation of Shakespeare but incorporates some themes from *The Merchant of Venice*. The play that the school children are participating in within the movie works well.

VK With *Noblemen* I went back to the interpretation that I always had of the text. In my story, Shay is the Shylock of the school. He's the gay and the non-macho minority. I chose the names carefully. Shay [played by Ali Haji] is Shylock, Arjun [played by Mohammed Ali Mir] is Antonio, Baadal [played by Shaan Groverr] is Bassanio, Pia [played by Muskaan Jaferi] is Portia. I skipped the rest, instead I added Murli [played by Kunal Kapoor], the teacher, who doesn't exist in the original text.

I think the use of the Founder's Day play is simplistic, but it helped give my characters motivation. In the Shakespeare text you have two main goals – the winning of the girl, and Shylock wants to make a profit. In the movie, Baadal still wants Pia, but what my Shylock wants is to prove himself on the stage on Founder's Day. It was a quick way to increase the stakes in a school setting. The person who's usually speaking Shakespeare is Shay, and he's always muttering Bassanio's lines. He's not muttering Shylock's lines because he's practicing for Bassanio.

TG It's a theatrical device, and you use it effectively.

VK It was an easy way to show that he's extremely invested in the school play, and that he's constantly rehearsing it. I end with Shay doing a monologue on stage, which is Bassanio's monologue of choosing one of the three boxes to win Portia's hand in marriage. But I use that speech in a very different context, and I only used a section of it.

To be honest, I was very worried that the Shakespeare *bhakts* [disciples] would be angry with me for the twist. Even the famous Shylock 'shall we not revenge?' speech that Murli does, I've conveniently just used one section of it and not the entire thing. I'm relieved nobody has criticized me for it.

TG I thought the teenage actors are very natural in *Noblemen*. How did you find them?

VK We looked everywhere – Delhi, Bombay, Calcutta, Bangalore, Pune. The kids we ended up with were really good, sincere, hardworking. I think they were drawn to the script. Shay's from Bombay, he's actually a child actor, and he had been acting since he was a six-month-old baby in ads and movies. But when we found him, he hadn't faced the camera for several years. Arjun is from Delhi. He is a theatre actor who had never faced a camera but has done a lot of Shakespeare and stuff.

Baadal is from Delhi. He moved to Bombay, wanted to act, but had never done anything except maybe a few ads. The girl who's Pia, Muskaan, her father is the comedian Jagdeep [Jaffrey]. She's a brilliant voice artist but had never acted before. Gunzo [another character that I added] has been doing TV for some time. He was my toughest because I had to keep telling him, stop acting.

TG Did you do workshops with them?

VK Yes, we workshopped about eight or nine days. I wish I had more time. Our workshop director Prashant Singh is a casting director, and an actor himself. He's very tough, but it's good because he really opens up the cast's vulnerabilities. They have to be willing to bare themselves, and that's actually easier the more untrained they are.

We did several exercises, making them write back stories for themselves, making them watch a few films that I thought were important – *Boys Don't Cry* [Kimberly Pierce, 1999], [*A*] *Clockwork Orange* [Stanley Kubrick, 1972], films from around the world. I spent a lot of time with them, so I became their friend, their confidant. I participated in some of the workshops, and I shared a lot of my experiences. My whole endeavour was trust building. I'm still friends with the kids, we chat, we talk.

TG It's excellent casting, and they make the film believable.

VK Yes, we were very methodical, and we shortlisted people, and did several callbacks. What also helped was that we all lived in Oak Grove boarding school where we were shooting. Our budget was really minuscule – 1.5 crores from blank page to final delivery – and we didn't have money for accommodation. The whole crew, the actors, all the light men, everyone, we all lived together. *Bachchon ke liye* [for the children] that became really good because many came from sheltered homes, and they didn't know what a boarding school is like. We were in January in Mussoorie, and it was snowing and hailing. We were in a dorm with no heating, windows broken, cold wind coming in. We would line up every day for a bucket of hot water to bathe. For me, it was going back to school. For the rest of the crew, it must have been torturous actually.

TG What was it like directing Kunal? Did you have to undo his Bollywood training?

VK We did some workshops with Kunal, although he didn't participate in the more serious ones. But I have a feeling, which I've discussed with Kunal, that *Noblemen* was more natural for him because it was in English. So, he was comfortable with the dialogues, and he wasn't paying attention to line *kaise bolni hai* [how to say the line]. But he disagrees and says that's not the case. We also did not get any costumes for him, and all his clothes in the movie are from his cupboard.

TG Your visual sense is excellent – the production design details, composition, et cetera.

VK Thanks! I will credit NID for it. My faculty for foundation studies were so good that my basic design, sensibility of colour, composition, framing, lensing, has become intrinsic. But writing, it's still a new skill and something I have to apply conscious effort.

I think my dad unknowingly created an interest in cinema long ago. He used to bring all kinds of cinema home on VHS tapes, since we were babies. I had seen *The Shining* [Stanley Kubrick, 1980], all of Hitchcock, etc. by the age of thirteen!

TG The first frame of *Noblemen* is in the pool and it's bookended with the end.

VK It's a homage to *Y Tu Mama Tambien* [Alfonso Cuaron, 2001]. You know sometimes an image just stays in your head, and then you end up expanding on it one day. It's more than a homage. I wanted the opening to be a little dreamlike, and the underwater sound is a certain way, so that at least for the first few minutes, you're wondering, is it something real or not?

TG It was beautifully shot and edited, so you must have story boarded it all, right?

VK Yes. On my technical recce, I do the blocking of the whole film with my ADs using the Artemis app on our iPad or smartphone. So, I have the lens information, framing, and everyone knows what we are going to shoot. This doesn't mean we are not allowed to change our minds during the actual filming. But this makes it much more organized, especially if you are shooting such tight schedules. I don't have any thinking time on set. One thing I learned is that I'll never shoot a film in twenty-two days!

TG You had an 'A' rating for the theatrical release, correct? Who is your audience?

VK Yes, and that's okay because the film is for adults. I wanted to show that there are three types of bullied kids – there is the fat kid [Gunzo], there is the girl [Pia] and there is Shay. They represent the three typical reactions to bullying – one kid tries to harm himself, which is the most typical reaction.

The girl wants to do the right thing, she wants to take legal recourse. And Shay has the worst kind of reaction, he turns evil and does something wrong.

Noblemen is about the making of an Arjun [Antonio]. No one, especially children of whatever age, hurts another person because they're feeling happy. They hurt another person when there's something happening inside them. That's why we start with that super – 'A monster left unchecked will create more monsters.' That was actually Kunal's idea. We added it just before the theatrical to make sure the message is clear.

Shay's going to grow up to be a really complex human being. He's changed for life. He has lost everything just like Shylock lost everything – his daughter, his estate, he got thrown out of Venice, all his money got taken away. Shay lost his play, he lost the teacher he loved, he's probably going to lose his friends, and he's lost the most important thing – his soul.

TG To bring it back to Shylock, Shakespeare's play is about Jews and Christians. But we don't really have that conflict in India, so you transferred that to sexual identity?

VK I think it's more than about being gay. It's about the bullied and the bullies who torment them. When I was researching the movie, I found out that kids with alternate sexuality are getting bullied a lot more these days. I wasn't really making a film about a gay person, which is why I don't fully spell it out. There are hints that Arjun might be homosexual himself. He is always touching Shay. He and Baadal also sit too close to each other, which is also part of the original text. Some people have thought that Antonio and Bassanio had undertones of being more than friends. The all-male-Venetian-world translated well into an-all-boys-boarding-school, with the same kind of complexities.

TG How did the movie do in its theatrical release?

VK It was the middle of the monsoon in Bombay, and everything was flooded like crazy so no one could go see it. But then the producers made the sales to Netflix very soon, and many more people have seen it online. We would never have done great business; it was an adult film in English, with violence, and all of that!

TG *Noblemen* has haunted me like nothing I've seen in a long time. I'd even say it's triggering for people like me who have been to boarding school. For full disclosure, both you and I attended Welham [Girls School] in Dehradun although at different times.

VK Yes, unfortunately I had not foreseen that impact. The film premiered at the KASHISH [Mumbai International Queer Film Festival] screening here in Bombay two years ago, and there were a lot of people who broke down actually. Grown up, 40-plus men who came to me, crying and saying that it brought back difficult memories.

Of course, I researched it for two months before writing it, and I spoke to students and teachers in boarding schools today. From Welham, Doon, Scindia, Sanawar, and others. I met a young boy maybe two or three years out of school, who was in Bombay trying to get into films. I was shocked to hear his stories of abuse with hockey sticks and other things. So, while I knew I was depicting something real, I didn't realize one would trigger people. That was never the intent.

TG It played at some American film festivals, right?

VK It played in NYIFF [New York Indian Film Festival], it played in Chicago [Chicago South Asian Film Festival]. It played in Nashville [Nashville Film Festival], and quite a few other American ones. It was in fewer European festivals, but it did play in a small Berlin film festival.

TG What was the audience reaction in the West?

VK They all get it. It seems to be very universal. I remember an old man getting up and saying in Berlin, 'Ma'am, this is what's happening on the streets outside right now.' I was like,

'Really? Tell me how you're making the connections?' You see, bullying is such a universal theme, it happens everywhere.

TG   Would you agree that indie filmmakers like you are now making films in English but it's still for an Indian audience, and whether the film has an impact in the West or not, is not important?

VK   Yes. I also think the world wide web has made us global, we are all watching a lot of content from all over the world.

Notes

1. Tula Goenka, *Not Just Bollywood: Indian Directors Speak* (Delhi, Om Books International, 2014).
2. Ashvin Immanuel Devasundaram, *India's New Independent Cinema: Rise of the Hybrid* (New York, Routledge, 2016).
3. William Shakespeare, *A Midsummer Night's Dream*.
4. William Shakespeare, *The Merchant of Venice*.
5. Poonam Trivedi, and Paromita Chakravati, eds. *Shakespeare and Indian Cinemas: 'Local Habitations'* (New York, Routledge, 2019).
6. Jonathan Gil Harris discusses the masala mixture of different religions and languages in *10ml Love* in *Masala Shakespeare* (New Delhi, Aleph Book Company, 2018), 58–65.
7. Varsha Panjwani provides a detailed materialistic critique of *10ml Love* in her essay 'Shakespeare and Indian Independent Cinema', in Trivedi, and Chakravarti eds., *Shakespeare and Indian Cinemas*.

References

Devasundaram, Ashvin Immanuel. *India's New Independent Cinema: Rise of the Hybrid*. Routledge, 2016.

Goenka, Tula. *Not Just Bollywood: Indian Directors Speak*. Delhi: Om Books International, 2014.

Harris, Jonathan Gil. *Masala Shakespeare: How a Firangi Writer Became Indian*. New Delhi: Aleph Book Company, 2019.

Panjwani, Varsha. 'Shakespeare and Indian Independent Cinema: *8 × 10 Tasveer* and *10 ml Love*.' In *Shakespeare and Indian Cinemas*. Routledge, 2019, 180–99.

Trivedi, Poonam, and Paromita Chakravarti, eds. *Shakespeare and Indian Cinemas: 'Local Habitations'*. New York and London: Routledge, 2019.

5

Vandana Kataria's *Noblemen*: Global Frames of Interpretation

Taarini Mookherjee

Early in Vandana Kataria's debut film, *Noblemen*, Baadal, a senior student who bullies, abuses and tortures his juniors, tries to bribe the drama teacher, Murli, into giving him the 'lead' role of Bassanio by offering his Bollywood star father's resources – sets, lighting, designers, choreographers, etc. Murli counters with this question: 'You do realize this is Shakespeare, not a Bollywood film, right?' Implicit in this rhetorical question is the perceived opposition between the elite high-culture Shakespeare and the for-the-masses Bollywood film industry. This is a perceived opposition that ironically reappears over and over again in Indian Shakespeare films, dating back to the maiden Merchant–Ivory venture *Shakespeare Wallah* (1965) where the film uses the opposition between the dying art of Shakespeare performed on stage and the emerging popularity of the film industry to narrate the end of the British Raj.[1]

In general, the pairing of Hindi popular cinema and Shakespeare seems unusual, if not antithetical, with the former associated with low-brow popular entertainment and the latter with high-brow literary culture. This is, of course a binary that does not hold up, and in many ways contemporary Bollywood is perhaps the closest modern analogue to the early modern theatre industry in terms of popularity among the masses, the quantity and speed of output and the unapologetic borrowing of source material. This similarity applies not just to the functioning of the industries but to the content, plots and narrative tropes used by both. The inception, development and consolidation of the Indian film industry (though it was not declared an industry until 1998) took place over the same period of time as the anti-colonial movement; the birth of Indian cinema occurred almost simultaneously with the birth of the Indian nation.

This persistence of a false separation between Bollywood and Shakespeare belies the plethora of commercially successful adaptations of Shakespeare in the twenty-first century Indian film industry. These are films that have been widely touted as evidence of Shakespeare's 'universality'. As Douglas Lanier argues, the globalization of Shakespeare film is one of the dominant twenty-first century trends in the field of Shakespeare adaptation, a trend that leads to the plays becoming 'increasingly detached from [their] imbrication in Britain's colonial past' and offering, therefore, the opportunity to '[relocalize] Shakespeare in new cultural contexts without filmmakers needing to address the politics of adapting the master texts of a former master' (Lanier 2010, 108). Lanier draws here on the example of the internationally successful auteur Vishal Bhardwaj, whose Shakespeare trilogy adapts the plays to a contemporary Indian context 'without engaging Shakespeare's place in India's colonial history at all' (109).

Ironically, however, in the Western and anglophone context, Indian Shakespeare is almost always conflated with 'Bollywood Shakespeare'. Bhardwaj's films have received perhaps the greatest critical and popular attention, and reviews of theatre productions that adapt Shakespeare to the Indian or diasporic context frequently describe them as 'Shakespeare goes Bollywood' or 'the bard in Bollywood'. Therefore, while on the one hand the union of Bollywood and Shakespeare is marketed as new and unique – when historical data suggests the opposite – Bollywood remains, particularly in the Western context, the dominant codeword for Indian performance. This has led to a flattening of the diversity of Indian engagements with Shakespeare which range from regional language films to urban theatre festivals, from school and college drama competitions to low-budget indies. If we consider Lanier's reading of Bhardwaj as solely representative of Indian engagements with Shakespeare, we lose sight of the ways in which colonial, post-colonial and neo-colonial networks inform and shape Shakespeare adaptations in India today and therefore we lose sight of the different frames that we can bring to bear in interpreting these films. In this chapter I deliberately provide multiple contexts for reading this film to prove that such cinema can lend itself to myriad research and pedagogical discussions that we overlook if we read these filmic products *only* as relating to Bollywood or Indian cinema.

In this collection, in Tula Goenka's interviews with the directors of indie films, *10ml Love* and *Noblemen*, both Sharat Katariya and Vandana Kataria describe some prior familiarity with Shakespeare. Shakespeare was something they read, watched and, importantly, studied; they do not tout his universal genius or the plays' innate resonances with the Indian context, but rather point to the indelible presence of Shakespeare in their broader cultural environment. Both directors also reference a mediated engagement with Shakespeare through popular abridged versions, such as Charles and Mary Lamb's *Tales from Shakespeare*, which condense the plays into short narrative prose pieces. Kataria explicitly distances herself from the 'Shakespeare *bhakts*' or 'bardolators', suggesting an approach towards Shakespeare that cannot be described as reification or critique. The ubiquity of Shakespeare, in a particular cultural and social milieu, certainly complicates questions of national ownership, yet the plays are neither entirely familiar nor entirely foreign but rather occupy an in-between space.

Despite the distinct lack of commercial advantage, both films explicitly acknowledge their Shakespearean antecedents. Sharat Katariya's *10ml Love* is instantly recognizable as an adaptation of Shakespeare's *A Midsummer Night's Dream*. The different social spheres and class hierarchies of the Shakespeare play lend themselves to the cosmopolitan urban milieu of a contemporary Indian city, and Katariya mobilizes the frictions between and within different social classes, religions and languages to generate a farcical comedy.[2] *Noblemen*, on the other hand, is part of a subset of Shakespeare film adaptations, which Richard Burt has termed 'the play-within-the-film genre' that places rehearsals and/or performances of a Shakespeare play within the plot of the film, compelling audiences to draw parallels between the actors and characters. While this is certainly an established genre in the field of Shakespeare films, it is also one that is popular within the more specific branch of Indian Shakespeare films including films like *1942: A Love Story* (for *Romeo and Juliet*), *Shakespeare Wallah* and *In Othello*. In all these iterations, the inset play serves as a means of allegorizing the plot and characters of the frame; what happens on stage provides insight or guidance for our analysis of the dynamics between characters, their motivations, as well as their ultimate fates. There are very few scenes in *Noblemen* that explicitly deal with the Shakespeare play itself as the film is concerned more with the lives of the teenaged students and the rigid hierarchies and cliques of high school where the relatively minor question of who gets to play the role of Bassanio assumes gargantuan proportions. The planned Founder's Day performance of *The Merchant of Venice*, the focal event of the academic year, becomes for some students a means of asserting and consolidating their position in the school's pecking order, while for others it is a marker of success in an environment that otherwise seems designed to decimate their self-confidence.

However, unlike many other Shakespearean plays-within-films, *Noblemen* does not lend itself to an easy analogy between the Shakespearean characters and the teenage actors. Instead, the movie traces a cycle of repeated and incessant abuse, within the frame of an-eye-for-an-eye justice introduced in an early classroom discussion of *The Merchant of Venice*. In a dimly lit and dusty rehearsal room, crowded with props and set pieces from performances past, the drama teacher poses a question to the teenagers gathered around a square green stage: '*The Merchant of Venice* is basically a tale about?' The answer that this question receives is a unanimous one: the play is about revenge. It is this single-word encapsulation of the Shakespearean comedy that then defines the relationship between the early modern text and its contemporary adaptation. The drama class continues, the teacher asking his students to flip the script, to think about how life might imitate theatre and to envisage the ways in which they might avenge themselves on someone who has wronged them. Collectively, the class comes up with four different answers. Pia, one of the school's only female students, who plays the role of Portia suggests 'an eye for an eye'; Baadal, the Bollywood star's son, seeks to recruit others to exact his revenge for him; Shay, the film's young protagonist, believes in a karmic balance, that those who wrong you will receive their just desserts; and Murli, the drama teacher, ends by saying that 'forgiveness is the sweetest revenge'. These four approaches structure the rest of the film, and the viewer is left attuned to the connective thread between moments that might otherwise be seen as markedly distinct. The movie zooms in on Baadal and three outsider figures – Murli, the drama teacher with no background in education; Pia, the daughter of a teacher and the only female student; Shay, the literature-loving adolescent coming to terms with his sexuality – and, like Portia in the Shakespeare play, we are left questioning: 'Which is the merchant here and which the Jew?' (4.1.172). Part of what the film tries to forward is a reading that suggests that the merchant and the Jew, the oppressor and the oppressed, the perpetrator and the victim, the bully and the target are not simply dialectically bound but also tied together in a cycle of inescapable replication. The film is clear about its pedagogical function – to reveal that revenge only breeds more revenge – and it does not allow for a space in which revenge can be justified, romanticized or idealized.

Beyond brief references to the play, the film does not visibly resemble Shakespeare's *The Merchant of Venice* in terms of plot. There are, however, some distinct parallels that tip the viewer invested in finding Shakespearean analogues in one direction or another. Arjun and Baadal, the two senior students who bully, abuse and torture their juniors are clearly versions of Antonio and Bassanio and their close personal friendship – lying in bed together – ironically provides the setting for their homophobic speculations about the drama teacher, Murli, and his favourite student, Shay. Baadal is also trying to steal the lead role of Bassanio from Shay, partly because he feels as the son of a famous actor he is entitled to it and partly because he is interested in Pia, one of the only girls in the school, who will be playing Portia. Similarly, Shay's close personal friendship with Ganzu could be seen as an analogue to Shylock and Tubal, though perhaps Ganzu has more in common with the clowning Launcelot Gobbo. These two younger students support and back each other through the film as they are mocked for their 'girlish' qualities. This also means that they are each treated as targets to punish the other, a pattern that eventually leads to Ganzu – chubby, fun-loving, and filmsong-singing – attempting to kill himself. The clearest analogue, simply by virtue of gender, is Pia. Having propelled her mother out of an abusive marriage, Pia appears to be the only figure that is offered some sort of moral redemption as she repeatedly takes a stand, encouraging others to do the same, to hold the bullies accountable for their actions.

Ultimately, a viewer who can identify these resonances must come to the film with some prior familiarity with *The Merchant of Venice*. As Kataria points out in the interview, because of its content, its 'A' rating and the fact that it was in English, the film already had a limited viewership in India. While the Shakespeare label has no commercial impact in the Indian context, it carries a cultural cachet in the global context and the film was screened at several international film festivals.

Given it was soon available on Netflix, it automatically reached a much broader global anglophone audience, one that was at least partially primed to recognize the Shakespearean echoes.

It is, perhaps unsurprisingly, in Indian Shakespeare films that utilize English as one of the dominant languages that there is some degree of acknowledgement or influence of a colonial history. Their engagement with Shakespeare, therefore, continues to reinforce a cultural hierarchy, from *Shakespeare Wallah* (1965) to Rituparno Ghosh's *The Last Lear* (2008). While only a brief reference in *Noblemen*, the distinction between Shakespeare and Bollywood movies expands outward to the rest of the film in the derision and mockery attached to mispronouncing English words. Scholars who work on Shakespeare in India have traced two separate but related avenues through which Shakespeare entered the Indian cultural consciousness, what Poonam Trivedi has termed 'an "academic" literary Shakespeare' that evolved from the classroom and 'a popular Shakespeare on stage, transformed and transmuted in translation' (15). The former, where Shakespeare was taught as literature and his speeches were memorized for the purposes of elocution and declamation was part of the early nineteenth century education policy of British India. This move, to include Shakespeare in college curricula, well before Shakespeare was taught in British universities, served to further the British imperialist agenda. This history is particularly pertinent for *Noblemen* because one can trace a fairly straightforward lineage from those early colonial colleges, designed to produce Macaulay's Men, to schools like the one in this film, built on the model of British public schools like Eton and Harrow. Ultimately, *The Merchant of Venice* is a text that is being taught, performed and adapted in this environment of simultaneous privilege and exploitation. While the only scene of theatrical performance in the film suggests a fairly straightforward and normative approach to the play, the rest of the film, in delving into the ways in which the characters conceive of this play and its relationship to their everyday lives, motivations and aspirations, pushes back against this approach. *The Merchant of Venice* thus functions as an intertext not simply for viewers of the film, but for its primary protagonists as they ignore, grapple with, adapt, recite and wilfully misinterpret lines from the text.

The film also deals, albeit tangentially, with questions of pedagogy and what it means in the context of this film to study and perform a Shakespeare play. Apart from the first conversation about revenge, there are no other discussions about the play itself, its characters, their motivations, its setting or its politics. While there is one episode where Murli calls on his students to shed their inhibitions and treat the actor's body as a neutral machine, it is an episode that is immediately rendered uncomfortable as he strips down to his boxers while performing the Prince of Morocco's 'mislike me not for my complexion' speech. This brief scene brings to the surface Shay's sexual awakening as he realizes he is attracted to his teacher, but it is also a scene that renders apparent a skewed gender and power dynamic in the classroom, one that Murli appears utterly oblivious to.

For most of the film, however, student engagement with the text of the play appears limited to a rote memorization and recitation of lines, often at seemingly incongruous moments as they go about their everyday lives. This memorization and recitation serves more to depict the advancing rehearsals of the play and less as a means of interpretation of the lines themselves, but there is one very important exception. Shay, bullied by Arjun and Baadal, is ostensibly being made to practice his marching for the upcoming parade at Founder's Day, but it is also a torturous exercise that they hope will push him into handing the role of Bassanio over to Baadal. As he marches, he recites to himself: 'Is every hate an offence at first?' This deliberate misquotation of Bassanio's line 'Every offense is not a hate at first' is one of the most explicit indications of the Shakespearean lines coming to bear on Shay's own reflections of his experience as a victim of bullying in school (4.1.68). To start with, he flips the positions of 'hate' and 'offense', turning a statement into a question. Whereas in the Shakespearean text, Bassanio argues, in rapid stichomythic back-and-forth with Shylock, that not every minor affront is equivalent to or builds up to hatred, also seeming to suggest simultaneously that not every minor affront is born from a deep-seated hatred. In contrast, Shay's question depicts a boy trying to make sense of the illogical pain he is being subjected to, a questioning that also uncovers the progression of his own hatred towards the bullies, building from the litany of humiliation, abuse and mockery they inflict on him.

The last and perhaps most normative extended engagement with Shakespeare in the film is the performance of the opening of Bassanio's speech from the casket scene:

> So may the outward shows be least themselves.
> The world is still deceived with ornament.
> In law, what plea so tainted and corrupt
> But being seasoned with a gracious voice,
> Obscures the show of evil? (3.2.73–7)

Shay performs this scene on dark stage with a single spotlight. He is dressed as Bassanio, complete with ruff, velvet cloak and powdered face. However, this soliloquy is intercut with the film's most climactic scene. By this point, Shay has been repeatedly abused and raped. In a shocking twist, the soft-spoken and gentle Shay deliberately orchestrates an episode that ensures a clash between the senior students and Murli, where the latter gets beaten up after confronting the students about the rape. Shay, who waits in the shadows until they abandon the bleeding Murli in the leaf-covered unused swimming pool, then proceeds to drown his beloved teacher, eventually pinning the blame for his death on Arjun and Baadal. Bassanio's speech, from a scene where he must successfully interpret the riddle of the caskets in order to secure Portia as his bride, seems a somewhat strange choice of Shakespearean text as a means of granting access into the mind of a teenager seeking revenge. But the film utilizes these brief snatches of Shakespeare to demonstrate the ways in which the system continues to fail students like Shay. Shay, with the calculated caution of his military mother, sets up a clash where his two enemies – the bullies who have made his life miserable and the teacher who rejected his advances and who knows his deepest secrets – cancel each other out. By the end of the film, it is Shay who has transformed the most, the repeated mistreatment at the hands of the other boys creating a monstrous figure capable of murder, a Shylock who can demand his recompense. However, the analogy does not hold. This is not Shylock exacting his pound of flesh, it is instead Bassanio deliberately orchestrating the scene, obscuring his evil intent by playing both sides against each other. He has internalized what it means to be and behave like a 'nobleman' in the contained world of this boarding school, suppressing his sexuality and sensitivity for a coldly calculated revenge.

While the film's paratextual materials foreground its relationship to Shakespeare, Kataria's interview reveals that there are several other vectors of influence, both Indian and global, and how we approach these films depends on the context[s] in which we encounter them.[3] A particularly compelling intertext for *Noblemen* is Peter Weir's 1989 film *Dead Poets Society*. It is set in a similarly elite and homosocial context of an all-boys' preparatory school; it engages with Shakespeare through an inset performance of *A Midsummer Night's Dream* and through the unusual pedagogy of literature teacher John Keating (played by Robin Williams); and it introduces gay desire if only to eventually supress it under the guise of heteronormative masculinity. I do not draw out this comparison to forward an uncritical universalization but rather to open up the possibility of an intertextual analysis that decentres the Shakespeare text and that takes into account the impact and limits of local context in an increasingly global world. *Dead Poets Society* is concerned with the American classroom and the 'reproduction of heteronormativity' and by placing this film in conversation with *Noblemen* we can ask questions not just about the film's adaptation of Shakespeare but also about its claim to a particular national identity (Burt 1997, 268).[4]

Noblemen is part of an expanding group of 'women's revisions of Shakespeare' in the Indian context (Novy 1999, 1). These include *Arshinagar* (Town of Mirrors), a 2015 Bengali musical adaptation of *Romeo and Juliet*, *The Hungry*, a 2017 British-Indian film adaptation of *Titus Andronicus* and *We That Are Young*, a 2017 English novel adaptation of *King Lear* whose directors and author are all women. These adaptations also depict strikingly similar narratives of the effects of global capitalism, the glaring disparity between working classes and the uber-rich and the power of this massive gulf to destroy lives and communities. *Noblemen* might appear on the surface to have little to do with women, capitalism or nationalism, but it similarly forwards an intersectional approach to Shakespeare adaptation. In exploring issues of rampant bullying, homophobia and abuse in an elite all-boys boarding school in northern India, it compels us to address the persistent presence of toxic masculinity and arrogant paternalism in the contemporary Indian context.

Notes

1 Several scholars have since questioned the historical accuracy of this enforced split, pointing to Shakespeare's prominent role in the inception of Hindi film, as well as the striking parallels between the functioning of the early modern theatre industry and the contemporary Indian film industry. For extended analyses of *Shakespeare Wallah* see Nandi Bhatia, 'Imperialistic Representation and Spectatorial Reception in *Shakespeare Wallah*,' Modern Drama 45, 2 (2002): 61–75; Lubna Chaudhry and Saba Khattak, 'Images of White Women and Indian Nationalism: Ambivalent Representations in *Shakespeare Wallah* and *Junoon*,' in *Gender and Culture in Literature and Film East and West: Issues of Perception and Interpretation*, ed. Nataya Masavisut, George Simpson and Larry E. Smith, Honolulu, University of Hawaii Press, 1994, 19–25; Dan Venning, 'Cultural Imperialism and Intercultural Encounter in Merchant Ivory's *Shakespeare Wallah*,' Asian Theatre Journal 28,

1 (2011): 149–67; Valerie Wayne, 'Shakespeare Wallah and Colonial Specularity', in *Shakespeare: the Movie: Popularizing the Plays on Film, TV, and Video*, ed. Lynda E. Boose and Richard Burt, New York: Routlege, 1997, 95–102; Richard Burt, 'All that remains of Shakespeare in Indian Film', in *Shakespeare in Asia: Contemporary Performance*, ed. Dennis Kennedy and Yong Li Lan, Cambridge: Cambridge University Press, 2010, 73–108; Parmita Kapadia, 'Bollywood Battles the Bard: The Evolving Relationship between Film and Theater in *Shakespeare Wallah*' in *Bollywood Shakespeares*, ed. Craig Dionne and Parmita Kapadia, New York: Palgrave Macmillan, 2014, 45–60.

2 For a sustained materialist reading of *10ml Love* see Varsha Panjwani, 'Shakespeare and Indian Independent Cinema': *8 × 10 Tasverr* and *10ml Love*,' in *Shakespeare and Indian Cinemas: 'Local Habitations'*, ed. Poonam Trivedi and Paromita Chakravarti, New York, 2019, 180–99. For a description of *10ml Love*'s multilingual features see Jonathan Gil Harris, *Masala Shakespeare: How a Firangi Writer Became Indian*, New Delhi: Aleph, 2018, 58–65. Note that Harris slots *10ml Love* into the category of a Bollywood film whereas Panjwani argues that the film is materially and aesthetically distinct from a commercial Bollywood film.

3 For instance, Rajat Kapoor, who plays Ghalib in *10ml Love* is perhaps best known to a Western audience for his performance as the paedophilic uncle in Mira Nair's *Monsoon Wedding*, a film that shares striking resonances with *10ml Love* and, to an extent, with *A Midsummer Night's Dream*. Kapoor is also, however, a mainstay of the Indian English theatre circuit and known for his experimental melding of Shakespeare, clowns and gibberish in *Hamlet the Clown Prince*, *I Don't Like It As You Like It*, *Nothing Like Lear* and *What's Done is Done*.

4 See Richard Burt, 'The Love that Dare Not Speak Shakespeare's Name: New Shakesqueer Cinema', in *Shakespeare, the Movie: Popularizing the Plays on Film, TV, and Video*, ed. Lynda E. Boose and Richard Burt for a more detailed queer reading of the film.

References

10ml Love. Directed by Sharat Katariya, Dirt Cheap Pictures, India, 2012.

Burt, Richard. 'The Love that Dare Not Speak Shakespeare's Name: New Shakesqueer Cinema', in *Shakespeare, the Movie: Popularizing the Plays on Film, TV, and Video* ed. Lynda E. Boose and Richard Burt. New York: Routledge, 1997, 246–74.

Burt, Richard. 'Backstage Pass(ing): *Stage Beauty, Othello* and the Make-up of Race', in *Screening Shakespeare in the Twenty-First Century*, ed. Mark Thornton Burnett and Ramona Wray. Edinburgh: Edinburgh University Press, 2006, 53–71.

Lanier, Douglas. 'Recent Shakespeare Adaptation and the Mutations of Cultural Capital.' *Shakespeare Studies* 38 (2010): 104–13.

Noblemen. Directed by Vandana Kataria, Saregama India, 2018.

Novy, Marianne. 'Introduction' in *Transforming Shakespeare: Contemporary Women's Re-visions in Literature and Performance*, ed. Marianne Novy. New York: St. Martin's Press, 1999.

Shakespeare, William. *The Merchant of Venice* in *The Norton Shakespeare* ed. Stephen Greenblatt, Walter Cohen, Suzanne Gossett, Jean E. Howard, Katharine Eisaman Maus and Gordon McMullan. New York: WW Norton & Company Incorporated, 2015.

Trivedi, Poonam, and Dennis Bartholomeusz, eds. *India's Shakespeare: Translation, Interpretation, and Performance*. University of Delaware Press, 2005.

6

Chutzpah: The Politics of Bollywood Shakespeare Subtitles

Varsha Panjwani[1]

Let us think about the multimodality of language both within a Shakespeare play and on a film screen. Language manifests through dialogue and songs, gesture and body language, and written language in the form of epistles and street names amongst other things. Even if we concentrate on spoken or sung language only, there are a host of nuances to consider from dialects to accents which are indicators of gender, class, geography, and nationality. When we go and see a Shakespeare film from a culture that is foreign to us, we rely on subtitles to transmit a huge proportion of this information. So, Shakespeare Film Studies should pay regard to the practice and research of subtitles to examine how subtitling relates to all these modalities and variations, and to study how subtitlers negotiate the demands placed on them in each project within the constraints of technology, time, and budget. However, my purpose in this chapter is not so much to examine comprehensively how subtitlers navigate each of these issues but rather I want to probe the ideology and the cultural politics of the practice and reception of English subtitles of Bollywood Shakespeare in particular and intralingual Shakespeare subtitles in general.

English subtitles of Bollywood Shakespeare films present a curious case of double translation. First, the Bollywood scriptwriters and directors translate Shakespeare's plays, written in Early Modern English, into Indian languages and then, the subtitlers translate these Indian translations into English. Lawrence Venuti has drawn attention to the tendency of translators in general to privilege the target/receiving culture, and an overwhelming majority of English subtitlers of Bollywood, as I will demonstrate, share this proclivity.[2] This raises serious concerns about the politics of English subtitles of Bollywood Shakespeares as it threatens to undo the diversifying of Shakespeare achieved through the scholarship and practice of Global Shakespeares. In other words, if the aim of Global Shakespeare Studies is to acknowledge that anglophone nations such as the UK and the US do not have a monopoly on Shakespeare, then the domestication carried out by the subtitlers, who often wipe out traces of the non-anglophone language when they provide English subtitles, works in the opposite direction towards a monolingual, monocultural, anglophone Shakespeare. Although translation theorists, including those working on Shakespeare, have discussed the issue of domestication of historically marginalized cultures into English, they have taken little notice of Shakespeare subtitles. On the other hand, scholars such as Abé Mark Nornes, Atom Egoyan and Ian Balfour have discussed the practical and theoretical aspects of subtitles in general, but this scholarship is yet to be taken into account in discussions of non-anglophone Shakespeare films.[3] Thus, Shakespeare subtitles are a blind spot in Shakespeare Studies despite the field's recent interest in mapping transcultural flows through Shakespeare films. By establishing Shakespeare subtitles as a significant site of study, this chapter not only redresses this neglect but it also thinks about more culturally ethical and productive approaches to subtitling.

Haider – a Hindi/Urdu Bollywood adaptation of *Hamlet* – is notable for several reasons and one of those is the subtlety of its dialogue.[4] In a scene which depicts the funeral of Parvez [Polonius], a brief but bristling exchange takes place between Ghazala [Gertrude] and Khurram [Claudius]:

> Khurram: *Aap ka beta uss taraf chala gaya hai Ghazala . . . Vaishi bhediya ban chuka hai*
> Ghazala: *Shukr hai aasten ka saanp nahi bana*

The subtitles that one reads will depend upon the platform on which one were watching the movie. If the viewer chose to stream the film via Netflix UK, this is the translation that they would read (Figure 6.1):

> Khurram: Your son is across the border, Ghazala. He's become a bloodthirsty animal.
> Ghazala: At least he's not a cold-blooded snake.

FIGURE 6.1 Film still: *Netflix Subtitles,* Haider, *directed by Vishal Bhardwaj © UTV Motion Pictures 2014. All rights reserved.*

However, if the viewer were old-fashioned and had access to a DVD player and were able to source a DVD of *Haider* (not easily available in the UK), they would derive a slightly different meaning because the same dialogue is subtitled thus:

Khurram: Your son has crossed over to the other side . . . He's become a bloodthirsty animal.
Ghazala: Yes . . . but at least he's not a snake in the grass.

For the Netflix viewer, Ghazala appears to be suggesting that whatever her son might be, Khurram is calculating, callous, or a 'cold-blooded' snake. However, as far as the sense is concerned, the DVD version is a better translation. The DVD spectator would rightly infer that Gertrude is implying that Khurram is akin to a snake hiding in the grass to sting its unsuspecting prey. If this hypothetical viewer happens to be a Shakespeare scholar, they might also appreciate the way in which scriptwriters Vishal Bhardwaj and Basharat Peer have digested and re-worked Shakespeare's language. In *Hamlet*, the Ghost reveals that, "Tis given out that, sleeping in my orchard, / A serpent stung me . . . But know, thou noble youth, / The serpent that did sting thy father's life / Now wears his crown' (1.5.35-40).[5] In *Haider*, the DVD-watching Shakespeare scholar might register both the serpent/snake echo to refer to Claudius and grasp that the sense of betrayal expressed in the Ghost's language has been carried over into Ghazala's words.

And yet, in making the meaning clear, the subtitles have drained what Koichi Iwabuchi terms the 'cultural odor' of the film's dialogue.[6] What Ghazala literally says is this: 'thankfully he hasn't become a snake in the sleeve'.[7] While 'snake in the sleeve' is a popular Hindi/Urdu idiom, 'snake in the grass' is an English idiom so replacing the Hindi/Urdu idiom with the English one dilutes the local Indian flavouring of the dialogue. Bhardwaj and Peer had made Shakespeare's language Indian but the subtitler here anglicizes their language. I will refer to this type of subtitling as 'assimilative subtitling'. As Nicki Lisa Cole explains, assimilation is a political strategy which is used 'when little to no importance is placed on maintaining the original [immigrant] culture, and great importance is put on fitting in and developing relationships with the new culture. The outcome is that the person or group is, eventually, culturally indistinguishable from the culture into which they have assimilated'.[8] Likewise, the practice of 'assimilative subtitling' is a concerted effort to make the dialogue of the film more attuned to the idioms, phraseology, and vocabulary of the host culture *at the cost of* the originating linguistic milieu.

Assimilative subtitling is common practice in the Hindi/Urdu film industry but a rather extreme instance of this can be observed in the DVD and Netflix subtitles for *Maqbool* – Bhardwaj's adaptation of *Macbeth* set in the Mumbai underworld.[9] Here, the subtitler translates '*salaam*' to 'greetings', '*chikne*' to 'princess', '*sharara*' to 'trousseau', '*Abbaji*' to 'the father', '*seviyan*' to 'dessert', and phrases such as '*Razia phas gayi hai gundon mein*' to 'trapped in a den of thieves'. *Salaam* is a Muslim greeting and the fact that two Hindu inspectors (the witches of this *Macbeth* adaptation) offer a '*salaam*' to *Abbaji* (the criminal Duncan in this re-working) helps to establish the power dynamic between them because the Hindu inspectors are adapting their language to the Muslim gangster. Similarly, *chikne* is not really 'princess' but slang for a young, attractive, possibly effeminate guy and here it connotes a catamite; *sharara* might be a part of 'trousseau' as the subtitles would have it but it would be more precise to describe it as a rather elaborate outfit consisting of a long skirt or skirt-like trousers with a long top and a scarf or stole; *Abbaji* could be loosely translated as the Godfather but the underworld of Mumbai depicted here is far from the stylish world of the Italian mafia that the reference to the Godfather might conjure, and *seviyan* is not just any dessert but vermicelli in sweet milk, served during the Muslim festival of Eid. Finally, the phrase '*Razia phas gayi hai gundon mein*' used by Maqbool (Macbeth) to describe the tricky situation that he has just landed in, is not just about being 'trapped in a den of thieves' but rather it is a popular idiom that asks the hearer to imagine the terror that a pious woman like Razia might feel if she is entrapped by a gang of goons. The remark, therefore, is comic because Maqbool is imagining himself as the innocent Razia even though he is a prominent mobster. For a Shakespeare scholar, this might be of further interest because it enables them to align Maqbool's wry sense of humour with Macbeth's sardonic wit exhibited in moments such as when he responds to Lenox's lengthy description of the horrors of an unruly night with "Twas a rough night' (2.3.60).[10] As might have become apparent from my glosses on these words and phrases, they are untranslatable unless they are accompanied by extensive cultural information that the subtitles simply cannot be expected to carry. What is remarkable, however, is that even though these words and phrases have no equivalents in English, instead of leaving them untranslated, the subtitler tries so hard to assimilate these into English that they become unmoored from the cultural geography of the Mumbai underworld in which this film is set.

In describing this kind of subtitling as assimilative subtitling, I deliberately borrow political terminology because such a subtitling practice is not just about aesthetic changes of local colouring or flavour but raises issues of cultural power relations. Just as a policy of cultural assimilation requires immigrants to shed traces of the home culture and re-make themselves into the image of the host culture thereby maintaining the dominance of the latter, I want to draw attention to the way in which 'assimilative subtitles' labour to reproduce the immigrant non-anglophone Shakespeare in the image of the anglophone Shakespeare of the host culture thereby upholding the supremacy of the latter. Nornes, who theorizes subtitles in his influential essay 'For an Abusive Subtitling' and subsequently in his book *Cinema Babel*, decries this subtitling practice which 'domesticates all otherness while it pretends to bring the audience to an experience of the foreign' and argues that it is, therefore, a 'corrupt' practice.[11] Amresh Sinha builds on Nornes' critique of such subtitling which provides the 'foreign in one's own idiom' and traces its dangerous implications especially when, as is the case here, the language of a previously colonized country is being translated into the language of an imperial culture. In these instances, he links this subtitling practice with 'cultural imperialism' because it ensures that the imperial/formerly imperial country 'maintains and preserves its cultural discourse along with its aggressive defence of economic, political, social, and religious identity'[12] even as it erodes the cultural assertion of the formerly colonized country.

However, as the subtitles from *Haider* and *Maqbool* attest, the critical rebellion against such subtitling has not discouraged it in practice but I want to contemplate the alternative to this predominant mode. For instance, what might have happened if the subtitlers had translated Ghazala's dialogue as 'snake in the sleeve'? From the image that is conjured, it would be clear to the audience that treachery by someone close is implied. The viewers might have then made the connection between 'snake in the sleeve' and 'snake in the grass', or another, albeit dated English idiom, 'growing a snake in one's bosom' themselves. The Shakespeare scholar would still hear the echo between the Shakespeare and the Bollywood texts, and all viewers would have been introduced to a Hindi/Urdu idiom. Similarly, perhaps, *salaam*, *Abbaji*, *seviyan*, and *sharara* might have been added to a viewer's vocabulary if they had remained untranslated in the subtitles. Inciting curiosity by creating a distance between the audience and the movie might have given an interested viewer a chance to research and find out things for themselves thereby providing an opportunity for exploring another culture. This is why I would call these type of subtitles 'intercultural subtitles'. Explaining interculturalism, Ali Rattansi writes that 'what is involved here is the positive encouragement of encounters between different ethnic and faith groups and setting up of dialogues and joint activities'.[13] Intercultural subtitles work along the same lines and, in this specific case, would have produced encounters between the English-speaking viewers and the Hindi/Urdu film, and by extension between two different cultures, leading to a dialogic approach which puts the onus on both participants to work towards understanding the other.

So far, I have been entertaining the scenario that intercultural subtitling, which does not try to domesticate or overly explain, would encourage viewers to explore and learn another language and culture. But, what if the viewer does not perceive the gap in their comprehension at all and misses the nuances of the film's language at best and interprets their lack of understanding as a flaw in the film at worst. This is what happened with the viewers of *Goliyon Ki Rasleela Ram-Leela* (henceforth *Ram-Leela*) – a Bollywood adaptation of *Romeo and Juliet* directed by Sanjay Leela Bhansali.[14] In this film, instead of a masquerade ball, Ram [Romeo] and Leela [Juliet] meet for the first time during Holi – a Hindu festival which is celebrated by people throwing coloured powders at each other. In a sequence which parallels the first meeting of the lovers in Shakespeare's play, Ram and Leela flirt with each other gesturally. Farah Karim-Cooper and Miranda Fay Thomas have pointed out the importance of attending to gesticular performance in Shakespeare and their work has proved that the long histories and connotations of gestures make powerful sociopolitical statements in performance.[15] Romeo and Juliet's first meeting, which, as Karim-Cooper explains, draws the eyes of the spectators to their palm-touching and lip-locking is particularly suffused with gestural language.[16] This choreography is also present in the *Ram-Leela* meeting scene – but with a modification. Unlike Shakespeare's play where the dialogue between the leads glosses their actions, a non-diegetic song plays when Leela and Ram begin communicating with gestures. So, here the subtitler had a choice: they could translate the gestures and/or the song lyrics. They chose to translate the song lyrics only. If one watches the movie on Netflix, the subtitles translate the song lyrics, '*lahu munh lag gaya*' to 'I've tasted blood'. Just as Shakespeare's language puns, so do the lyrics of this song. It is a critical commonplace that the phrase, 'a pair of star-crossed lovers take their life' (prologue.6), that the Chorus uses to describe Romeo and Juliet, suggests both that the lovers are born in this city that is riven by rival families and that they would end their life here.[17] 'I've tasted blood', similarly, intimates both the beginning of the 'real' thing but also foreshadows that the lovers will end up with a taste of violence and enemy blood. However, while the verbal nuances are captured by the subtitling, a significant portion of the gestural dialogue is left untranslated. First, Leela teases Ram by bringing some red coloured powder in her hand and suggestively applying the powder on her neck. Then, Ram suggests that she should apply the red powder on her lips by kissing him – and she does. These gestures are overtly flirtatious and easy to comprehend. However, just before the kiss, Ram gestures to Leela that he wishes to take some of the red powder that she is holding and put it in her hair. Although Leela, with her expressive eyes, dares him to do it, he refrains at this moment and challenges her to kiss him instead. To a culturally informed spectator, it would be clear that Ram has proposed getting married on the spot and Leela has urged him on because the ritual of *mang bharai* which involves the groom filling the bride's hair parting with vermilion-coloured powder is one of the most significant Hindu marriage rituals and is often used in movies as a shorthand for the entire marriage ceremony.

Culturally specific gestures pose a dilemma for subtitlers. In an interview with Uday Bhatia for *Mint*, Francois-Xavier Durandy, a French subtitler for Hindi films, describes how he had to 'cheat a little' when he was dubbing a Bollywood film, *Masaan*, in French. He describes how, in one scene in that movie, the love-interest replies to the offer of friendship from the romantic lead with a 'couple of head tilts' which any Indian would infer as a 'yes'. Durandy decided to add a spoken 'oui' in the frame where her face was not showing rather than risk any 'wrong conclusions' on the French viewers' part.[18] In this instance, the technology of dubbing and the frames of the film allowed this moment to be expounded but this would simply not be possible for the subtitler of *Ram-Leela* because, when the marriage gesture is made, the subtitles are translating the background song's lyrics. In the movie, however, this gesture acquires significance through accumulative echoes. For instance, in a later song, Ram and Leela solemnize their secret marriage by performing the *mang bharai* ritual and subsequently Leela refuses to wipe out the vermilion when her confidante suggests that she forget Ram and get married to the groom chosen by her family. Just as Shakespeare speaks powerfully in gestures, Bhansali's film, too, creates gestural patterns that echo across various scenes. Though the subtitles can enable a viewer to observe verbal patterns, they cannot help to decode the gestural language if the gestures are culturally specific ciphers. For this, the viewer needs to explore further but that does not always happen. Critiquing *Ram-Leela* in *Shakespeare's Cinema of Love*, Robert S. White describes the lovers' meeting scene that I have been recounting as follows:

> In the 'ballroom' scene (here a spectacular Bollywood dance ensemble) there is a visual equivalent of 'palm to palm is holy palmers' kiss' ... 'O then, dear saint, let lips do what hands do', as Ram takes red powder from the palm of Leela and they smear it over each other's face. [19]

Although White dwells on this moment and the gestural language of the scene, he does not register that this needs further translation, thereby missing the way in which this non-verbal language resonates through the film.

Besides the verbal and gestural, as the introduction to this chapter points out, the screen is replete with modalities of language that can only be translated partially by subtitlers as they must make decisions about what writing from the mise-en-scene should be translated. More specifically, for *Ram-Leela*, there is a scene towards the end of the movie which is set in Leela's bedroom where she has been writing Ram's name over and over on her mirrors in Hindi. Here, the subtitler could have chosen to indicate that Leela has inscribed Ram's name as this would not be apparent to anyone who cannot read the Devanagari script in which the Hindi language is written but, in this instance, the Netflix subtitler did not (Figure 6.2). Decisions such as these have an impact on the reception. In his review of the film in *Variety* magazine, David Chute opines that Ram and Leela are 'too down to earth, too level-headed, to be convincingly star-crossed'.[20] However, Bhansali's film

FIGURE 6.2 Film still: *Mirrors in Leela's Bedroom*, Goliyon Ki Rasleela: Ram-Leela, directed by Sanjay Leela Bhansali © Eros International 2013. All rights reserved.

meshes Shakespeare's *Romeo and Juliet* with the Hindu mythological epic, *Ramayana*, and it is through the latter that the director brings in the questions of fate and destiny into this love story. As I have argued elsewhere, gestures such as Ram unpinning Leela's hair, or the fact that Leela has emblazoned Ram's name over and over on her dresser are key to appreciating this linkage which brings forth the star-crossed aspect of this adaptation.[21] When Chute does not encounter this information in subtitles, he fails to realize the metaphysical aspects of this re-working and considers it a failing of the script.

In contrast to the viewers, most subtitlers are quite aware of their role as partial interpreters. Henri Behar, who has subtitled a number of English films into French, unequivocally states that 'your job is not that of the literary translator, it is to give the *Cliff Notes* to a movie'.[22] Nasreen Munni Kabir has had a long career in Bollywood and has subtitled hundreds of Bollywood movies into English. In an interview with me, she admits that she refrains from over-translating because 'when audiences go to see an Indian film, they want to see an Indian film. And they will accept the fact that they don't know the actors necessarily, they don't know the language, and they will accept the fact that every single line when it is translated to subtitles will not be easily comprehensible to them'.²³ However, from the accounts above, it is evident that even though subtitlers are aware of the incomplete nature of their translation, the viewers do not perceive or engage with the gap in the subtitle translations. To paraphrase Disney's Pocahontas, viewers and critics seem to leave the film never knowing what they never knew.

Perhaps the most glaring instance of not examining this gap occurs in Ryan Gilbey's review of *Haider*. This adaptation of *Hamlet* is embedded in Kashmir – a territory that has been caught in the political impasse between India and Pakistan since India's independence from the British colonial rule and the creation of Pakistan in 1947. It has seen an unpreceded abuse of human rights so Kashmir at the peak of militancy in the mid-nineties is the real 'rotten state' which stands for the fictional 'rotten state' of Denmark in this movie. The script, as mentioned before, is co-authored by Bhardwaj and Peer, who, like Haider (Hamlet) in the film, was born in Kashmir and wrote a memoir, *Curfewed Night*, recording the brutal conflicts in this area.²⁴ One of the ways in which Bhardwaj and Peer creatively reshuffle Shakespearean words, tropes and narratives, or 'Shake-shift', as Diana E. Henderson terms it, is by repetitions of the play's most famous soliloquy, 'To be or not to be'.²⁵ Translated differently each time, it shows up at various junctures in the movie in the mouths of several characters. In one of the versions, Haider stands in Lal Chowk – an area of political significance in Kashmir – and delivers this speech to a standing crowd from a raised platform. The staging strongly evokes Hamlet on the stage of the Globe playhouse, talking to ordinary people in the audience. Haider starts listing the whips and scorns of time in Kashmir which, he insists, have created a culture of 'chutzpah'. Explaining the concept of 'chutzpah', he narrates the following (real or allegorical) anecdote: a bank robber points a gun at the cashier's head and loots all the money, then he nonchalantly walks to another counter and asks to open an account because there is so much money that he needs to deposit, such is this proud man's contumely, such is his 'chutzpah'. After thus entertaining the audience, he concentrates on the insolence of office or the corruption of 'law and order' in Kashmir by quoting the highly controversial and much abused act from the colonial-era: the 'Armed Forces Special Powers Act' which gives 'armed forces' the right to 'fire upon or otherwise use force, even to the causing of death, against any person who is acting in contravention of any law or order'.[26] In what, according to me, is a linguistic coup, Haider proceeds to rhyme the 'Armed Forces Special Powers Act' or AFSPA (pronounced af-spa) with 'chutzpah', except he pronounces the 'ch' as it is pronounced in chai, change, or cheat. Articulated thus, the word sounds like a commonly used profanity in India, *chutiya*, and sounds especially close to the abstract noun that is derived from this, *chutiyapah*. It is a coarse swear word, employed to denote silliness and stubbornness to the point of audacity and senselessness. The exact line that Haider delivers in the film is worth noting. He says: '*Yeh hota hai chutzpah. Besharam, gustakh, jaise AFSPA*' which the subtitles translate as 'That is chutzpah. Such audacity, such stupidity, like the AFSPA' (Figure 6.3). By connecting AFSPA and chutzpah, Haider draws attention to the arbitrariness and stupidity or perverse audacity of the Act through a bilingual pun. This fooling with language to critique the abuse of power is an important characteristic of Hamlet, who is no stranger to coarse language in Shakespeare's play, and this is mirrored in Haider's temperament.[27] However, Gilbey, reviewing the movie for *The New Statesman* in the UK makes it a point to flag the actors' inability to pronounce chutzpah properly. He writes that: '"Chutzpah" is a word that crops up repeatedly in the script and that none of the actors has been told how to pronounce it properly doesn't detract from its pertinence here.'[28] So, rather than exploring the reason for the mismatch between actors' pronunciation and the subtitles, Gilbey is content with assuming that the subtitles translate exactly what is being said and blames his misguided superiority over the English language and reluctance to work harder to understand Shakespeare from another culture on

FIGURE 6.3 Film still: *Haider's Chutzpah*, Haider, directed by Vishal Bhardwaj © UTV Motion Pictures 2014. All rights reserved.

actors' unwillingness to perfect their English pronunciation. In doing so, he does not recognize one of the most subversive wordplays in the film.

The kind of reviews written by Chute and Gilbey are the very reason why I have argued elsewhere that the Shakespeare reviewing sector in the UK and the US – both academic and journalistic – needs to diversify urgently.[29] However, here I want to examine an underlying issue with the way in which subtitles operate ideologically that has perhaps contributed to such reviews. Ask any number of subtitlers and they would stress the importance of their invisibility. Behar, for instance, remarks how 'our task as subtitlers is to create subliminal subtitles so in sync with the mood and rhythm of the movie that the audience isn't even aware it is reading. We want *not* to be noticed.' So prominent is this invisibility that an overwhelming majority of Bollywood films do not name their subtitlers in the end credits. Also, as Behar argues, the desire to produce a seamless experience where the audience 'isn't even aware it is reading' is made possible by the technology of subtitling as it has been perfected in the cinema.[30] The very first step in subtitling is 'spotting'. This is the process of defining the in and out times of individual subtitles so that they are synchronized completely with the audio and the shot changes of the movie. Commenting on this practice, Trinh T. Minh-ha argues:

The duration of the subtitles ... is very ideological. I think that if, in most translated films, the subtitles usually stay on as long as they technically can – often much longer than the time needed even for a slow reader – it is because translation is conceived here as part of the operation of suture that defines the classical cinematic apparatus and the technological effort that it deploys to naturalize a dominant, hierarchically unified worldview. The success of the mainstream film relies precisely on how well it can hide [its articulated artifices] in what it wishes to show. Therefore, the attempt is always to protect the unity of the subject; here to collapse, in subtitling, the activities of reading, hearing, and seeing into one single activity, as if they were all the same. What you read is what you hear, and what you hear, is more often than not, what you see.[31]

So, together the industry practices, the technology, and the propensity for assimilative subtitling are geared towards eliding the mediation of subtitles, thereby lulling the viewers into thinking that very little labour is required on their part to grasp the language of the foreign film. As David MacDougall warns in *Transcultural Cinema*, subtitles 'may induce in viewers a false sense of cultural affinity, since they so unobtrusively and efficiently overcome the difficulties of translation. They may reinforce the impression that it is possible to know others without effort.'[32]

Effort is precisely what is required for interculturalism to work. Like any good relationship, the onus needs to be on both parties to endeavour to learn. There are several ways to signal this requirement. One option is to make the audience aware of the mediation and partial nature of the subtitles. Increasingly, subtitlers such as Durandy are campaigning to be accredited for their work and have their name included in the credits. Another option was offered by the Criterion Collection when they released *Throne of Blood* – Akira Kurosawa's celebrated 1957 Japanese adaptation of *Macbeth* on DVD. Paying due regard to subtitling, they took the unprecedented step of including two separate subtitle tracks, by two different translators. Moreover, the two subtitlers, Linda Hoaglund and Donald Richie, explained 'their approach to translation and interpretation of the film' in a booklet included in the DVD package.[33] As Daniel Martin explains, 'the Criterion Collection edition of the *Throne of Blood* thus offers its audience a choice of translation depending on personal tastes and prejudices, and by including two contrasting sets of subtitles, it refutes the idea that any one translation can ever be truly definitive'.[34] By foregrounding mediation, the DVD release made the audience hyper aware of the distance between the film's language and the linguistic habitat of its audience. Nornes has also argued for what he terms 'abusive' subtitling in which he encourages subtitlers to 'embrace' moments of 'untranslability' in order to celebrate 'privileged encounters with the foreign' to shake viewers out of their sense of complacency.[35] I agree with Nornes but I reject his term 'abusive' and instead refer to these subtitles as intercultural because it is hardly abusive to ask and expect English-speaking spectators of Bollywood/Global Shakespeare to labour in trying to understand what they are watching. Sinha argues that subtitlers should translate in a way that 'the foreignness is not made ours, on the contrary, in subtitles, what is ours, our own language, is made foreign'.[36] Unless we are ready to let go of our stranglehold over Shakespeare ownership in the West, unless we use Global Shakespeare not to domesticate foreign Shakespeare but to expand and change our definition of Shakespeare, and unless we are ready to train ourselves into foreign ways of thinking and experiencing Shakespeare, all we will hear and see is: chutzpah.

Notes

1   I would like to thank Dr Courtney Hopf. Her insightful question on my paper about Bollywood Shakespeares at NYU London is what led me to research subtitles in the first place. Gratitude is also owed to Dr Robert Stagg who invited me to present a

version of this essay as a part of the Oxford Renaissance Online Seminar so that I could benefit from the feedback of the generous audience that attended.

2 See Lawrence Venuti, *The Scandals of Translation: Towards an Ethics of Difference* (London: Routledge, 1998).

3 See Abé Mark Nornes, *Cinema Babel: Translating Global Cinema* (Minneapolis: University of Minnesota Press, 2007); Atom Egoyan, and Ian Balfour, eds. *Subtitles: On the Foreignness of Film* (London: The MIT Press, 2004).

4 *Haider* (2014), [Film] Dir. Vishal Bhardwaj, India: UTV Motion Pictures.

5 Unless otherwise noted, all in-text citations of *Hamlet* are from William Shakespeare, *Hamlet*, eds. Ann Thompson and Neil Taylor (London: Bloomsbury, 2006).

6 Koichi Iwabuchi, *Recentering Globalization: Popular Culture and Japanese Transnationalism* (Durham: Duke University Press, 2002), 27.

7 All translations are mine.

8 Nicki Lisa Cole, 'Understanding Acculturation and Why It Happens', *ThoughtCo,* available at: www.thoughtco.com/acculturation-definition-3026039 (2018), accessed 25 September 2019.

9 *Maqbool* (2004), [Film] Dir. Vishal Bhardwaj, India: Kaleidoscope Entertainment.

10 Unless otherwise noted, all in-text citations of *Macbeth* are from William Shakespeare, *Macbeth*, eds. Kenneth Muir (London: Methuen, 1951).

11 Abé Mark Nornes, 'For an Abusive Subtitling', *Film Quarterly* 52, 3 (1999): 18. Also see Nornes, *Cinema Babel*.

12 Amresh Sinha, 'The Use and Abuse of Subtitles', in *Subtitles: On the Foreignness of Film*, eds. Atom Egoyan, and Ian Balfour (London: The MIT Press, 2004), 182.

13 Ali Rattansi, *Multiculturalism: A Very Short Introduction* (Oxford: Oxford University Press, 2011), 152.

14 *Goliyon Ki Rasleela: Ram-Leela* (2013), [Film] Dir. Sanjay Leela Bhansali, India: Eros International.

15 See Farah Karim-Cooper, *The Hand on the Shakespearean Stage: Gesture, Touch and the Spectacle of Dismemberment* (London: Bloomsbury, 2016); Miranda Fay Thomas, *Shakespeare's Body Language: Shaming Gestures and Gender Politics on the Renaissance Stage* (London: Bloomsbury, 2019).

16 Karim-Cooper, *The Hand on the Shakespearean Stage*, 176–81.

17 Unless otherwise noted, all in-text citations of *Romeo and Juliet* are from William Shakespeare, *Romeo and Juliet*, eds. David Bevington, Barbara Gaines, and Peter Holland (London: Methuen, 2005).

18 Uday Bhatia, 'Parlez-vous Bollywood?', *Mint*, available at: https://www.livemint.com/Leisure/2VlDlKjGY4G78kgP8gFARN/Parlezvous-Bollywood.html (2018), accessed 25 September 2019.

19 Robert S. White, *Shakespeare's Cinema of Love: A Study in Genre and Influence* (Manchester: Manchester University Press, 2016), 205.

20 David Chute, Film Review: '*Ram-Leela*', *Variety*, available at: https://variety.com/2013/film/reviews/film-review-ram-leela-1200841506/ (2013), accessed 25 September 2019.

21 See Varsha Panjwani, 'Juliet in *Ram-Leela*: A Passionate Sita', *Shakespeare Studies* 46 (2018): 110–19.

22 Henri Behar, 'Cultural Ventriloquism', in *Subtitles: On the Foreignness of Film*, eds. Atom Egoyan, and Ian Balfour (London: The MIT Press, 2004), 84.

23 Nasreen Munni Kabir, personal interview, 25 November 2019.

24 Basharat Peer, *Curfewed Night: A Memoir of War in Kashmir* (London: Harper Collins, 2010).

25 See Diana E. Henderson, *Collaborations with the Past: Reshaping Shakespeare Across Time and Media* (London: Cornell University Press, 2006), especially 1–38.

26 This dialogue is from the film itself in which Haider quotes the Act in English.

27 Hamlet's use of rude punning is quite evident in 3.2 when he is determined to embarrass Ophelia by asking her if her mind was on 'country matters' (3.2.110) and telling her that it would 'cost you a groaning to take off mine edge' (3.2.242).

28 Ryan Gilbey, 'To Pout or Not to Pout: *Hamlet* goes Bollywood', *The New Statesman*, available at: https://www.newstatesman.com/culture/2014/10/pout-or-not-pout-hamlet-goes-bollywood (2014), accessed 15 September 2015.

29 See Varsha Panjwani, 'Britain, India, Shakespeare, and the Nightwatch Constabulary', *Shakespeare en devenir* 13 (2018): https://shakespeare.edel.univ-poitiers.fr/index.php?id=1493.

30 Behar, 'Cultural Ventriloquism', 85.

31 Trinh T. Minh-ha, *Framer Framed* (New York: Routledge, 1992), 207.

32 David MacDougall, *Transcultural Cinema* (New Jersey: Princeton University Press, 1998), 175.

33 Criterion Collection, *Throne of Blood* package insert (New York: Criterion Collection, 2003).

34 Daniel Martin, 'Subtitles and Audiences: the Translation and Global Circulation of the Films of Akira Kurosawa', *Journal of Film and Video* 69, 2 (2017): 29.

35 Nornes, 'For an Abusive Subtitling', 28.

36 Sinha, 'The Use and Abuse of Subtitles', 189.

References

Behar, Henri. 'Cultural Ventriloquism', in *Subtitles: On the Foreignness of Film*, eds. Atom Egoyan, and Ian Balfour. London: The MIT Press, 2004.

Cole, Nicki Lisa, 'Understanding Acculturation and Why It Happens', *ThoughtCo,* available at: www.thoughtco.com/acculturation-definition-3026039 (2018), accessed 25 September 2019.

Criterion Collection, *Throne of Blood* package insert, New York: Criterion Collection, 2003.

Egoyan, Atom, and Ian Balfour, eds. *Subtitles: On the Foreignness of Film*. London: The MIT Press, 2004.

Goliyon Ki Rasleela: Ram-Leela (2013), [Film] Dir. Sanjay Leela Bhansali, India: Eros International.

Haider (2014), [Film] Dir. Vishal Bhardwaj, India: UTV Motion Pictures.

Henderson, Diana E. *Collaborations with the Past: Reshaping Shakespeare across Time and Media*. London: Cornell University Press, 2006.

Iwabuchi, Koichi. *Recentering Globalization: Popular Culture and Japanese Transnationalism* (Durham: Duke University Press, 2002).

Karim-Cooper, Farah. *The Hand on the Shakespearean Stage: Gesture, Touch and the Spectacle of Dismemberment*. London: Bloomsbury, 2016.

MacDougall, David. *Transcultural Cinema*. New Jersey: Princeton University Press, 1998.

Martin, Daniel. 'Subtitles and Audiences: The Translation and Global Circulation of the Films of Akira Kurosawa.' *Journal of Film and Video* 69, 2 (2017): 20–33.

Maqbool (2004), [Film] Dir. Vishal Bhardwaj, India: Kaleidoscope Entertainment.

Minh-ha, Trinh T. *Framer Framed: Film Scripts and Interviews*. New York: Routledge, 1992.

Nornes, Abé Mark. *Cinema Babel: Translating Global Cinema*. Minneapolis: University of Minnesota Press, 2007.

Nornes, Abé Mark. 'For an Abusive Subtitling.' *Film quarterly* 52, 3 (1999): 17–34.

Rattansi, Ali. *Multiculturalism: A Very Short introduction*. Oxford: Oxford University Press, 2011.

Panjwani, Varsha. 'Juliet in *Ram-Leela*: A Passionate Sita.' *Shakespeare Studies* 46 (2018): 110–12.

Panjwani, Varsha. 'Britain, India, Shakespeare, and the Nightwatch Constabulary', *Shakespeare en devenir* 13 (2018): https://shakespeare.edel.univ-poitiers.fr/index.php?id=1493.

Peer, Basharat. *Curfewed Night: A Frontline Memoir of Life, Love and War in Kashmir*. London: HarperCollins, 2011.

Sinha, Amresh. 'The Use and Abuse of Subtitles', in *Subtitles: On the Foreignness of Film*, eds. Atom Egoyan, and Ian Balfour. London: The MIT Press, 2004.

Thomas, Miranda Fay. *Shakespeare's Body Language: Shaming Gestures and Gender Politics on the Renaissance Stage*. London: Bloomsbury, 2019.

Venuti, Lawrence. *The Scandals of Translation: Towards an Ethics of Difference*. London: Routledge, 1998.

White, Robert S. *Shakespeare's Cinema of Love: A Study in Genre and Influence*. Manchester: Manchester University Press, 2016.

PART TWO

Recontextualizing the Stranger

7

Curating Indian Shakespeares at the BFI in 2016

Helen de Witt in conversation with *Anne Sophie Refskou*

In 2016, the British Film Institute (BFI) launched a major programme dedicated to Shakespearean cinema with multiple screenings at their London Southbank venue as well as a national and a worldwide tour. The programme was curated by a team led by Robin Baker, head curator at the BFI National Archive, and included a special section on Indian Shakespearean cinema co-organized with the 'Indian Shakespeares on Screen' project run by Koel Chatterjee, Varsha Panjwani, Preti Taneja and Thea Buckley.[1] The Indian section became a significant feature in the Southbank programme, which included screenings of Vishal Bhardwaj's acclaimed Shakespeare trilogy – *Maqbool* (2004), *Omkara* (2006) and *Haider* (2014) – with introductions by the organizers of 'Indian Shakespeares on Screen' as well as in-depth Q&A with Bhardwaj and scriptwriters Abbas Tyrewala and Robin Bhatt. The trilogy is a long-standing favourite across Shakespearean cinema studies and has had significant global audience reach whilst also helping to extend the global reach of Bollywood cinema in general.[2] Yet, the BFI screenings and additional events organized by 'Indian Shakespeares on Screen' made the films accessible – in more ways than one – to new audience groups in the UK.

The screenings were sold out and, even more significantly, interviews with audience members which were carried out by the 'Indian Shakespeares on Screen' organizers demonstrated the presence of a diverse cultural demographic, with many audience members entirely new to Bollywood or Indian cinema. The same interviews also showed a range of positive responses to experiencing Shakespeare through Indian cinema from audience members in varied age-groups.[3] It is highly interesting that the screenings, judging by a number of interview responses, appear to have created a temporary sense of community between regular BFI members who were new to Indian cinema, but familiar with Shakespearean cinema, and audience members of Indian or Pakistani heritage, who were very familiar with both the spoken and the visual language of Bhardwaj's films, but found the opportunity to share the experience – and the enjoyment – with a mixed British and international audience engaging in new and unexpected ways. Thus, certain kinds of bilateral processes of defamiliarization seem to have taken place, in which both Shakespeare's plays and Bhardwaj's films were mutually reinvigorated for – and by – the audience. This represents a potentially positive intercultural exchange, which is often the aim, but not always the wholly successful result for international Shakespearean projects.

On the other hand, a danger still lurks of relegating screenings of non-anglophone Shakespearean cinema to a niche or 'foreign' category, when curating a programme such as the BFI's Shakespearean programme in 2016. Especially, if audience expectations, or the context of a certain cultural moment, require more recognizably national products to take centre-stage. Curating means having to negotiate such fault-lines between celebrating – and making accessible – international Shakespearean cinema, while also to some extent promoting a British cultural agenda, both at home and abroad. The Indian section of the BFI's Shakespearean programme in 2016 in certain ways highlighted such questions and contradictions, but in productive ways that spark reflection and dialogue.

In the following conversation, film curator Helen de Witt, who worked closely with the organizers of 'Indian Shakespeares on Screen' in her role as head of cinemas at BFI Southbank, discusses the delivery and impact of 'Indian Shakespeares on Screen'.

Anne Sophie Refskou (ASR) Mark Burnett has said about global Shakespeare and cinema that 'what is required to support an intellectual appraisal of this material is an approach that takes us away from the separate bracketing of the "foreign Shakespeare" and towards a new sensibility' (2013: 3). Poonam Trivedi and Paromita Chakravarti address the same issue, albeit in slightly stronger terms, when they describe how, despite a rapid growth in the academic interest in Shakespeare on film and media, 'interest in the range of the international Shakespeare film has been slow to take off. Entrenched conservatism towards what constitutes the "authentic" Shakespeare has relegated a vast number of innovative and transgressive "foreign" reappraisals of Shakespeare on film to the margins of this new discipline' (2019: 3).

In other words, over the last decade or so, it has become increasingly clear that we need to challenge entrenched ways in which non-British Shakespeare (on screen and the stage) is categorized as 'foreign' and 'particular' (as opposed to British or anglophone Shakespeare as a normative and universal). This is sometimes easier said than done, however, as the above statements also indicate. And if it is difficult within academic and educational environments, it is possibly even harder within commercial setups, when you need to cater to a wider audience who may represent a variety of understandings and appreciations of Shakespeare's position in a global context. What are your initial thoughts on this, and what do you think film festival programming and curating can do?

Helen de Witt (HDW) This is a complicated issue, yes. On the one hand, even when there is a clear wish to create a programme that is global and highlights Shakespeare's iterations in a range of other cinematic cultures, the proverbial umbilical cord is always there, somehow. However autonomous or culturally specific such projects might be – and even when there is a sense of limited accessibility to a British audience – there is still a sense of Shakespeare as something that Britain gave to the world. That seems to be the fundamental problem, and I think it applies to Shakespeare more than to any other cultural figure. In terms of the Indian context, the colonial history becomes an additional issue, and there is a danger of implying a certain kind of patronising attitude that Indian Shakespeares are a result of what the British gave to India. Of course, several discourses are trying to break that down, including the examples you mention here, but it does still underwrite certain traditional assumptions. We are also having this conversation in the context of Brexit, where we are seeing a certain nostalgic reinstatement of 'Britishness' and are constantly made aware of how contingent these formations of nationalism are.

Yet, speaking generally of Shakespeare on film, cinematic tradition, at least, has provided an alternative way into Shakespeare, including for me personally. What I mean is that, if you have in any way a radical, cultural outlook, the way in which British bourgeois culture venerates Shakespeare might make you want to reject him along with other elements. But through films – for example, the brilliantly imaginative Shakespeare adaptations by a director such as Derek Jarman – interest in Shakespeare can be rekindled and you can come to appreciate the complexity of his plays in a new way. Anecdotally, I've always loved Jarman's comment that 'Shakespeare would have loved cinema' in all its casual simplicity (and I think he was right). It is also interesting that a Shakespearean cinema programme in some way allows to break with the well-established tradition of curating seasons that showcase the work of either a star director or a star actor (data has shown us that these seasons do better at the box-office than thematic ones, which is also the reason why they feature so frequently). Of course, this is because Shakespeare comes to stand as the uber-author, but at least it means that you can include a range of very different films.

ASR I appreciate what you say about cinema making us look at Shakespeare afresh, and in that sense, cinema is doubly helpful in that it will almost inevitably include international filmmaking too, right? Which can make you discover unexpected complexities, not just about a range of non-British native cultural contexts, but about Shakespeare. Varsha Panjwani has often said that we need to stop thinking in terms of what Shakespeare does – or has done – for non-British cultural contexts, but what they do for 'him'. Which also underwrites the overarching discursive shift promoted throughout this book, of course.

HDW Absolutely. Cinema is one of the richest areas for thinking in those terms, because international and intercultural relations are at the core of how films work. Sir Ian McKellen, who was the cultural figurehead of the BFIs Shakespeare Programme in 2016, began one of his talks with a list of films that he felt should be within the pantheon of great adaptations and, not surprisingly, they were not all British (the ones he mentioned were Kurosawa's *Throne of Blood* and *Ran*; Welles' *Chimes at Midnight*; Zeffirelli's *Romeo and Juliet* and Polanski's *Macbeth*). It's also interesting to note that the two most booked films on the national touring part of the Shakespeare programme were Baz Luhrmann's *Romeo and Juliet* and Wise and Robbins' *West Side Story*, both English-language films, certainly, but not British either. They're also films that speak about global youth culture, in their own time, about poverty and class and, to some extent, about diversity.

ASR So, it seems as if the BFI may have an advantage in some ways when it comes to thinking globally about Shakespeare (which other British institutions may not necessarily have, even if global Shakespeares have gained considerably more focus in recent years), because cinema already is global and in putting together a Shakespeare on film programme you simply can't ignore that?

HDW Yes, and in that sense, it may be called the 'British' Film Institute, and it is of course in Britain, but it is really about promoting international cinema as an art form as well as British filmmaking and production, so it is a dual emphasis. And although many of the programmers are highly aware and knowledgeable about British film history, most people are there because of film in a much broader and international sense, so they would be thinking 'what are the best film options for a particular programme and how do we represent British film within that' rather than 'we'll start with British film and then we'll add some foreign ones as well'.

ASR I find that another helpful and significant description. Especially because it has sometimes been the case with other Shakespearean projects – including some in 2016 – that you start with British Shakespearean events/productions/scholarly production etc. and then add 'the foreign ones' later, separately or by extension, which, despite good intentions, fundamentally confirms a centre-and-periphery perception, where a British, Shakespeare remains at the centre, both culturally and economically and in terms of symbolic status. What you are describing is a more inclusive approach that slightly inverts that perception.

HDW I think that came through in the overall structure of the 2016 BFI Shakespearean programme too. We, the team led by Robin Baker, had a clear sense that the audience expectations to the programme would be about the classics, but it was equally clear that the curating process and decisions would also be about subverting those expectations; you can't just show the Branagh or Olivier films and leave it at that. I think we wanted to show that there is a rich and imaginative world of Shakespearean cinema beyond the immediate reference frame of the establishment, and that that richness can be in part ascribed to the Shakespearean source material, but also to the vision of film directors and their creative teams *and* not least to the local cultural specificities which they draw on. Thus, while Part One of the programme included many of what we might call expected classics of Shakespearean cinema, it was still highly international, showing Grigori Kozintsev's *Hamlet* and *King Lear*, for example, or Roman Polanski's *Macbeth*. And then Part Two broadened the scope even further to include international films more loosely based on Shakespearean sources. At the same time, it is important that the films are allowed to speak for themselves, rather than solely representing the curators' views.

ASR Turning then to the Indian section of the 2016 BFI Shakespearean programme and the collaboration with the 'Indian Shakespeares on Screen' project, how did it begin and how did it become such an important feature?

HDW When we (Robin Baker and I) were approached by Varsha Panjwani as one of the organizers of the 'Indian Shakespeares on Screen' project, we jumped at the idea immediately. We were already wanting to create an international Shakespeare programme, but we certainly did not want to take an approach based on a 'Britain and the rest of world' attitude, nor did we necessarily want to do a play by play order, or even an auteur-focused presentation. Vishal Bhardwaj actually became the only director to be presented in a focused way, which, in terms of the overall project, is important, I think. In terms of audiences, we knew that the BFI already has quite an extensive London-based audience for Indian cinema and that there is a longstanding close relationship with the London-Indian Film Festival, but the challenge is always to convert such specifically focused audiences into coming to see other kinds of films. 'Indian Shakespeares on Screen' and the Bhardwaj film screenings in some ways gave us an opportunity to speak to different kinds of audiences; to people who are dedicated fans of Indian cinema and who would know exactly what they were coming to see, and to people who might be Shakespearean theatregoers, or indeed Shakespeare fans who might have committed to seeing the whole Shakespeare programme at the BFI and would therefore include the Indian films in their bookings too. I remember that the range of questions during the Q&A sessions after the Bhardwaj screenings demonstrated this audience diversity, in the sense that there were some highly specific questions, clearly being asked by Indian cinema experts or devotees, as well as specifically 'Shakespeare-related' questions on processes of adaptation, but also questions that implied a first-time encounter with either Indian cinema or Shakespeare and showed real curiosity and interest. Another important thing to mention here was the fact that, thanks to the collaboration with the 'Indian Shakespeares on Screen' project, we could include the screen-writers in the conversations too. So, it didn't only become a conversation about the director's re-imagining of Shakespeare, but also about how the plays were being re-written as Indian cinema. Generally during the 2016 Shakespeare programme, I learnt a great deal about how Shakespeare's plays have been adapted in many countries, including India, in order to speak to the political/cultural/social concerns relevant to their time and place. I knew this already, but the chance to see the films and hear such speakers as Bhardwaj and scriptwriters Abbas Tyrewala and Robin Bhatt, made me understand much more about the specificities of contexts and processes of adaptation.

ASR   The screenings were sold out, isn't that correct?

HDW   Yes, they were, and it helped immensely that we had the introductions provided by Koel Chatterjee, one of the organizers of the 'Indian Shakespeares on Screen' project, which I thought were superb, because they found such a good balance between being informative on a high level, without being overly 'academic'. They managed to contextualize and explain the films and make them accessible to a diverse audience.

ASR It also seemed like an exemplary partnership between a cultural institution and academics, which of course isn't always such a smooth relationship.

HDW Yes, I think because cultural institutions work simultaneously from top-down and bottom-up, it can be difficult to assess how much freedom there is regarding decisions and collaborations. Sometimes there are big agendas, so, for instance, the BFI had to do something with Shakespeare in 2016, and that was decided at the top. At the middle layer, it was more a question of how do we do that exactly – what form should the Shakespeare programming take – while at the bottom there can be room for inserting elements and events that might be slightly more risk-taking or subversive. Screening the Bhardwaj trilogy actually worked across different layers of the decision-making process, because it became – in a very positive way – a slightly subversive intervention within a programme that could have been very conventional 'Shakespeare on film' programme. It also related to a Global Shakespeare Study Day the following month during which Varsha Panjwani and Koel Chatterjee returned as speakers.

Finally, it is also worth mentioning that I think the Bhardwaj trilogy screenings prepared audiences for the BFI's subsequent Indian cinema programme, in the sense that the Shakespearean films might have made some audience members reconsider their expectations of Indian cinema in general. I hope that it deepened the understanding of Bollywood as not being so single note or stereotypical as some people sometimes think. In another sense, it also generated more knowledge of Indian film within the BFI and helped stimulate interest in it in greater depth, as well as inspire some programming and event ideas.

Notes

1 The 'Indian Shakespeare on Screen' project ran as a conference at London's Asia House from 27 to 30 April 2016 and included – in addition to the BFI screenings – workshops, talks and exhibitions of film archive materials. Many of these were also recorded by Backdoorbroadcasting and can be accessed on https://backdoorbroadcasting.net/2016/04/indian-shakespeare-on-screen/.

2 See for example Chakravarti and Trivedi: 'if today Bollywood has acquired a global recognition, the Shakespeare trilogy by Vishal Bhardwaj has had a salient role in it' (2018: 6).

3 I am grateful to the organizers of 'Indian Shakespeares on Screen' for sharing the recorded interviews with me for the purpose of this chapter. The range of interviewees include university students, long-standing BFI members, school teachers, as well as Shakespearean and film scholars.

References

Burnett, M. *Shakespeare and World Cinema*, Cambridge: Cambridge University Press, 2013.

Chakravarti, P. and P. Trivedi, eds. *Shakespeare and Indian Cinemas: 'Local Habitations'*. New York and London: Routledge, 2019.

8

'Travelling' with Shakespeare through Bhardwaj's *Haider*: From US Classrooms to the Global Shakespeare Movement

Jyotsna G. Singh

It would be fair to say that Shakespeare's works continue to maintain their presence in a humanistic curriculum in US universities. However, the humanities project itself is being re-examined from varied perspectives: on the one hand, we are witnessing empirically-driven technical intrusions of the 'digital humanities', which seem to repress direct affective engagements with literature; and on the other hand, the more accessible appeal of popular contemporary culture (as in films and graphic novels) and identity politics (in terms of the race and ethnicity of demographic groups) are further alienating students from canonical 'white' authors such as Shakespeare. In the latter response, Shakespeare's works are often associated with 'whiteness' and its attendant class privileges. Yet in a complex, perhaps over-determined, field, as the trends of multiculturalism are taking hold, the idea of a canonical Shakespeare is also losing influence. Interestingly, Global and Race studies have now been increasingly coming to the aid of Shakespeare. Thus, it has been heartening to see the emergence of the new, evolving subfield of Shakespearean Race and Postcolonial Studies in which Shakespeare's plays are contextualized within historicized, Anglo-American racial discourses and 'race-thinking' of the early modern period, through the emerging colonial and subsequent post-colonial era. The conceptual breakthrough of this field means that the critics can no longer elide race within general considerations of human nature; rather they see it as a shifting category in multiple locations in which categories such 'race' and ethnicity perform different cultural functions. This has provided a useful answer and pushback to presentist identity politics. Instead it offers a more fluid vision of identity and location.

In tandem, another burgeoning trend of global, often non-Western, adaptations of Shakespeare, intersecting with post-colonial perspectives, are re-inventing his works in vibrant and significant ways; movements variously labelled as 'Native Shakespeares', 'Bollywood Shakespeares', 'Arab Shakespeares', 'Chinese Shakespeares,' and the broader category, 'Global Shakespeare', among others, are indeed a welcome development in making the field more inclusive and multifarious. In stage and film performances as well as in critical engagements, Shakespearean idioms and themes are being given new meaning within non-metropolitan and non-Western modes of knowledge and experience. The trend in 'Shakespeare and World Cinema' (also the title of Mark Burnett's book), has brought to the fore cinematic interpretations of his works in locations and cultures far afield and beyond Western representations. Why has this idea or field of 'Global Shakespeares' caught on? How does it 'register the shifting locus of anxiety between cultural particularity and universality'? (Huang 2013, 273) These are pertinent questions that force us to re-think whether the hallowed Bard is universal, culturally neutral or can be assimilated within different cultures and histories.

First let us acknowledge, again drawing from Huang (2013), that '"global Shakespeares' operate as a transnational brand," and have gained a "critical mass of participants, from the arts, academe, and public and private sectors ... visible in publications, at conferences, at festivals, and in institutions' (274). But, even as we stress the transnational networks of the plays travelling through disparate cultures and societies, often eschewing or bypassing state power and endorsements, I believe that we are in danger of eliding the divide between the global north and south, or between Anglo-American classrooms and the 'native', 'non-metropolitan knowledges' that are intertwined into global Shakespeares as they make their way into the West. Martin Orkin (2005) raises the important question about who are Shakespeare's 'local readers'? He first reminds us of what constitutes local readers in Western, metropolitan locations: who 'in their encounters with the texts have shared and continue to share a common bank of Shakespeare scholarship and knowledge. Constituting the centre of Shakespeare studies, they may be thought of as the Shakespeare metropolis' (3). Yet by now, in our post-colonial world, 'as a result of the processes of colonization and globalization, Shakespeare's texts have long since travelled further afield'. Thus, he provocatively asks: 'what may recognition and exploration of ... markedly dissonant locations contribute to the understanding of the text and its locations?' (4). 'Non-metropolitan knowledges', he argues, 'offer additional opportunities for thinking about Shakespeare's plays (and Shakespeare's readers)', which are crucial in bringing in new perspectives to the scholarly Shakespeare metropolis (3). What Orkin proposed here in 2005 has been further articulated by other intercultural critical works, mining the plays for new meanings in non-western contexts, and in excess of their canonical, western uses (Dionne and Kapadia 2008, 2).

While the critical trend is loud and clear in proposing a global, intercultural Shakespeare in general, with its corollaries in subfields such as comparative race theory and post-colonial studies, among others, we must ask further, what happens 'on the ground' in Anglo-American university courses that deploy these approaches? What meanings in excess of canonicity and what expressions of subalternity can non-western appropriations of Shakespeare yield within the status quo of educational transactions in the classroom in the US? These issues have gathered more complex urgency in the 'Black Lives Movement' that has currently swept the world. How do we align this movement that stemmed from anti-black racism in America to other subaltern, global movements – including efforts to interrogate colonial history? Addressing such questions through the instance of teaching *Hamlet* and its Indian film adaptation *Haider* in an American classroom, as I demonstrate, unveils a complex two-way transaction. On the one hand it shows students how Shakespeare goes 'native' with the tragic, poetic language and representations in a play such as *Hamlet* giving us a distinct emotional language to understand the disintegration of the characters caught up under the surveillance state of Kashmir in the film adaptation of *Haider*. On the other hand, it highlights how Vishal Bhardwaj's film in turn offers us an emotional language to understand the characters in the midst of betrayal and violence in Denmark.[1]

A pedagogy of cultural intelligibility

When I talk of the American classroom, I approach it on two levels: on one hand, the broad humanistic investments in teaching Shakespeare as a marker of universal cultural value and experiential perspectives; and on the other hand, reflecting demographics of racial and ethnic difference in the contemporary US. Of course, as Renaissance teachers in this US classroom, our task is to recover racialized discourses in the rich body of earlier work – lyrics, plays, travel accounts, religious treatises, aesthetic theories – which can uncover the powerful discursive mechanisms energized by resilient tropes of otherness, often in binaries of black/white. Shakespearean race studies (with an emphasis on 'blackness'), beginning with Kim Hall's seminal *'Things of Darkness'* to the 2016 issue of *Shakespeare Quarterly* on 'Rereading Early Modern Race', and the 2017 edited collection by Delia Jarrett-Macaulay, *Shakespeare, Race, and Performance: the Diverse Bard* have provided pedagogical support for such intellectual inquiries. However, it is a critical commonplace that students bring their own histories into classroom discussions; in the contemporary US climate, an awareness of race and ethnic histories dominates, with accompanying recognition and interrogation of 'white privilege'. Thus, in teaching a work like *Othello* and *Oroonoko*, one can often observe how Caucasian, 'white' students may more often find it easier to relegate early modern representations of 'race' and racism to the past, marking easy historical divisions between 'then' and 'now'.[2] Though this demarcation is not static either. As we can see from the intermingling of different races in rallies for Black Lives Matter, responses to the plays do not neatly line by racial/ethnic lines. However, given fraught racial histories in the US, students of colour as historians of the early modern period engage in a process of 'domestication', according to racial and ethnic divisions in the contemporary US: 'by the different questions they raise and by the continuities and discontinuities they perceive between past and present racial inequities' (Singh, 1998, 75).

Thus, early modern Shakespearean race studies as they emerge in American classrooms often take on *local dimensions*, addressing concerns of contemporary race struggles that easily lend themselves to plays like *Othello, The Tempest, The Merchant of Venice* and *Titus Andronicus*. Of course, critics often point to interconnections between racial tropes and intimations of England's proto-colonial forays into the early modern period. Students productively engage with Shakespearean plays about 'race', more strongly evident in uses of *Othello*, but works like *Titus Andronicus*, *The Merchant of Venice* and *Antony and Cleopatra* are also often viewed through a critical race lens. In sum, however, the dominant imperative in US classrooms, among all students, irrespective of their colour, race or ethnicity, is always cast in domestic, US-centred terms.

However, when the intercultural perspectives of the Global Shakespeare movement enter the curriculum, they call for new, culturally diverse, and yet specific, perspectives on ideological struggles around issues of race, gender, ethnicity, religious and national identity, among others, in global contexts. Here I would like to call for a dialogue between US race studies and the Global Shakespeare movement that can run in tandem, and in the process offer us deeper, intersectional views of global race and identity struggles. A group of foreign film adaptations that have emerged as an important intercultural phenomenon encompass the *oeuvre* of Indian film director Vishal Bhardwaj; *Maqbool* (*Macbeth*) *Omkara* (*Othello*); and most recently *Haider* (*Hamlet*). The term 'Bollywood Shakespeare', often used to describe these films, is somewhat strained, complicated and cross-hatched, as perceptively explored by Craig Dionne and Parmita Kapadia in their topical and timely anthology, *Bollywood Shakespeares*.[3] While the term, when applied to Bhardwaj's film, may suggest (to many Western readers) a kind of 'watering down' of the sacrosanct, canonical bard, these films have nonetheless created a critical 'buzz' in various reviews and cultural debates.[4] Demonstrating the reach of Shakespeare, these films fuse the global dissemination of Bollywood Hindi cinema with local, non-Western contexts. Academic colleagues and cultural critics often cite Bhardwaj's film versions so the next question to ask is: Through what kind of trajectories of exchange does global Shakespeare intercultural work enter the US classroom in Bhardwaj's films such as *Haider/Hamlet*?

The story of Kashmir's long political and cultural struggle as played out in the 1990s insurgency offers a challenging and unfamiliar context for students' experience of perhaps Shakespeare's most famous and iconic play. Despite the challenge of the language, most students in mainstream American universities find Shakespearean plots engaging – with varying degrees of familiarity – and mostly, though unevenly, can be encouraged to do the work to master the difficult language and vocabulary of the plays and poems. My assertion does not only come from experience, but the fact that typically some contact with Shakespeare's plays is intrinsic to the curriculum of English literary studies in some form in many, if not most, high school and Higher Educational institutions. Even with all the challenges to the humanities, the cultural capital accruing to the signifier 'Shakespeare' makes students open the Bard's works. The world of *Hamlet* with all its moral pitfalls and ambiguities has become domesticated in the Western imagination. Denmark and Elsinore do not evoke a precise topicality, but carry an emotional and affective charge as a tragic drama about a riven kingdom and family. In Bhardwaj's film, he problematizes the role of the tragic protagonist Haider, the Hamlet figure, showing how his personal traumas are imbricated in the political, cultural and historical undercurrents that shaped the Kashmir civil conflict and occupation until the mid 1990s. So, is this still Shakespeare's play? Or some rendering of the story in an 'exotic' locale?

Let us consider how the play is refracted through the Kashmiri conflict. 'Kashmir' only offers a very vague name recognition in the US, often elided with Cashmere, or even if recognized as a historical entity, it figures in loose associations with India and possibly Pakistan. In the past year, while the Indian occupation of Kashmir has received some coverage in the international and global media, it does not loom large in the US imaginary. Though in general terms, in the collective imagination of the Indian subcontinent, the disputed border territory is closely associated with the lingering traumas of the 1947 Partition and its aftermath. The 1990s, as captured in the film, was a particularly bloody period with direct occupation of the Indian Army and a regime of surveillance and division of families. The emotional charge that drew Bhardwaj and Basharat Peer, the co-scriptwriter, to use Shakespeare's *Hamlet* as a template for a story of a fractured Kashmir and its denizens is often inaccessible to students in an American classroom, given that Kashmir rarely figures in US news (in comparison, say to Afghanistan). Thus, when I include Bhardwaj's *Haider* alongside *Hamlet*, radical cultural fault-lines appear in the classroom as students try to engage with Shakespeare in Kashmir. They can often enthusiastically relate to the love story of Haider and Arshia, an Ophelia figure who differs from her Shakespearean model in that she is represented as an independent woman journalist with agency and resolve. She openly defies her family to attach herself to Haider and join in his cause of finding his father. Overall, students can easily relate to the family dramas, the brother Khurram who betrays the older brother Dr Meer, and the woman at the centre of the drama, Ghazala/Gertrude, who marries the younger after the death of her husband. The Polonii family, in this case Arshia's father Parvez, an agent and informer of the State, and a hectoring brother Liyaqat/Laertes, who leaves Kashmir to return after her death, echo the original. The complexity in the treatment of this history is also made accessible in the ancient universal, archetypal story of a brother betraying a brother in a time of a divisive war. A story as old as Cain and Abel, this carries a familiar resonance.

Beyond these familial, emotional arrangements, one can often sense among Western students a typical, and often predictable resistance to topical specificity about the India–Pakistan Partition, the Kashmiri conflict, the 1990s Indian occupation and the ensuing civil conflict. Typically, American students, though covering a range of ethnicities, races and religions, do not wish to 'travel' with *Haider* through Kashmir in any sustained way. I recognize that this broad, experiential claim may not apply in every classroom setting, but using this as one template, I want to explore ways in which students can be trained to read global cultural difference with contextual depth (including local cultural languages), as well as offer a pedagogy that uses the 'local' 'non-Western' culture to read Shakespeare and vice versa.

In the case of *Haider*, I call this approach a *pedagogy of cultural intelligibility* – which requires of the students a reading of the Shakespearean language and plot by refracting it through the tragic historical conflicts faced by Bhardwaj's protagonist in 1990s Kashmir. I use the term "intelligibility" with a deliberate sense of sustained effort to decipher seemingly opaque cultures. How does any text or film become intelligible? How do we break down terms and concepts – with differing affective charges – into cultural, social and affective terms that become domesticated and culturally akin to our own? While Anglo-American academia and culture in general often bandy about the term 'cultural literacy', I deliberately eschew that label as it implies a general knowledge, or a check list, rather than a sustained engagement and struggle for understanding. Such a pedagogy of 'cultural intelligibility' eschews any 'pure' identity, while recognizing the hybrid post-colonial world.

Locating the film in the period during a time of a collective trauma, the director presents it in terms of a suggestive analogy: 'In my film, in a way, Kashmir becomes Hamlet' (Bhardwaj, 'Interview', Harmeet Singh 2014). I use this ingenious, though somewhat strained metaphor as an entry point into the play for students to unpack the fault lines between an individual and collective trauma. Kashmir is not simply Elsinore. The latter is a barricaded, closed domain of surveillance, with action fairly contained – in the court, in closets, battlements, and a cemetery scene. There is a reference to Ophelia drowning, but we do not see it. Kashmir in *Haider* invokes vast, sweeping landscapes, cemeteries, gardens, rivers, villages, as well as incarceration camps and town squares. This insistent landscape also enables students to focus on Shakespeare's 'travels' in the world, in dissonant locations such as a fractured Kashmir, while re-thinking their relationship to the 'original' text. Students learn in the process to travel globally and yet become 'local readers'. In doing so, we also address the sources of the film, most notably the co-scriptwriter, Basharat Peer's *Curfewed Night* which forms the basic framework of the film. In a 2010 interview, Peer observes, 'Kashmir is a place where there have been too many deaths', thus providing a context for poignant representations of cemeteries and graveyards, with the film's extended finale taking place amidst a landscape of graves and continuing violence. It is useful to read *Haider* in conjunction with Peer's memoir, showing how the brutal history of Kashmir permeates Shakespeare's play. To this contextual reading, I further add the poetry of Agha Shahid Ali, the Kashmiri poet whose work resonates in Peer's memoir, which takes its title from Ali.

Return to Shakespeare's *Hamlet*

Finally, in our explorations of how Kashmir becomes Hamlet, we return to Shakespeare's play to consider how our journey into Kashmir may offer additional opportunities for rethinking the play. Students are now asked to unpack the depth and breadth of Hamlet's experience of tragic loss at the death of his father and the aftermath of his mother's marriage, as in this passage below:

> How weary, stale, flat and unprofitable
> Seem to me all the uses of this world!
> ... 'tis an unweeded garden
> That grows to seed, things rank and gross in nature
> Possess it merely.
>
> *Hamlet* (1.2.133–6)

In these iconic lines from Shakespeare's *Hamlet*, we see Hamlet's psychic struggle to locate his personal grief into the world metaphorically conceived as an 'unweeded garden', which seems 'weary, stale, flat, and unprofitable' to him but the larger world remains within the confines of Elsinore, even though Denmark is conceived of as a 'prison'. References to outside locations such as Wittenburg or England remain elusive markers than any 'real' locations until the end, when Fortinbras enters the stage as the conqueror. If Shakespeare's *Hamlet* is the ultimate metonymy for the tragic early modern – and for the formation of the individual subject as we see in Hamlet's psychic struggles – Bhardwaj's *Haider* creates a tragic subjectivity in which the personal is repeatedly imbricated in the historical, cultural and political currents that both underlie and shape the Kashmir militancy and occupation. Herein lies the challenge to make the Kashmiri locales, history, language and culture intelligible to the students. We address questions about the 1990s insurgency in Kashmir against the national Indian government and its military, about Pakistan's involvement across the border, and of the brutal repression of local Kashmiris under the guise of suppressing terrorism. Thus, in *Haider*, Shakespeare's play is refracted through post-colonial history of the subcontinent, with a close-up of the ravaged beauty of Kashmir.

So why, students ask, do we need this Shakespearean template within which to represent this land far removed from the story with only a few broad echoes? Shakespeare's *Hamlet*, in fact, offers a distinct emotional language to understand the disintegration of the characters caught in sundered relationships in the midst of betrayal and violence in *Haider*. Furthermore, it also contributes to the primal story of 'brother against brother' to formulate and envision the workings of a surveillance state. Thus, considering *Hamlet* through the prism of the contextual histories of *Haider*, students cannot have the luxury of tracking the lives of small familial units. Instead, they begin to track the poetic resemblances between Shakespeare's play and the film: 'all of Kashmir is a prison' or 'Kashmir becomes Hamlet', and the resonances between the two works proliferate into a complex tragic experience. Despite the multiple dead bodies strewn on stage, and the impending conquest of Denmark in Shakespeare's *Hamlet*, it is in the end largely only the protagonist's tragedy, summed up by Horatio in these elegiac lines:

> Now cracks a noble heart. Goodnight, sweet Prince,
> And flights of angels sing thee to thy rest.
>
> (5.2.343–5)

This contrast between the two works, when addressed in the classroom, leads the students to recognize that they cannot identify with and relate to Haider, in whose language the original soliloquies are incorporated into dialogues and public addresses with similar ease as they can do to Shakespeare's Hamlet who beckons them into his inner psychic space in his soliloquies.[5] Thus, Western epistemological certainties are disrupted in *Haider*, as Western students attempt to understand his motivations and experiences within unfamiliar historical traumas.

Another productive area of inquiry into the echoes and distinctions between *Hamlet* and *Haider* in the classroom concerns the differing treatments of the central theme of revenge in both works. The template for *Hamlet* is the classical, Senecan revenge tragedy as well as Nordic sources that highlight the bloody mechanics of revenge. Revenge as a timeless plot device becomes a useful entry for students' engagement with the play, given the fare of violence and revenge in Western-themed contemporary popular culture. The iconic scene recognized by all students is when Hamlet faces the Ghost in the image of his father who calls for revenge: 'If thou didst ever thy father love ... Revenge his foul and most unnatural murder" (1.5.757–62). With confident resolve, Hamlet declares: 'Haste me to know't, that I, with wings as swift/As meditation or thoughts of love, / May sweep to my revenge' (1.5.763–5). We all know that unlike the more predictable avengers in early modern revenge tragedies, ranging from Thomas Kyd's *The Spanish Tragedy* to Thomas Middleton's *The Revenger's Tragedy*, and even Laertes and Fortinbras in *Hamlet*, violent action for revenge eludes Hamlet as he drifts in the posturings of his 'antic disposition'. The generic compulsion of the Renaissance revenge tragedy focuses on the revenger as an individual, once-noble protagonist, who is called to commit revenge but fails or falters in his task. Shakespeare offers us a more complex view of a revenger in *Hamlet*, who grapples with moral questions and philosophical inquiry, but dies with his credentials of 'nobility' as 'sweet Prince' intact.

The treatment of revenge in *Haider*, however, reveals different cultural investments in the history of the subcontinent, in that not only is Haider, the tragic protagonist-cum-avenger, but Kashmir itself embodies histories of revenge and retribution in the India–Pakistan conflict. For American students comparing the two works, Haider's search for his missing, and later murdered, father has an unfamiliar political, communal resonance in repeated shots of cemeteries in the film – leading to the climactic ending of the film in a cemetery (rather than the palace duel in *Hamlet*). They are drawn into the local world of Kashmiri society and culture. Thus, Haider's angst-ridden trauma is but a mirror for horrors visited upon the denizens of the land in torture chambers, police raids, check points, blasted homes and graveyards. The film also creatively translates the original ambiguity regarding the Ghost in Shakespeare's play by replacing the ghost of Hamlet's father with the presence of a phantasmal militant, hiding his bruises under dark glasses, aptly called *Roohdar* (soul/spirit retainer), played by the charismatic actor, Irfan Khan. He brings the message of revenge (*Intiqam*) from Hamlet's dead father (Dr Meer) whom he knew in the torture chambers of the Indian military. Revenge as a theme veers away from the English revenge genre in *Haider*, as the call to revenge (*Intiqam*), both for Haider and the Kashmiris, including resistance fighters, brutalized by the occupying forces, is tempered by a call for true freedom or *Azaadi* – here specifically implying a freedom from violent retribution. In a surprise twist at the end of the film, Haider refuses to fire the final shot on his traitorous uncle Khurram (Claudius), after a skirmish between insurgents and the police in the final graveyard scene. Haider rejects the course of individual vengeance as the screen shot widens into a larger frame of the snowy, bloodied landscape of Kashmir. The communal vision of loss and tragedy that shapes the final vision of *Haider* invokes mourning for a land carrying the burden of the traumas of multiple generations in the Indian subcontinent. Shakespeare's iconic *Hamlet* enables Bhardwaj to tell a compelling and lyrical history of Kashmir's partitions.

The film, the students learn, opens an intercultural perspective on the thematic conflicts and selected images drawn from Shakespeare's play, for example, graveyards, prisons and bed chambers, among others. Thus, in its best pedagogical possibilities, local and global and early modern and post-colonial converge in the film's impact on learning audiences, both in the Shakespearean world and beyond. Global Shakespeare (like race studies) can offer students a chance to explore a more nuanced understanding of Shakespeare, the world, and themselves.

Notes

1 For a discussion of the relation between the film and the play, see Singh, *Shakespeare and Postcolonial Theory*, chapter 7.
2 For a full discussion of racialized responses in contemporary classrooms to early modern texts, see Singh (1998): 72–5.
3 See Dionne and Kapadia (2014), 'Introduction,' 1–15.
4 As examples, see Singh (2019) and Charry and Shahani (2014).
5 This has interesting parallels with Abhishek Sarkar's article which asserts that *Haider* 'decisively jettisons this radical interiorization of action in favour of a wider communal focus that has a direct bearing upon Haider's personal travails . . . It is evident that the film does not deploy the human crisis of Kashmir only as a convenient objective correlative of Haider's problems. On the contrary, it seeks to project Haider's sufferings as symptomatic of, and objectively continuous with, the vexed reality of Kashmir.'

References

Ali, Agha Shahid. *The Country without a Post Office*. New Delhi: Ravi Dayal, 1997.
Bhardwaj, Vishal, and TRM Editors. 'Decoding Shakespeare: Vishal Bhardwaj on *Haider* at NYIFF', *The Review Monk*, 15 May 2015. Available online: https://thereviewmonk.com/article/

decoding-shakespeare-vishal-bhardwaj-haider-nyiff/ (accessed 29 April 2018).
Charry, Brinda, and Gitanjali Shahani. 'The Global as Local: *Othello* as *Omkara*', in Craig Dionne, and Parmita Kapadia, (eds.), *Bollywood Shakespeares*. New York: Palgrave Macmillan, 2014, 107–23.
Dionne, Craig, and Parmita Kapadia, eds. *Native Shakespeares: Indigenous Appropriations on a Global Stage*, Aldershot, UK: Ashgate, 2008.
Dionne, Craig, and Parmita Kapadia, eds. *Bollywood Shakespeares*. New York: Palgrave Macmillan, 2014.
Hall, Kim. *'Things of Darkness': Economies of Race and Gender in Early Modern England*. Ithaca: Cornell University Press, 1995.
Hall, Kim, and Peter Erickson. '"A New Scholarly Song": Rereading Early Modern Race.' *Shakespeare Quarterly* 67, 1 (Spring 2016): 1–13.
Huang, Alexa. *Chinese Shakespeares: Two Centuries of Cultural Exchange*. New York: Columbia University Press, 2009.
Huang, Alexa. 'Global Shakespeares as Methodology', *Shakespeare* 9, 3 (2013): 273–90.
Jarrett-Macauley, Delia. *Shakespeare, Race, and Performance: The Diverse Bard*. London: Routledge, 2017.
Orkin, Martin. *Local Shakespeares: Proximations and Power*, London: Taylor & Francis, 2005.
Peer, Basharat. *Curfewed Night*, New York: Scribner, 2010.
Sarkar, Abhishek. '*Haider* and the Nation State: Shakespeare, Bollywood, and Kashmir.' *South Asian Review*, 37, 2 (2016): 29–46.
Simon, Scott. 'Interview with Basharat Peer: New Shakespeare Movie Puts *Hamlet* in Kashmir', National Public Radio, 25 October 2014. Available online: https://www.npr.org/2014/10/25/358789984/new-shakespeare-movie-puts-hamlet-in-kashmir (accessed 14 April 2018).
Singh, Harmeet. 'Interview: "Kashmir is the *Hamlet* of my Film," says Vishal Bhardwaj on *Haider*', *The Indian Express*, 5 October 2014. http://indianexpress.com/article/entertainment/bollywood/kashmir-is-the-hamlet-of-my-film/ (accessed 28 April 2018).
Singh, Jyotsna G. 'Racial Dissonance/Canonical Texts: Teaching Early Modern Literary Texts in the Late Twentieth Century'. *Shakespeare Studies*, 26 (1998).

Singh, Jyotsna G. *Shakespeare and Postcolonial Theory*. London: Arden Bloomsbury, 2019.
Singh, Jyotsna G. and Abdulhamit Arvas. 'Global Shakespeares, Affective Histories, Cultural Memories', *Shakespeare Survey*, 68 (2015) 183–96.

9

Understanding Nimmi: Tracing Interpretations of Vishal Bhardwaj's *Maqbool*

Ana Laura Magis Weinberg

Perhaps I should begin by showing my hand: this essay has been with me for almost a decade, since I began exploring the world of adaptation theory, Bollywood, and Shakespeare on screen. It stems from emotional affect, informed by personal experience. The reader will find an anomalous term here used frequently, 'love'. But I cannot express my feeling for *Maqbool* in any other terms. Pretending that I do not have a deep emotional attachment to this movie would be, I believe, dishonest. We have long laboured under the presumption that academia is objective and that there is no place for the personal within the critical – a view which dismisses that, for most of us, our career in literature arose from a love of reading and is strongly linked to our deepest affinities. In this decade of living alongside this careful examination of Nimmi, the female protagonist of Vishal Bhardwaj's *Maqbool* (2004), my interpretation of the character has changed. I have grown from an indifferent bystander in Indian cinemas into an avid Bollywood fanatic. My Hindi, through disuse, has grown noticeably worse, and my interpretations of Shakespeare on the Indian screen have evolved, especially as I inform them more and more with their contexts of production. Some things have not changed, however, and those are the same underlying affects – those 'unacademic' chords that have been struck. Vishal Bhardwaj remains my favourite Shakespeare director, and Nimmi looking into Maqbool's eyes and asking him *hum pagal ho rahe hain na?*, at the end of the film still moves me to tears.

This essay is a soliloquy where I, Macbeth-like, try to make sense of my own thoughts by speaking, sometimes to myself, sometimes in conversation with other Shakespeare and Bollywood scholars, in order to understand, exactly, why my single state of mind is shaken so whenever I watch *Maqbool*. Bhardwaj managed to do what I have not come across anywhere else on screen when he created a Lady Macbeth that one empathizes with, and all my considerations on this film are investigations into how the director, screenwriter, producer and composer managed to do this. On exploring further, and after years of watching and rewatching the film, I have come to the perhaps controversial conclusion that *Maqbool* is many things – a Bollywood crime drama heavily influenced by *Scarface*, a homage to Akira Kurosawa's *Throne of Blood*, a tradaptation of Shakespeare's *Macbeth*. But, above all, *Maqbool* is a tragedy of love. In her seminal essay on Bhardwaj's female protagonists, 'Woman as Avenger: "Indianising" the Shakespearean Tragic in the Films of Vishal Bhardwaj', Poonam Trivedi wrote that: 'While there has been considerable comment on his films, what has been little noticed is how he has modified the configuration of the genre, mainly through changes in the endings and the role of women' (23). This change in the roles of women is no small thing: by carefully altering the roles of female protagonists and adding more women with agency, Bhardwaj 'rebalances Shakespeare' (as Trivedi would have it), managing to 're-textualize' 'submerged meanings' (24). In *Maqbool*, the meaning that comes to light is the love within the Macbeth couple. By bringing it to the forefront, Bhardwaj re-genred the film, making it into a love tragedy closer to *Antony and Cleopatra* or *Romeo and Juliet*, where conflict stems from 'the power relation between the amorous couple and the outside world' (Callaghan 1994, 81). Bhardwaj found the thread of the love between the Macbeths, strong but woven into an intricate tapestry, and brought it to light. Beyond the ambition to climb to the top of an illicit empire and weïrd policemen who read horoscopes, is not *Maqbool* about the struggle of Nimmi and Maqbool to be together, and once they do so, their inability to be happy, due not to them but to the outside world?

How to proceed? Starting off with a conclusion and then fitting the facts to confirm it is not scientific. It is not academic. But what else is it that we do if not that? It might be my intersectionalities that give me pause, or my experience as a *videshi* in India,[1] with that constant feeling of not understanding the codes of conduct, of never *really* knowing what was happening around me. A misreading is a disservice to the text, but above all, it is also a form of imperialist violence: violent in that it imposes a foreign framework on a text without questioning its validity, and imperialistic in that it assumes that the Western modes of interpretation are universal, and that all modes of representation adhere to it, ignoring the internal workings of the culture that text was produced in and for.

How to ensure, then, a 'correct' interpretation? Coming from a marginalized Western country, Mexico, I am familiar with these misreadings and misinterpretations, and was wary of perpetuating the same forms of violence that I have been subjected to, academically. However, I still love this film, still want to discuss it, and still feel that my contributions are valuable. My love for this film began after my deep-running love for India and Indian literature, and my living in the country for almost a year. I felt, at the same time, deeply attached to it, while feeling as if a barrier, almost physical, stood between me and a 'fair', 'correct' or 'academic' interpretation. So, I decided to contextualize the film and, when in doubt, contextualize some more. I began this by looking at non-literary theory that could help me understand Nimmi as an Indian woman, with all the realities that this entails. Armed with this, I made the effort to closely examine the character, relying especially on subtitling and my own knowledge of Hindi. I was also fortunate enough to meet with Bhardwaj in 2014 and interview him on both *Maqbool* and his adapting process. On several occasions I consulted native-speaking friends to clarify certain aspects (particularly when Nimmi uses *hum* to refer to herself in the plural instead of the singular first person, something that I believe subtly but crucially affects the interpretation of the film). I have continued to share my research, particularly with Indian colleagues, in an attempt to amend any misreadings.

Nimmi

Nimmi, interpreted by Tabu, is the female protagonist in *Maqbool*, and follows a character arc analogous to Lady Macbeth's in that she incites her partner to murder the king (here tradapted as the head of a Muslim Mumbai mafia), falls into an altered perception of reality, and dies before the end of the text. Importantly, however, Nimmi is *not* Maqbool's wife: at the beginning of the film she is Abba-ji (Duncan)'s mistress,[2] which shifts the motivation for the couple. It is not because of a power-hungry scramble to become king and queen hereafter that they shoot (rather than stab) the reigning monarch, but because they need to remove him in order to be together. This first intuition was confirmed by Bhardwaj, who told me that he did not find much of this love in the play, but rather he had to write it into the story, noting that for Maqbool, 'the Lady Macbeth becomes the throne'. But the two aspects that truly differentiate Nimmi from other Lady Macbeths, be it on the stage, the screen or even in rewritings, is that this Lady Macbeth has a child during the course of the film.[3] Naturally, analyses of *Maqbool* have focused on this child, who has been interpreted as everything from an instrument for manipulation to an atoning presence.

However, the thing that I believe most sets this Lady Macbeth apart from all others is her capacity for inflicting violence. Lady Macbeth is famous for declaring that she would pluck the babe that suckles her and dash its brains out (a declaration of violence that is proven to be hollow once she is confronted with the deed itself) while Nimmi allows violence to be performed unto her (being physically assaulted by Abba-ji, Guddu, Sameera, and even her love Maqbool), and is willing to perform violence unto herself. When at Maqbool's doubt over the paternity of her child she says, 'I will get an abortion', rather than making grand declarations of commitment, she is offering to sacrifice a (very real) child for Maqbool's benefit. This capacity for self-harm is also manifested when she unflinchingly steps barefooted on a rusty nail in order to make Maqbool tend to her, and when she not only enters the room where the king sleeps but lies next to him in bed. Although Maqbool pulls the trigger, it is her face which is splattered with the don's blood as she calmly walks to the window and shoots into the air in order to alert the sleeping household of the killing.

There is a great sense of urgency underlying *Maqbool*. Indian screen adaptations tend to extend the narrative, usually giving backstories to characters who did not have them in the originating texts or choosing to start the films decidedly not *in medias res*. For Bhardwaj, this has meant extending the events before the beginning of Shakespeare's plays (*Omkara* (*Othello*) shows us Dolly falling in love with Omkara and the warrior passing over Langda for a promotion, while *Haider* (*Hamlet*) starts with a very much alive Dr Hilal Meer and devotes some time to show the return of Haider and the search for his father). In *Maqbool* the originating play's plot does not really begin until after the intermission: in a film with a runtime of over two hours, most of *Macbeth* takes place in its final forty minutes. But urgency, most notably, is brought by the murder of Abba-ji. The key question I have asked myself through my interpretation of Nimmi has been why they kill Abba-ji when they do. In the originating play, the timing of the assassination is decided because of its convenience, as the king will be spending a night under their roof. But in *Maqbool* this is not a consideration, as Nimmi spends every night with Abba-ji, and Maqbool, as a trusted underling, can easily contrive to also spend the night under that same roof. The assassination happens after Sameera's engagement party: although the couple have begun a physical affair in the previous days, it is not until Abba-ji starts hinting that he will replace Nimmi with a younger Bollywood up-and-comer, Miss Mohini, that the couple decide to kill him. Maqbool is not convinced by his Lady asking him to screw his courage to the sticking-place, but rather by Nimmi's putting into perspective what Abba-ji leaving her (or rather, throwing her out) would mean. Trivedi has identified this sense of urgency in the film, which I ascribe to the couple – and Nimmi in particular – being in a literal life- or death situation.

The sacrifice scene takes place after a musical number, as Nimmi places flower garlands around the necks of the goats that are to be slaughtered for the feast. The butchers take the animals and Nimmi puts the remaining garland around her own neck, while telling Maqbool, 'It's time you sacrificed me too...Jahangir [Abba-ji] has got his new mistress' (77). Nimmi has transformed completely, and for the first time shows herself to be vulnerable, without the illness that has so far attended her. She cries, imploringly, but her words do not seem to have any effect on Maqbool until she says, 'Can't even go back home...Everyone knows I am Jahangir's concubine. He looks so repulsive naked...must be as old as my father' (78). These words reveal that Nimmi ran away from home and does not have her family's protection. With this, the Indian audience would immediately understand that Nimmi is in real danger and that breaking up with Abba-ji would mean being left homeless and without the means for subsistence. In Nimmi's situation, and considering the desperation she is going through, the only option seems to be to get rid of Abba-ji. Nimmi asks Maqbool to choose: '*Hum ya Jahangir*'. In the film's high register with a strong Urdu presence, *hum* means simply 'me'. However, in the popular Hindi that most of the film's target audience would speak, *hum* means 'us'. This word can be heard and interpreted both ways simultaneously, without one excluding the other; however, the meaning that would be most easily accessible to the audience would be the plural. This dilemma, 'us or him', comes close to the rhetoric of love tragedies where the couple must face the world.

As a foreigner, one of the most important points in my research was contextualizing Nimmi's position. For this I had to resort to sociological texts that would discuss the situation of women in India – texts that, in 2014 in Mexico, were not particularly easy to come by. I found texts that describe motherhood or the role of women during the movement for Independence, but the lack of bibliography on women who are in illicit relationships was telling. Nimmi (and this bears insisting upon) is not married to Abba-ji at the beginning of the film. Even before we meet Nimmi, the film presents us with Abba-ji looking at the photograph of his dead wife, Rukhsana.[4] That the betrayal onto Abba-ji was done by Rukhsana's brother shows how deep those kinship ties still are. Maqbool, on hearing the prophecy that he will take over the brother-in-law's business, does not respond awe-struck that Asif lives and is a prosperous gentleman. Rather, his disbelief lies in the fact that Abba-ji would never move against this man. It is only his betrayal of the don that drives Abba-ji to execute him and elevate Maqbool to his rank.

Nimmi is Abba-ji's mistress, a position so precarious that all relevant information I could find revolved around prostitutes or widows: women whose guardianship (if not legally, at least socially) has been removed from their fathers but is not in the hands of a husband, making them quasi-ghosts who inhabit a liminal and precarious place. Legally and socially, Nimmi has no standing. In the sacrifice scene, where she equates herself with a goat to be slaughtered, she reminds Maqbool that she had run away from her home (in far-away Lucknow, while the film takes place in Mumbai): she cannot go back to the paternal home nor be expected to be taken in by any family. The power dynamics that are evinced in the film show that, although she leads a comfortable life, everything around her belongs to

Abba-ji (as opposed to Lady Macbeth, who is mistress of Inverness). The way others react once Abba-ji has been killed and Nimmi 'goes to' Maqbool[5] makes it clear that the couple could not have been together even if Abba-ji had discarded Nimmi: she would always remain the don's property, not to be picked up by anybody else. When Nimmi tells Maqbool, in the sacrifice scene, 'you must kill either him or me', she means it in the most literal sense: if Abba-ji is permitted to supplant Nimmi with Miss Mohini, Nimmi will be left completely destitute.

However, social contextualizing did not end there. There is another sub-text running in Indian culture, and that is the woman's role as outlined by sacred texts, such as the *Ramayana*. In this epic, Sita's chastity is of such extraordinary importance that she is constantly questioned until she goes through fire as proof that she remained virtuous through her imprisonment. That Sita was a prisoner and the victim would not have mattered: it is her responsibility to be faithful to her consort, implying that rape by the demon Ravana would still have been Sita's fault. It was through Farhat Jahan's historical survey of how womanhood has been constructed in India that I discovered the importance of female chastity in the Indian context: there seems to be the underlying narrative in the Indian cultural imagination that women are by nature polluting, and that their only redemption lies in being good wives and mothers.

Love

There are two scenes that show how we should interpret Nimmi. As opposed to the overt descriptions of her as a bewitching evil influence, it is in two key moments, guided by very subtle performance, where the film hints at the truth behind both Maqbool and Nimmi. One such moment happens at the end of the song '*Jhini mini jhini*', which portrays engagement rituals in the women's quarter interspersed with Miss Mohini seductively dancing for Abba-ji. The two scenes overlap until the men walk into the women's tent and the actual engagement takes place, where Nimmi stands behind Sameera as a mother would: she still retains a position of power within the household. But when the ceremony is over, Miss Mohini takes Abba-ji's hand and begins to dance with him in front of all the guests. Nimmi stands to the side, and in a few seconds her facial expression changes. In the following scene we see Miss Mohini sitting next to Abba-ji while Nimmi, who has changed out of her elegant outfit, waits on them like a servant. This is what gives way to her realization that either she or Abba-ji must die, a realization which she expresses melodramatically by placing a sacrificial wreath around her neck.

The other scene I am referring to takes place early in the film just before the pilgrimage song (which the script tells us is a Sufi song in praise for the Almighty but is also 'implying Maqbool's feelings for Nimmi' (40)), a scene that is widely ignored by criticism and seems to be coloured by the previous instances of Nimmi's 'manipulation' of both Abba-ji and Maqbool. The scene begins with Nimmi on the road, arms crossed, standing motionless until Maqbool is forced to save her from being run over by a vehicle. After this she tells him, 'That astrologer Inspector Pandit of yours ... he's a goddamn liar ... You'll never take Abba ji's place', and when he asks her why, she replies, 'You are a wimp [...] you'd burn in my love but you'd never have the guts to touch me' (38). This exchange is subtle but crucial to the film. Nimmi refers to the prophecy made by Purohit regarding Maqbool's future, who declared him 'King of kings'. Some consider that Maqbool is not in love with her, like William C. Ferleman, who says that 'Nimmi cunningly tempts Maqbool into an illicit and amorous love affair', suggesting that Maqbool's tragic flaw is falling into this trap: 'Macbeth indeed "murdered himself when he murdered Duncan"; in the film, Maqbool murders himself when he agrees to "fall" in love with Nimmi'. However, this interpretation completely ignores that Nimmi already knows the prophecy, as is clear by Irrfan Khan's performance, where his lack of surprise acknowledges the constant conversations between the two. Bhardwaj chooses to suggest an offscreen moment that corresponds to the greatest point of intimacy in the couple – the letter where Macbeth informs his wife of what has happened with the witches. This small scene proves that Maqbool and Nimmi have more exchanges than those we are witness to: perhaps, as she says, he dares not touch her, but he makes her his partner of greatness by informing her of the prophecy.

Academic criticism amongst Shakespeare scholars tends to refer to Nimmi as one of the many Lady Macbeths who use sexuality to manipulate her husband, as is shown by Ferleman's view that 'Maqbool is unmarried and ostensibly uninterested in women; he must be seduced into a transgressive affair by Nimmi'. Trivedi notes that 'Bhardwaj makes Nimmi the aggressor in love, and she unabashedly pursues her sexual attraction for Maqbool' (29), and while it is true that Nimmi appears to be the pursuer, this does not mean that Maqbool is not interested in her. Lady Macbeth manipulates her husband when he changes his mind and decides not to kill Duncan, while Nimmi's manipulation lies in her forcing Maqbool to acknowledge his feelings for her and, in her own view, stop being 'a wimp' who 'does not have the guts to touch her', be it holding her hand, calling her 'darling' or having sex. Never does she force him to have a relationship he does not want. As she tells him, 'You never had the guts to even look at me but I knew what you wanted [...] You can die for me at this very instant...and kill for me as well...Tell me if that's a lie' (39).

Despite these elements that hint to the closeness of the couple, many critics have chosen to focus only on Nimmi's overt acknowledgement of her love for Maqbool, discussing the relationship in terms of 'the seduction of Maqbool into treachery by Abbuji's mistress Nimmi' (Singh, 4), or fixating on her as a manipulating seductress: 'the loaded gun in Nimmi's hand speaks to Maqbool's helplessness relative to the intimate, intimidating presence of Nimmi's seductive sexuality' (Ferleman). This last reading is particularly worrying, since it negates the full range of violence that Nimmi is subjected to throughout the film by Abba-ji, Guddu and especially Maqbool. In particular, when referring to the firearm, one must remember that Nimmi playfully points it at Maqbool (and is subsequently beaten with it), but some scenes later (just before they go through with the assassination), Maqbool not only presses the gun to her temple but actually pulls the trigger.[6] While Macbeth and Lady Macbeth are together from the beginning of the play, Nimmi and Maqbool spend the first part of the movie establishing their relationship. Vishal Bhardwaj acknowledged that this changes the motive behind Abba-ji's murder, stating that he made this alteration because of the requirements of the plot: 'I was just thinking: "what will make my film work?" Not *Macbeth* the play but my *Maqbool* the film...Films should have some love and not just lust...Now in retrospect, when I see, I think the boldest step was to change the character of Lady Macbeth'.

Abba-ji

Interpreting Nimmi hinges entirely on interpreting Abba-ji. Some critics see him as an idealized father figure: 'we first see Abbaji as a father. We are introduced first to the benevolent paternal aspect of the sinister conqueror and thus shown that even within this vicious despot, there is some kind of balance' (Croteau 2010, 5), but I find that these readings lack a more critical interpretation of the performances in the film. In contrast, for example, to how Amitabh Bachchan would depict a dignified older man, Pankaj Kapur is shown slurping, picking his teeth, and spitting. During a meeting with his underlings, the camera follows his greasy hand and lingers as he wipes it on his hair, forcing us to witness each of his unsavoury habits. When we see his naked torso, Kapur has hunched his back and exaggerated his paunch. Abba-ji's characterisation has been calculated to elicit our disgust: 'The paan chewing don's gruff voice betrays an inner sickness; his gait, slowed down by flab, his concupiscence, is marked by a sense of the decay of flesh' (Biswas 2006, 8). As if zooming in on Nimmi's revolted face when he gets into bed was not enough, Nimmi will later confess her disgust: 'The Don, Abbuji, is old and obese, and she confesses she is repulsed by his corporeality' (Trivedi 2019, 29). This king, as opposed to Duncan, is also riddled with moral defects: 'In such manipulations of the source-text, Bhardwaj effectively shifts the weight of the moral flaw of Macbeth, as Abbaji is no benevolent Duncan; none is better than the other' (Dutta 2013, 41). Abba-ji has been interpreted in the light of gangster film traditions with a heavy focus on *The Godfather*. However, the best correspondence I can trace is to Brian de Palma's *Scarface*, which presents many analogies to *Maqbool*: a young upstart is taken affectionately in by a mafia don, he is dangerously attracted to the don's mistress and his desire for her leads in part to his killing his mentor, and this upstart is left completely isolated by the end. A parallel can be seen in *Maqbool*, especially in how the upstart has to kill the Don to move ahead and how instrumental his mistress is in his desire to usurp the Don's place. There is a visual echo of Tony Montana's mansion, which plays with the audience's expectations: when we expect the storming of the house (which fulfills the prophecy that the sea will come knocking at Maqbool's door) and the protagonist's death as he defends his home, we instead find him gone.

Seeing Abba-ji thus, instead of in Don Corleone's idealized image, can help shed light on *Maqbool*. In *Scarface*, Montana, despite admiring Frank Lopez, recognizes that he cannot continue to co-exist with his mentor, breaking their bond when Lopez orders a hit on Montana and later lies about it, thus becoming a 'cockroach' in the criminal's eye. This de-idealizing of the Don also operates in *Maqbool*. Maqbool, just as Macbeth, has to be talked into killing the king. However, it is not the promise he has made his wife that convinces him, but rather, as in *Scarface*, the de-idealization of the mafia boss.[7]

Child

Nimmi is, to date, the only Lady Macbeth who has become a mother on screen. Ferleman takes Nimmi's pregnancy as another of her strategies to manipulate Maqbool, and states that 'Nimmi cunningly tempts Maqbool into an illicit and amorous love affair, the result of which is her pregnancy', while Trivedi sees the child as an atoning element: 'Nimmi, who leads Maqbool into treachery and murder, through her babe, redeems him from them' (2019, 32). The pregnancy has several functions within the film. On one hand, it leads to the disarticulation of the couple, since they cannot agree on the child's paternity: 'The film brings in the element of suspense about the father of the child, and this doubt becomes a key reason for the breakdown of Maqbool's and Nimmi's relationship' (Sapra 2012, 6). It is also used to signify Nimmi's 'sleepwalking' when she confesses that the fetus's crying does not let her sleep. Instead of a tyrannical and paranoid Macbeth we get an overwhelmed Maqbool: when he chooses to look after Nimmi his empire begins to crumble, and at the moment he tries to tend to the business Guddu and Boti break into his (once Abba-ji's) home and Nimmi is harmed. Maqbool is forced to accept a risky deal but abandons it to rush to Nimmi's side at the hospital, where the child has been born prematurely. As Maqbool strokes Nimmi lovingly, the intimate tableau is interrupted by a man who barges into the room: Maqbool listens to him while holding on to Nimmi, and there is a clear dilemma between the public and the private in a scene that echoes *Throne of Blood* when Washizu must decide between being with his wife or defending his castle: Khan even mimics Toshiro Mifune's head movements as he violently turns from one to the other.

It is here that I have felt the most barriers to my *videshi* understanding. While I do not believe, as Ferleman, that the child is a manipulative ploy, I was surprised when an Indian colleague pointed out that Nimmi had been redeemed by virtue of giving birth. I have always interpreted Nimmi's redemption as stemming from her becoming a love heroine. It makes sense, however, that in a culture where women can only be absolved of their evil by becoming mothers, Nimmi giving birth to a child will automatically redeem her.[8] I was also oblivious to the religious importance children (particularly male children) have, especially since both in Hinduism and Islam sons are expected to perform certain rites that will help the deceased soul ascend to Heaven or break free from the wheel of life. Beyond any social or religious interpretation, Trivedi (2019, 32) identifies the child's presence in a more dramatic context:

> Nimmi's child is central to the resolution posed by the film; it becomes the instrument of the tragic catharsis. Maqbool gives up his life of bloodshed, abdicates violence, is killed soon thereafter, and appropriately, seems at peace. Nimmi's child brings about a reprieve: as Maqbool falls to the ground and his eyes shut, the camera swivels up to show a blue sky, and birdsong and spiritual music flooding in.

Reading the film

Rahul Sapra states that 'Nimmi is portrayed as a victim of the underworld don' (2012, 4), while Amrita Sen contextualizes her in a larger filmic tradition: 'Abbaji's mistress shares much in common with the fallen women who emerge as love interests of rising gang lords' (2009, 4–5). However, despite my original interpretation of Nimmi as a love heroine, the character remains much more problematic than this, which can be understood through other filmic influences, particularly Bhardwaj's own *Omkara* and the portrayal of 'seductresses' in Bollywood cinema. Nimmi shares much with Bhardwaj's interpretation of Desdemona in Dolly, who has also been plucked out of her context, isolated in a world that completely belongs to her partner where she is expected to become the obedient housewife. Despite Dolly being more developed on screen than her Shakespearean counterpart, innocence remains her defining characteristic (not only sexual but also as child-like naïveté). Even as she is conscious of the noose that is slowly tightening around her, she knows there is nowhere for her to go. As she tells Omkara when he accuses her of giving his family heirloom away, 'Who do I have besides you anyway . . .? Have left the whole goddamn world to be with you' (120).

It may not be that Nimmi was crafted through Desdemona,[9] but rather that Bhardwaj is interested in exploring the same social complexities regarding women: all his Shakespearean heroines (Ghazala, Dolly, Nimmi) exist in a traditional society that allows them very little agency. These women try to escape their circumstances and find a semblance of happiness (in each case by marrying the man they love despite social constraints) but instead discover that there is no escaping the web they are enmeshed in, as if Bhardwaj's corrupted and isolated India is a nightmare from which they are trying to awake. On finding out the inevitability of their situation, the three women resign themselves to their fate.[10] In the case of Nimmi, this is manifested when Sameera and Guddu throw her to the ground, throttling her as they call her a witch. From then on, Nimmi will be a sleepwalking shell of herself, with a single last lucid moment before her death. Dolly's father tells Omkara 'may you never forget the two-faced monster a woman is...she who can dupe her own father will never be anyone's to claim' (29), and this phrase is also applicable to Nimmi. When she tells Maqbool that she ran away from her father's home, the target audience doubly understands that she is essentially destitute and that she is a bad daughter (and therefore a bad woman), who deserves all ill that can befall her.

My interpretation of Nimmi as a love heroine is confirmed by the Bollywood traditions that Bhardwaj uses: particularly in the love songs that are interspersed through the first part of the film, we see the convention of romantic performance in Bollywood, whether it is the pious woman performing a religious ceremony that the male protagonist looks on, the celebratory song in the woman's quarter filled with gestures of complicity between Sameera and Nimmi (as if the plot revolved around two couples in love) or the song where the man has hurt the woman and is trying to win her forgiveness. However, these conventional representations of Bollywood love are purposefully equivocating: each of these scenes is sinisterly punctuated with violence and manipulation (during the pilgrimage Nimmi hurts herself, the fight that Maqbool is trying to make amends about started with him pointing a gun at Nimmi and then physically assaulting her, and the celebratory song is interspersed with Miss Mohini dancing for Abba-ji).

Nimmi is problematic as a Bollywood heroine. Despite having been interpreted as a film 'in which for the lovers to unite, the villain, the obstacle in their path, needs to be eliminated' (Sapra 2012, 3), where 'The figure of the fallen woman as the love interest is quite common in underworld movies, but Nimmi is no common prostitute. She is "a mistress performing the wife's role"' (Dutta 2013, 41), characters in the film continuously refer to Nimmi as a witch and a whore, which cannot be disregarded as they bring to light elements that cast Nimmi as a villain. My original interpretation hinged upon feeling pity for Nimmi, finding her vulnerable and adrift in a world where she is reduced to performing domestic and sexual work for a man who can (and hints that eventually will) discard her and leave her without any protection. But as I have grown familiar with Bollywood I have come to understand her in the filmic context she exists in, especially those films where female characters are seen as bewitching the protagonists.

Perhaps not the only one, nor the most influential, but Dimple Kapadia's character in *Dil Chahta Hai* (released just three years before *Maqbool*) presents a character that is echoed in Nimmi. This is an older, troubled woman with whom one of the young protagonists falls in love. Although she does nothing to 'seduce' the young man, he still falls in love and this ruins his relationship with his mother and friends, as well as his future prospects. The film treats her as a villain, whose only redeeming quality is that she dies and sets her admirer free. This character can guide the interpretation of Nimmi for an outsider (the two characters, with their long dark hair flowing freely and dressed in salwar suits, even look similar). Tabu is not much older than Irrfan Khan, but she *is* older. In the scene where Nimmi denies Maqbool the jug of water until he confesses his love for her, we see echoes of this older seductress who leads a character into a dark, dangerous web. Kapadia's divorced woman who cannot see her daughter and who, distraught, sinks herself in alcoholism, is not treated with sympathy but is instead portrayed as a villain, and is held accountable for the young man's infatuation with her. Nimmi, after all, 'seduces' Maqbool. Despite the many clues given in the film that this is not the case, she can still be interpreted as the seductress, responsible for his downfall.

In the midst of all these avenues for (mis)interpretation, I have decided to follow the characters in order to interpret them. Abba-ji is not characterized by Kapur as being benevolent, but rather as an old man capable of a lot of violence under the seemingly calm surface he presents. Maqbool's real, deep love for Nimmi is present in how Khan breaks down upon her death, and Nimmi's desperate situation can be seen in the scene where she is in bed with Abba-ji and the camera zooms in on her disgusted expression, and particularly at the split second where we see her heart breaking as she comes to the realization that her life is about to end.

But if I interrogate what moves me every time I watch *Maqbool*, the answer does not lie in any of the reasons I have here given: these are facts that confirm my initial reaction, one that is brought about by the scene near the end where Nimmi dies in Maqbool's arms. The 'Tomorrow and tomorrow' state is not brought about by Maqbool's learning that the queen is dead. Finding himself cornered, in a last effort Maqbool drags Nimmi (and notably, not their child) from the hospital. As he is scrambling to get their passports, Nimmi begins washing the walls where she sees and smells blood. At this, instead of preparing to bear-like, fight the course, Maqbool lets himself fall to the floor and takes Nimmi in his arms. Any doubts regarding what they have felt for each other are put to rest once we see them, with her asking repeatedly *'hum pagal hain?'* (again, *'hum'* is doubly 'I' and 'we,' and the phase can be translated as 'was I / were we mad?') as she desperately tries to make sense of the end that has befallen them, her tears leading to Maqbool's own.

The treatment of the characters turns the movie into a love story, and this makes Nimmi closer to Juliet than Goneril. However, despite her becoming a love heroine and later a 'proper' Indian woman by having a child, different Bollywood tropes are used to override the subtle hints at her tragedy, leading instead to two readings: a conscientious interpretation of gestures, portrayals, cultural contextualizations and linguistics, or a broader reading influenced by tropes of seductresses, men who must be good because they are referred to as 'father', and the constant use of the word 'whore'. Which is correct? Perhaps a 'true' understanding of Nimmi does not lie in one interpretation or the other. Perhaps, just as with the word *hum*, we need to understand both realities simultaneously. Just as Nimmi can concentrate both the singular and the plural in her use of the first person, Bhardwaj has managed to compress a myriad of realities within this one character. *Maqbool* has proven to be a complex film that, in its turn, can illuminate Shakespeare's originating play, casting a new light through which we can interpret its maligned female protagonist. Nimmi is both Desdemona and Lady Macbeth, both sinned against and sinning. Our understanding of the character lies neither in one or the other, but in our ability to interpret her as both at the same time.

Notes

1. From 'vi-' which is a negative and 'desh', which means country, this term is a casual, perhaps endearing way of referring to foreigners in Hindi.
2. Other changes in character gender and configurations are also in operation. Notably, the Weïrd Sisters are portrayed by two male policemen who do not hover into the fog and filthy air but rather work with the mafia; Kaka (Banquo)'s son, Guddu, is also the one who orchestrates Maqbool's downfall and ultimately succeeds as the new head of the gang, and Sameera (Malcolm) is a daughter, rather than a son, who by marrying Guddu legitimizes him as the heir.
3. I have got to this conclusion after following William C. Carroll's survey of recent recastings of the character on the screen, stage and page in 'The Fiendlike Queen: Recuperating Lady Macbeth in Contemporary Adaptations of *Macbeth*'.

4 By this point in the film, we have already seen a woman call Maqbool after the assassination of the rival gang leader; however, her face remains in shadowy profile. The conversation is very short, with her only asking him if he is alright before quickly hanging up. We will not learn her identity or that she is Abba-ji's partner until much later.

5 Inspector Pandit clarifies that 'the rules of the business dictate that whatever was Abba jis's once, is now Maqbool's to keep ... be it daughter or whore' (93).

6 The gun was not loaded, but neither Nimmi nor the audience knew this beforehand.

7 This is of course an echo of Kurosawa's *Throne of Blood*, where Washizu's outlook changes on being told his lord assassinated his own predecessor. With *Maqbool*, many things can function doubly at the same time, and this revelation of Abba-ji's climb to the top functions as a reference both to Kurosawa and De Palma.

8 Gandhi, for example, wrote that only through motherhood can a woman 'forget she ever was or can be the object of man's lust' (1938, 36).

9 One should remember how adamant Bhardwaj is in denying his 'faithfulness' or 'reverence' towards Shakespeare, especially since he claims he has had little contact with the author beyond Lamb's retellings.

10 Gazala is the most proactive of the three and decides to kill herself and Khurram in an effort to undo her misdeeds instead of letting herself be fortune's fool.

References

Bhardwaj, V. 'Vegetarian Tacos in Paris' [interview]. Interviewed by A. L. Magis Weinberg, Paris: May 2 and 3 2014.

Biswas, M. (2006) 'Mourning and Blood-Ties: *Macbeth* in Mumbai', in *Journal of the Moving Image*. Available online at http://www.jmionline.org/article/mourning_and_blood_ties_macbeth_in_mumbai.

Callaghan, D. 'The Ideology of Romantic Love. The Case of Romeo and Juliet', in *The Weyward Sisters. Shakespeare and Feminist Politics*. Cambridge, MA: Blackwell Publishers, 1994.

Carroll, W. C. 'The Fiendlike Queen: Recuperating Lady Macbeth in Contemporary Adaptations of *Macbeth*', in *Borrowers and Lenders: The Journal of Shakespeare and Appropriation*, 2014. Available online at http://www.borrowers.uga.edu/1077/show.

Croteau, M. 'Colonial Negotiations, Intertexts, and 'Strange Garments' in *Maqbool*', paper for Shakespeare and World Cinema delivered at Shakespeare Association of America Annual Meeting, Chicago, April 1 to 3 2010.

Dutta, S. 'Shakespeare-wallah: cultural negotiation of adaptation and appropriation', in *The South Asianist* 2, 3 (*Celebrating a Century of Indian Cinema: Passions, Pleasures & Perceptions*), 2013. Available online at http://www.southasianist.ed.ac.uk/article/view/292.

Ferleman, W. C. 'What If Lady Macbeth Were Pregnant?: Amativeness, Procreation, and Future Dynasty in *Maqbool*', in A. C. Y. Huang, ed., *Asian Shakespeares on Screen: Two Films in Perspective* (special issue). *Borrowers and Lenders: The Journal of Shakespeare and Appropriation* vol. IV no. 2 (spring/summer 2009). Available at http://www.borrowers.uga.edu/1422/show.

Gandhi, M. K. 'What Is women's Role?', in *Woman and Social Injustice*. Ahmedabad: Navajivan Publishing House, 1938.

Bharadwaj, V. and Tyrewala, A. *Maqbool. The Original Screenplay with English Translation*. Noida: Harper Collins, 2014.

Bharadwaj, V., Bhatt, R., and Chaubey, A. *Omkara. The Original Screenplay with English Translation*. Noida: Harper Collins, 2014.

Trivedi, P. 'Woman as Avenger. "Indianising" the Shakespearean Tragic in the Films of Vishal Bhardwaj', in P. Trivedi, and P. Chakravarti (eds.) *Shakespeare and Indian Cinemas. 'Local Habitations'*. New York and London: Routledge, 2019.

Sapra, R. 'The Criminal Shakespeare', [paper] in *Shakespeare and Hollyworld: 40 Annual Reunion of the Shakespeare Association of America*, Boston, 1–4 April 2012. Available at http://killwill.wikispaces.com/Shakespeare+and+Hollyworld.

Sen, A. '*Maqbool* and Bollywood Conventions', in A. C. Y. Huang, ed., *Asian Shakespeares on Screen: Two Films in Perspective*. (special issue) *Borrowers and Lenders: The Journal of Shakespeare and Appropriation* vol. IV no. 2 (spring/summer 2009). Available online at http://www.borrowers.uga.edu/.

10

'Nainā ṭhaga lemge': Visual Uncertainty in *Othello* and Vishal Bhardwaj's *Omkara*

Shani Bans

'*Nainā ṭhaga lemge*' ['The eyes will deceive you'], is the first song in *Omkara* (2006), Vishal Bhardwaj's Indian adaptation of Shakespeare's *Othello* (*c*.1606).[1] As the first song, '*Nainā*' imbues an atmosphere of visual distrust similar to *Othello*. While Othello insists to 'see before [he] doubt[s]', '*Nainā*' warns both Omkara (Othello, played by Ajay Devgn) and Dolly (Desdemona, played by Kareena Kapoor) – as well as the audience – to 'doubt *what* you see' (III.iii.193). Eyes in *Omkara* behave roguishly: Gulzar's lyrics to '*Nainā*' describe how the eyes can take you night-walking into heaven ['*Nainā rāta ko calate calate / svarga mem le jāve*']. Similar to Mercutio's depiction of Queen Mab, 'the fairies' midwife', who 'gallops night by night / Through lovers' brains, and then they dream of love', Gulzar personifies the eyes as mischievous and seraphic spirits who take you night-walking into your most desired and ethereal dreams (*Romeo and Juliet*, I.iv.54, 70–71). Much like Iago's counselling of Othello to 'wear your eyes thus', as the opening song to *Omkara*, 'Nainā' resoundingly warns against visual credulity (III.iii.201; Shakespeare, 1997).[2]

This chapter offers a close reading of *Omkara*'s language, especially Gulzar's lyrics to 'Nainā', alongside Shakespeare's language of visual uncertainty in *Othello*. More attention needs to be paid to the language of Shakespearean film adaption in order to facilitate cross-cultural engagement. By translating the language of *Omkara*, this chapter aims to eliminate the language barrier and, in doing so, not only offers a case study in how translating the language of *Omkara* can open up the film to further interpretation (for example, specific thematic issues such as visual uncertainty) but also demonstrates what is at stake if we ignore the word choices of such adaptations. More broadly, this chapter encourages Shakespearean adaptation studies to move beyond subtitles and commission more accurate and rigorous translations and, thereby, incite further dialogue and bolster the study of Indian film adaptations of Shakespeare in syllabi and critical discourse.[3] Unable to convey the linguistic nuances of *Omkara*'s language, the subtitles have led critics such as John Milton to assume 'that language is the one area where *Omkara* differs most from *Othello*' and to argue that, '*Omkara* is typical of adaptations of Shakespeare in losing much of the original language' (Milton 2014, 93). Reading the language of *Omkara* beyond the subtitles, however, allows us to not only interpret but to enrich and illuminate Shakespeare's language. In short, this chapter sets out to encourage scholars, practitioners and teachers of Shakespeare adaptations to break down the assumption that non-anglophone Shakespeares are hermeneutically sealed off from anglophone Shakespeares and to promote a cross-cultural re-imagining of Shakespeare studies, one that opens outwardly in its efforts of interpretation rather than closing its borders.

'Scattering and unsure observance' in *Othello*

Othello's demand for 'ocular proof' is a testament to the play's scepticism towards reported narratives (III.iii.363). For example, in the opening Act, the Duke dismisses the reported letters that claim the Turks' fleet towards Rhodes as nothing but 'thin habits and poor likelihoods / Of modern seeming' since 'to vouch, is no proof, / Without more wider and more overt test' (I.iii.108–10). Under the Duke's inflicted scepticism, to vouch, to witness and/ or to testify is no longer sufficient proof. Similarly, Othello positions himself as a sceptic who insists on 'see[ing] before I doubt; when I doubt, prove' (III.iii.193). Therefore, it is not enough to report Desdemona's infidelity, Iago must provide 'some proof' for Othello to be 'satisfied' with his narrative (III. iii.389–95). In its preoccupation with empirical evidence, *Othello* raises a crucial question about the possibility of seeing proof. What does it mean to *see* proof? Observing a friendly interaction between Desdemona and Cassio, Iago admits to 'know[ing] not if't be true / But I, for mere suspicion . . . / Will do *as if for surety*' (I.iii.387–89; my emphasis). Taking 'mere suspicion' – something without any evidence – and treating it 'as if for surety', Iago begins fabricating his own artificial proof (I.iii.389). In Iago's hands, the 'antique token', originally a symbol of Othello's mother, is converted to a malign handkerchief drenched with the artificial proof of Desdemona's infidelity (V.ii.214). Rather than confirm certainty, empirical tokens (such as handkerchiefs, eyewitnesses and testimonies) in *Othello* fuel further doubt.

Act II of *Othello* begins with an off-stage storm. Montano and the three gentlemen stand at the shore, attempting and failing to 'discern' what lies beyond the 'high wrought flood' (II.i.1–4). In his attempts to catch sight of Othello, Montano describes how they would 'throw out our eyes for brave Othello / Even till we make the main and the aerial blue / An indistinct regard' (II.i.37–39). As 'the main and the aerial blue' blur into one another, Montano and the three gentlemen touch on two central, and arguably interchangeable, preoccupations of the play: the frustrating inability to see and the restless desire to know what is beyond the eyes' capability.[4] As a play preoccupied with the optically indeterminate, it is fitting that the titular protagonist increasingly distrusts his own vision in favour of Iago's visual guidance. Mistaking Cassio and his officers for Brabantio and his men, Othello turns to Iago for confirmation, 'is it they?' (I.ii.32); unable to catch sight of Cassio parting from Desdemona, again he relies on Iago, 'was not that Cassio parted from my wife?' (III.iii.37). Time and again, Othello's impaired eyes seek Iago's guidance. Iago reciprocates and eagerly guides Othello's vision, constantly instructing him to 'mark the fleers, the gibes, and notable scorns / That dwell in every region of [Cassio's] face / . . . I say, but mark his gesture. . . / Did you perceive? . . . / And did you see?' (IV.i.86–170). In doing so, Iago establishes visual dependency whereby Othello relies on him not only for visual but epistemological confirmation, 'Why dost thou ask? / . . . Why of thy thought, Iago? . . . / Indeed? . . . / What dost thou think? / . . . what dost thou mean?' as he pleads Iago that 'if more thou dost perceive, let me know more' (III.iii.96, 98, 102, 158, 243). Thus, despite Iago's insistence that Othello 'take no notice, nor build [him]self a trouble / Out of [my] scattering and unsure observance', Othello's sight becomes increasingly conditioned by Iago's 'scattering and uncertain observance' (III.iii.154–5).

'Ocular proof' in *Othello* does not resolve epistemological doubt but propels a need for further excavation for truth (III. iii.363). In the so-called temptation scene (III.iii.90–281, 332–482), Othello's desire for 'ocular proof' is not satisfied but, instead, raises more questions (III.iii.363). A 'proof' (or 'curette'), was a medical instrument used by sixteenth century surgeons as a 'probe; an instrument wherewith he sounds the bladder, & gathers together such grauell, congealled blood, or other filth' (Cotgrave 1611, sig.Z3r). Indeed, instead of providing Othello with empirical evidence, 'ocular proof' acts as a sceptical probe with which Othello attempts to penetrate into a hidden interior of Iago's mind which is 'shut up' and 'too hideous to be shown'

(III.iii.363, 111). In *Othello*, what is 'too hideous to be shown' is hideous precisely because it is hidden from show. Iago's fabricated proof, his false narrative of Desdemona's infidelity, is so obscene that it cannot be seen; the obscenity of what remains unseen demands that what is 'ocular' is never sufficient 'proof' for Othello. His desire to spy, search and see that which is impossible or at the least improbable – Desdemona's infidelity – is a desire to access that which lies beyond the threshold of sight. Seducing him with a warning such as 'it is impossible you should see this', Iago weaves a narrative that imbues Othello with a desire to discern and descry into 'an essence that's not seen' (III.iii.405; IV.i.16); with each cautionary warning to *not* look, 'to scan this thing no farther', Iago persuades Othello to search further and, in doing so, exhausts Othello's vision (III.iii.249). Towards the end of the play, Othello is no longer concerned with understanding the visual world of representation but, rather, in navigating a world of uncertain meaning. Turning to Iago to inquire, 'discerns't thou ought in that?' Othello attempts to find 'ought' where there is none (III.iii.102). For Othello to assess what is 'vile and false' from what is 'apt and true' becomes a task as inscrutable as discerning 'the main [from] th'aerial blue' (III.iii.139; V.ii.173; II.i.38).

With *Othello*'s 'scattering and unsure observance' in mind, let us address *Omkara*'s 'Nainā', a song that teases out the visual uncertainties presented in *Othello* (III.iii.156). Much like Iago's opening confession that although he 'must show out a flag and sign of love / [It] is indeed but a sign' (I.i.154–55), 'Nainā' heeds against the visible and instructs Omkara and Dolly to treat outward signs and flags of love to be nothing more than signs.

Translating *Omkara*

Before examining how visual uncertainty depicted in *Othello* is translated in *Omkara*'s song, 'Nainā', it is important to register the problematic task of translation. In their decision to translate, interpreters are faced with a conflict between the risk of obscuring or losing sense of meaning or distancing from the original text and, yet, facilitating a richer understanding of the work. To translate any Shakespearean adaptation is to acknowledge that the translation is at least twice removed from the original play; therefore, *Omkara*'s language is once removed from Shakespearean English and my translation of 'Nainā' is twice removed from *Othello*.[5] That is not to say that my translation 'back' to English attempts to undo Bhardwaj's and Gulzar's work or to reclaim its English source but, rather, by offering an English translation as close as possible to *Omkara*'s language I aim to bridge *Omkara*'s and *Othello*'s language in order to facilitate cross-cultural and linguistic comparison; my intention is not to examine how close or successful *Omkara*'s language is to *Othello*'s but to demonstrate how Bhardwaj and Gulzar adapt and appropriate Shakespeare's language to convey political, cultural, and artistic nuances. If 'Shakeshifting', as Diana E. Henderson terms it, involves 'the creative reshuffling of Shakespearean words, tropes and narratives within modern media', a practice that is 'transmedial, transhistorical – and here [in *Omkara*], transnational' (Henderson 2016, 692), this chapter would like to include translation as a form of such 'Shakeshifting'; by making the song 'Nainā' more accessible, this chapter aims to encourage further investigation into *Omkara*'s creative and cultural appropriation.

In an interview with Vishnupriya Bhandaram discussing the influence of English on Indian vernacular literature, Gulzar (2012) notes that, 'English has now become a bridge language ... it is very important that [English] translations are made'. As such, the English subtitles to *Omkara* are necessary in making the film accessible to a wider international audience. However, due to the limitations and industry practices, the subtitles lose much of the poetry and rhetoric that brings *Omkara* closer to Shakespeare's language in *Othello*. For example, 'Iago's continually being referred to as "honest" is not eliminated from *Omkara*' (Milton 2014, 93), but Bhardwaj replaces 'honest' with '*jhūṭhā*' ('liar'). Despite Iago confessing his villainous intentions in his soliloquies, Othello repeatedly refers to him as 'honest Iago' (I.iii.295, II.iii.7, 173; V.i.31; V.ii.150); that Iago is anything but 'honest' contributes to the play's dramatic irony and highlights Othello's credulity. In *Omkara*, however, Bhardwaj does not provide Langda (Iago, played by Saif Ali Khan) with any soliloquies in which to confide to the audience; instead, characters repeatedly call Langda '*jhūṭhā*' in a teasingly mocking fashion, ironically to confirm their trust of him. Langda's double bluff is captured in the scene where he interrupts a police officer's announcement prohibiting contraband items; muting the microphone with his hand, Langda tells him that he is carrying all of the contrabands only for the police officer to laugh him off, 'Away with you, liar!'. '*Jhūṭhā*' is an endearing name for Langda until the end of the film, where his lies accumulate and, standing at the threshold of Omkara and Dolly's bedroom, Langda asserts: 'What you know, you know. There is no difference between my truths and lies.' Another example of such appropriation is seen in *Omkara*'s use of somatic language; if Othello demands to 'know [Iago's] thoughts' only for Iago to refuse, 'you cannot, if my *heart* were in your *hand*', Bhardwaj takes Shakespeare's corporeal metaphor and refigures it into its Hindi equivalent, 'No. Not everyone has the "*jigaar*" [courage/liver] to hear the truth' (III.iii.164; my emphasis). Or, again, in the naming of Langda, Bhardwaj hints at Iago's monstrosity; if Iago 'bring[s] th[e] monstrous ... to the world's light', Bhardwaj connotes such monstrosity within Langda's name (implying his limping gait and, albeit problematically, associating his disability with his moral malaise; I.iii.403). It is not simply in the dialogue and characterization, however, that Bhardwaj's adaptation appropriates *Othello*, but also through Gulzar's lyrics to *Omkara*. Therefore, rather than simply translate the song lyrics into English as a way of bridging between the two languages (Gulzar 2009, 77), this chapter homes in on the rhetorical ambiguity of Gulzar's '*śāyarī*' ['poetry'] in 'Nainā'. In order to situate 'Naina' in the wider cultural context of Indian cinema, a final note on the use of songs to the narrative of Indian cinema must be made before reading the lyrics to 'Nainā'.

Songs and narrative in Indian cinema

Typically, in Indian cinema, the music director collaborates with the director and producer before choosing the lyricist (Morcom 2007, 29). In his Shakespearean trilogy (*Maqbool/Macbeth* [2003], *Omkara/Othello* [2006] and *Haider/Hamlet* [2014]) Bhardwaj subverts this tradition by occupying the role of both director and music director and collaborating much more intimately with Gulzar thereby doing away with the hierarchical structures, in which the lyricist holds the lowest status (Morcom 2007, 29). Before his directorial debut in *Makdee* (2002), Bhardwaj was predominantly known as a music director and his first composition was *Maachis* (1996) where he initially collaborated with Gulzar. In an interview with Anna Morcom, prior to the production of *Omkara*, Bharadwaj explains the importance of keeping to the narrative demands of film when composing its music:

> ... it is film music, so everything depends on the film, the story ... I can't, I don't want to, you know, throw ... my music, my style on a film. Rather I'll try to adapt that film's region, the characters' mental state and the place it has been set in ... film music to me is like being part of the story writing team.
>
> (Morcom 2007: 35)

Indeed, songs in Indian films play an inherent part in the film's narrative and *Omkara*'s music, especially, functions as a metanarrative device. That is to say, the songs are inherently built into and propel the narrative forward; while 'Nainā' recounts the story of Omkara and Dolly's love, 'Beedi' replaces Iago's 'cannikin clink, clink' song (II.iii.65–70) as Langda gets Kesu (Cassio, played by Vivek Oberoi) drunk, 'Namak' is used as a honey trap for Omkara's men to round up the police officers and 'Jaag ja' replaces Desdemona's willow song (IV.iii.39–56). The film heavily associates songs with sex, where the dance numbers 'Beedi' and 'Namak' encode a certain eroticism into the narrative and sexualize Billo (Bianca, played by Bipasha Basu), while other characters use music as an innuendo for sex comparing Kesu and Billo's love making to 'composing duets under the sheets'. Both Omkara and Dolly use music as a means of communicating their affections, while Omkara sings Dolly a lullaby *'jaag ja'* ['wake up'], Dolly, eager to learn Western music, is adamant to learn Stevie Wonder's 'I just called to say I love you' on the guitar from Kesu in attempt to woo Omkara. Therefore, *Omkara*'s genre – the genre of Indian films, which demand songs to be part of a film's narrative – works to the adaptation's advantage. Thus, Gulzar's choice to write 'Nainā' with 'the folk flavour [in] the style of a "thumri", a genre of semi classical Indian music which connects dramatic gesture, evocative love poetry and folk song regional to Uttar Pradesh, Bhardwaj's home state and the setting of *Omkara*' (Morcom 2007, 75). Through the use of 'thumri' in 'Nainā', Gulzar subtly gestures toward the importance of storytelling in *Othello*, where Othello admits to how both Desdemona and 'Her father oft invited [him], / Still questioned [him] the story of [his] life' (I.iii.129–30).

Recalling his lyrics *'āṁkhoṁ kī mahakī khuśabū'* ['aroma of those eyes'] for the film *Khamoshi* (1970), Gulzar reminisces how he was 'heavily criticized and even teased [by the producer] for writing this kind of poetry' (Gulzar 2009, 25). During their collaboration on 'Nainā', however, Gulzar curiously describes the song's composition as 'shar[ing] poetry with Vishal' who, he admits, allowed him to 'tak[e] ... poetic liberties' that were 'unusual' for Indian films (Gulzar 2009, 75). Thus, in the composition of 'Nainā', Gulzar adopts the role of a poet rather than lyricist. Gulzar's lyrics to 'Nainā' reflect his poetry's preoccupation with vision. In his poem, 'It was Cold and Misty', for example, Gulzar describes how 'morning's eye ... / Was half shut, half open' making 'A settlement the size of a suitcase / A temple the size of a wallet' (*Neglected Poems*, 2012, 13). 'Morning's eye', either referring to the sun's rays or the speaker's eyes awakening from slumber, cause a shift in perspective and distorts the shape and size of objects seen from 'a settlement' to 'a suitcase' and 'a temple' to 'a wallet'. Similarly, in the poem

'Distance', the poetic figure reinforces the eyes' ability to distort what they see, requesting his beloved to 'move away a bit, / So that I can / hold your face / in my eager eyes' (Gulzar 1999, 35). Distance, here, is necessary for perspectival clarity. Gulzar goes on to incorporate his fascination with perspectives, distortions, and the dangers of vision into his lyrics to 'Nainā'.

As an integral part of the *Omkara*'s narrative, 'Nainā' is Bhardwaj's appropriation of Othello's 'round unvarnished tale' (I.iii.91). However, rather than have Omkara deliver the 'whole course of [his] love', as Othello does, Bhardwaj shifts the focus to Dolly who recounts to her father, Ragunath Mishra/ Vakīla Sāhaba (Brabantio, played by Kamal Tiwari) and Tewari Bhaisaab (the Duke, played by Naseeruddin Shah) how she 'lost [her] heart to Omkara' (I.iii.92). The song starts as Dolly begins the story and the lyrics, her interpolated dialogue, and imagery consist of several layers of seamlessly interwoven narrative; as the song lyrics warn against the dangers and distrust of vision, Dolly narrates her tale recounting how she fell in love with Omkara which further includes reading out a suicide note that she sent him. All this overlaps with her confession to her father, a monologue that synchronizes with and, yet interrupts 'Nainā'. Therefore, 'Nainā' is not only integral to *Omkara*'s plot but is used as a framing device for Bhardwaj's didactic narrative on the consequences of jealousy. The song permeates the film: it is the first song in the film, is repeated in fragments at vital moments of Langda's manipulation of Omkara, and replayed, hauntingly, during the closing credits after Omkara murders his wife. In what follows, I offer a translation, close reading, and comparative analysis of the song against the 'scattering and unsure observance[s]' in *Othello* (III.iii.156).

Dolly's deceiving eyes

'*Nainā ṭhaga leṃge*' ['The eyes will deceive, they will con']. The song's chorus insists upon the illusory and intoxicating, powerful and yet fickle nature of eyes. The etymological root of 'Ṭhaga' is 'Ṭhag', from which we derive the English word 'thug' (*Oxford English Dictionary*), meaning a cheat or swindler. 'Ṭhaga' re-occurs throughout *Omkara* and is most frequently associated with Dolly. As the central figure of her father's and later Omkara's doubt, it is Dolly's dubious '*nainā*' ['eyes'] that are constantly up for debate. By placing 'Nainā', a song about distrusting one's eyes, just after Dolly's first words, 'I am slave to my own will', Bhardwaj deliberately makes her the subject of visual scrutiny. As soon as Dolly clasps her hands for forgiveness and a tear trickles down her cheek, Rahat Fateh Ali Khan's voice interrupts with '*nainoṃ kī mata māniyo re*' ['don't believe the eyes'] – echoing Othello's dismissal of Desdemona's tears as feigned emotions, 'each drop she falls would prove a crocodile' (IV.i.245) – as if to caution us and Omkara against sympathizing with Dolly's tears. As Fateh Ali Kahn's leading male vocals are coupled with a chorus of men repeating 'don't believe the eyes', 'Nainā' sets the tone for the rest of the film as one of misogynistic distrust of women. Much like Desdemona's claim that she 'beguile[s] / The thing [she is] by seeming otherwise', from the outset, Bhardwaj initiates a visual ambiguity about how to read Dolly that preoccupies the film (II.i.122–3). Creating a discrepancy between outer gesture and inner emotion, the opening lines of the song warn Omkara, much like Brabantio warns Othello: 'Look to her, Moor, if thou hast eyes to see: / She has deceived her father, and may thee' (I.iii.293–4). *Omkara* places great weight on these lines which are first uttered by Dolly's father, 'Don't forget that women are two faced, she who can dupe [*ṭhag*] her own father, will never be anyone else's to claim'. Here, '*ṭhag*' is transferred from the song's emphasis on the eyes that can '*ṭhag*' ('con') you to Dolly as a '*ṭhag*' ('thug') who has duped her own father and may '*ṭhag*' ('deceive') Omkara. In *Othello*, Shakespeare uses 'deceive' to describe Desdemona – twice by her father and echoed again by Iago when he warns Othello that, 'She did deceive her father, marrying you' (III.iii.209) – for a similar effect (I.i.163; I.iii.294). Yet, whereas Othello begins with a sense of trust towards his wife, 'My life upon her faith!', only to later be persuaded by Iago, 'And so she did', Omkara becomes hooked to Vakīla Sāhaba's warning from the outset and obsesses over Dolly's ability to '*ṭhag*' him (I.iii.295; III.iii.211).

Throughout *Omkara*, Bhardwaj teases out the multiple meanings of '*ṭhag*', especially bringing forth the word's adulterous connotations. Moments before his wedding, Omkara confides in Indu (Emilia, played by Konkona Sen Sharma): 'this whole time her father's voice rings in my ears: "she who can dupe [*ṭhag*] her father, will never be anyone else's to claim"'. Replying to Omkara's concerns about Dolly, Indu explains how women 'leave our homes, lives, everything, and walk into your lives with bare empty hands' and, yet, are still subject to male scrutiny, 'even after the holy fires approve us, we are still regarded disloyal [*ṭhagī*] sooner than loyal [*sagī*]'. By placing '*ṭhagī*' and '*sagī*' (which not only means 'loyal' but also 'legitimate') as binary opposites, Indu feminizes the noun '*ṭhagī*', and places emphasis once again on the deceptive nature of women, and in doing so, she transfers the meaning of '*ṭhagī*' from 'con' or 'deceptive' to 'unfaithful' and 'illegitimate'. The consequences of this linguistic transformation from '*ṭhaga*' in the opening of 'Naina' ('*Nainā ṭhaga lemge*') to '*ṭhagī*' comes full circle in the final scene of the film where, after suffocating Dolly, Omkara turns to Indu, as if to justify his actions and repeats, 'she couldn't be loyal to her father nor could she be loyal to anyone else, "Two faced"'. For Omkara, women only have two faces, '*sagī*' ['loyal'] or '*ṭhagī*' ['disloyal']. Soon after Omkara discovers the truth of Langda's plot, 'Naina' plays again, however, this time the emphasis shifts away from Dolly as the object of visual uncertainty (as to whether she is '*ṭhagī*' [disloyal] or '*sagī*' [loyal]) to Omkara's own eyes and cautioning him, '*nainoṃ kī mata māniyo re / nainoṃ kī mata suniyo*' ['don't obey your eyes, / don't listen to them']. Whereas in *Khamoshi*, Gulzar fuses smell and sight in his lyrics '*āṁkhoṃ kī mahakī khuśabū*' ['the aroma of these eyes'] in order to heighten the sensuality of the love song, in *Omkara* Gulzar evokes synthesia between hearing and sight, warning Omkara not to listen to his eyes; here, the song not only challenges Omkara to be vigilant of 'ocular proof' but also – and, ironically through the medium of song – to be cautious of the dangers of hearing, overhearing, and receiving second-hand reports of events (III.iii.363). Thus, '*nainoṃ kī mata māniyo re / nainoṃ kī mata suniyo*' ['Don't obey your eyes, / don't listen to them'] conveys a sense of pathos and foreshadows the tragic consequences of Omkara's visual credulity.

It is not just Othello's 'round unvarnished tale' that the song transfers onto Dolly, but also the allegations of witchcraft (I.iii.91). The lyrics, '*jagate jādū phuṃkemge re / jagate jagate jādū*' ['These eyes will cast a magical spell, even when you are wide awake'], combined with a close-up of Dolly's eyes, convey a certain '*jādū*' ['magic'] that won over Omkara's love and not Othello whose 'charms ... / ... conjuration and ... mighty magic ... / ... won [Brabantio's] daughter' (I.iii.92–4). Bhardwaj removes all associations of witchcraft from Omkara and inflicts them onto Dolly. Later, in the interim of another song, '*O Sāthī Re*', Dolly holds a gun to Omkara's chest and playfully asks, 'Now tell me, why do you think I'm a witch?' only for Omkara to respond, 'In case your beauty hides some magical spell.' Rather than associate witchcraft with the handkerchief, which Othello's mother begets from an 'Egyptian ... / ... charmer', 'A sibyl' who 'On her prophetic fury sew'd the work', 'dyed in mummy' and 'Conserved of maidens' hearts', Gulzar's lyrics make Dolly's eyes the agents of witchcraft (III.iv.59–77). Whereas in *Othello*, Brabantio believes Desdemona to be the victim of Othello's witchcraft, 'abused ... corrupted / By spells' or made 'blind, or lame of sense / Sans witchcraft could not' (I.iii.61–65), in *Omkara* such magic spells are cast ['*phuṃkemge*'], through Dolly's eyes. '*Phuṃkemge*' means to literally blow or cast a substance and implies a materiality in the eyes which are thought to be capable of casting beams of physical matter onto the object of bewitchment. If repetition in *Othello* depicts Othello's loss of agency ('Oh, blood, blood, blood!' or the chiasmic 'But yet the pity of it, Iago! / O Iago, the pity of it, Iago!', III.iii.454;

IV.i.192–3), Gulzar's lyrics, in contrast, conjure a hypnotic control that Dolly's eyes have over Omkara through repetition of *'jagate jagate jādū'* ['wakeful wakeful magic'].

The intoxicating nature of Dolly's eyes is further established in the next verse, *'Nainoṃ ko to ḍasane kā caskā lagā re / Nainoṃ kā zahara naśīlā re'* ['These eyes are addicted to biting / Their venom is intoxicating']. Here, the word *'ḍasane'*, commonly associated with a snake bite, implies a piercing through and entering of the skin and carries a certain violence. *'Ḍasane'* is a violating and violent action that wounds as it pierces and thereby breaks down the barrier of exterior and interior in one swift jab. That is to say, these serpentine-like eyes will *'das'* ['pierce'] through you, they will poison you with their venomous bite. This snake like imagery is prominent throughout *Omkara*, from Langda, Kesu, and Billo's snake like dance during another song, 'Beedi', to a snake that casts a bad omen on Dolly's wedding, to Langda's phallic enactment of a snake when in bed with Indu. The intensity of this poison is reflected through the internal rhyme of *'ḍasane kā caskā'* [*'caskā'* meaning addiction], where Gulzar extends his metaphor of contagion by injecting it into the language itself. While 'Nainā' is primarily Dolly's account of how she fell in love with Omkara, Gulzar's lyrics enclose poisonous qualities we typically associate with Iago rather than Desdemona. In *Othello*, it is not Desdemona but the infectious Iago who takes his own envy, a 'poisonous mineral [that] gnaws [his] inwards' and infects others with it; it is Iago who intoxicates Cassio with the 'distempering draughts' and who infects Othello's vision with 'indirect and forced . . . / poison' (II.ii.295; I.i.98; I.iii.112–13). Some editors of *Othello* read 'medicine', in Iago's exclamation, 'Work on, / My medicine, work!', to mean 'poison' rather than antidote (IV.i.44–5).[6] However, Gulzar's appropriation, *'Nainoṃ kā zahara naśīlā re'* ['the venom of the eyes is intoxicating', where *'zahara'* means poison and *'naśīlā'* implies being drunk] captures this oxymoronic meaning of poisonous medicine; *'zahara naśīlā'* suggests a sense of poisonous pleasure where the eyes' poison works like alcohol and eases the pain that it inflicts. Like Iago, Langda infects Omkara, Dolly, Kesu and Rahjun (Roderigo, played by Deepak Dobriyal) with his poisonous thoughts; in the case of Kesu and Rahjun, he constantly poisons them with alcohol, as he observes Omkara doubt and Dolly pine, Langda penetrates and '*dasses*' like a serpent into their thoughts poisoning them with his own pharmaceutical conceits and doubts. Thus, Gulzar sustains Shakespeare's concept of sight as painfully infectious. If Lodovico closes *Othello* with 'this object poisons sight, / Let it be hid', 'Nainā' attempts to prevent such contagions from spreading by warning Omkara and Dolly against them (V.iii.362–63).

'To see rain . . . when its cloudless': *Omkara*'s ocular proof

'Nainā' further problematizes Omkara's relationship to what he sees through the lines, '*Bina bādala barasāve sāvana / Sāvana bina barasātā / . . . / nainā bāvarā kara dem̐ge*' ['With no signs of clouds, they will make you see rain, / rain will pour down when it is cloudless. These eyes will make you mad']. Here, Gulzar implies that eyes are susceptible to tears (rain) without cause of grief (clouds); more abstractly, the notion that the eyes 'see rain . . . when it is cloudless' connotes the eyes' ability to distort and deceive and trick us into seeing what is not there. In the line, '*Bina bādala barasāve sāvana / Sāvana bina barasātā*', '*sāvana*' ['rain'] doubles upon itself, imitating the pitter patter of rain, while '*bina bādala*' ['without clouds'] and '*bina barasātā*' ['without rain'] sit at either side of '*sāvana*' as if to question whether it is raining at all.[7] Indeed, Gulzar's use of chiasmus exemplifies semiotic ambiguities that are prevalent throughout *Omkara*; just as the signifier ('rain') occurs independent of the sign ('clouds'), Langda's accusations of Dolly's adultery occur without visible proof. Like Iago, Langda must 'thicken other proofs / That do demonstrate thinly', transubstantiating a 'something, nothing' into a material handkerchief (III.iii.432–33, 160).

Bhardwaj appropriates Othello's 'antique token', 'a handkerchief / Spotted with strawberries' into a '*kamarband*' that is typically worn around the waist by women (V.ii.214; III.ii.437–8).[8] We first encounter the '*kamarband*' as a treasured family heirloom that Omkara gifts to Dolly who mistakes it for jewellery. From its first appearance around Dolly's waist to Omkara's insistence that Dolly wear it during sex, from Indu's stealing of the '*kamarband*' as a sexual favour to her husband, to Kesu holding it up as a gift for Billo, the '*kamarband*' acts as a fetishized object that transmits jealousy from one couple to the next.

Henderson argues that the '*kamarband*' circulates from one character to the next 'as a means to gain favours' and, as such, is used by Langda as a 'commodity fetishism to blur boundaries in a more sinister way' (2016, 684, 675). Unlike Iago, who tells Othello that 'it is impossible you should see this' only to then create a desire to see into 'her honour[, which] is an essence that's not seen', in *Omkara* the overtly sexualized and expensive *kamarband* is constantly on display, either in Billo's dance numbers or through voyeuristic shots into bedroom scenes between each couple that strangely mirror each other (III.iii.405; IV.i.16). As Henderson observes, 'the object's circulation from body to body continues to be linked more logically and overtly to the main plot's development than in *Othello*' (2016, 685).

Much like the rain which appears without any clouds, Langda convinces Omkara of Dolly's infidelity chiefly in a scene which does not have the material, physical, and palpable proof of the '*kamarband*' present. Gathering Omkara and the other men around the fire, Langda tells them about how he 'hid in a blanket with a hole in it' to watch Kesu and Billo 'wrestle' under the sheets with nothing but the 'beautiful *kamarband*' between them. Curiously, Bhardwaj does not present the scene itself but chooses verbal rather than visual voyeurism to first convince Omkara of Dolly's betrayal.

Paradoxically, the *kamarband* is both proof of Dolly's infidelity and, as the object of tragic anagnorisis, acts as evidence to disprove such accusations. Omkara accuses Dolly of adultery without any legitimate proof just as the rain pours down 'with no sign of clouds'. Gulzar's lyrics can, therefore, be read as caution against 'ocular proof', whereby what is visible is but a hallucination of the real (III.iii.363); to extend the metaphor, Langda's visible and verbal proof is conjured out of thin air; 'with no signs of clouds', Langda coerces Omkara into believing that it is raining (i.e. Dolly is having an extramarital affair). The song's didactic tone heeds against empiricism whereby trust in vision will make you mad (*'nainā bāvarā kara demge'*).

'Nainā' further problematizes Othello's desire for 'ocular proof' by cautioning Omkara, 'Don't believe the language of these eyes / There is no written agreement, no receipt or record for what they say / They converse through the air' (*'Nainom kī zubāna pe bharosā nahīm ātā / Likhata-parhata na rasīda na khātā'*; III.iii.363). The song challenges Omkara to take heed of Langda and his claims of material proof (anything visibly written or recorded). If the Duke in *Othello* insists that 'to vouch is this, is no proof / Without more wider and more avert tests', 'Naina' dismisses the validity of all visual proof (I.iii.107–8). Just as Othello's need for 'ocular proof', his demand for a point of reference to confirm his suspicions, is met by Iago's endless deferral (from the outset of the play Iago admits that 'mere suspicions . . . / Will do as if for surety' [I.iii.388–9]), 'Nainā' adopts a sceptical voice that insists the impossibility of pinning down evidence since eyes 'converse through the air' (III.iii.363). Commenting on his collaboration with Bhardwaj on this verse, Gulzar notes, 'the line "*na raseed na khata*" is very unusual to be used in poetry, but working with Vishal, I have been taking these poetic liberties' (Morcom 2007, 75). '*Na rasīda na khātā*' is unusual because of its ambiguity in meaning, on the one hand, it can mean the eyes leave 'no receipt or record' (i.e. they leave no traceable evidence), in a similar vein, it is also the word for 'account', denoting both

Omkara's and *Othello*'s preoccupation with economic and monetary gain.[9] Yet, '*khātā*' also means to eat or consume so the eyes 'do not consume any written record' and carries echoes of consumption in *Othello*, where Desdemona's 'greedy ear / Devoured up [Othello's] discourse' and where Iago observes how Othello is 'eaten up with passion' (I.iii.150–1; III.iii.394). In these lines, Gulzar's poetic liberties can be read as a direct response to Othello's demand that Iago, 'Make me to see it; or at the least, so prove it' as if to counsel him that there are 'no receipts or records' of what is seen (III.iii.368). In *Omkara*, just as in *Othello*, what is seen is immaterial, imaginary and, therefore, without 'ocular proof' (III.iii.363).

Conclusion

Omkara's final song is the lullaby '*jaag ja gudiya*' ['wake up my doll'] the only song apart from '*Nainā*' that is repeated in the film. '*Jaag ja*' is *Omkara*'s version of the willow song but, once again, Bhardwaj inverses gender roles so that it is Omkara who sings it rather than Dolly. Playing with Dolly's name, '*gudiya*' meaning 'doll', the song conveys a rare moment of Omkara's outward possessiveness over his wife, '*Nainoṃ meṃ tere hama hī base the / Hama hī base haiṃ, hai nā?*' ['I'm the one who resides in your eyes / I'm the only one who resides in them, right?']. Here, Gulzar's chiasmus works effectively to change the tone from accusation to a playful teasing in its first recital when Omkara wakes Dolly from post-coital sleep and from playful teasing to tragic accusation, the second time, after he murders her. Indeed, the lyrics '*jaag ja mari*' ['wake up dead one'] used playfully at first, gain a macabre meaning the second time when Omkara pleads the dead Dolly to open her eyes. The eerie silence that follows Omkara's suicide, broken violently with the creaking sounds of the swing as both lovers lie dead, continues into the rolling credits only to be eased by '*Nainā*' playing one final time; ironically, this final recitation heeds the cinematic audience against the dangers of trusting what we have seen.

Notes

1 I would like to thank Thea Buckley, Koel Chatterjee, Varsha Panjwani and Preti Taneja for organizing the 'Indian Shakespeares on Screen' conference (2016), where I presented an earlier draft of this chapter. My heartfelt thanks to Siddharth for his help in ensuring the translations from Devanagari into The International Alphabet of Sanskrit Transliteration (IAST) are accurate. All translations are my own, as are remaining errors and deficiencies. I have used IAST transliteration throughout however some symbols do not have an IAST transliteration. In these cases I have used ISO 15919.

2 All subsequent references to *Othello* will refer to this edition and be given in parentheses within the text.

3 In January 2020 I co-taught *Omkara* with Professor Helen Hackett to third-year undergraduates in the English Department at UCL as part of a seminar course on 'Shakespeare and Intercultural Encounters'. During the film screening, the subtitles to the 'Beedi' song, 'Light your fags with the bosom of my heart' caused a few sniggers among students. The erotic imagery in Hindi becomes somewhat absurd and comedic in English which loses the provocative intensity of Billo's proposition. A more accurate translation of the line '*bīṛī jalaī le jigara se piyā jigara mā baṛī āga hai*' would be 'Come light your joint on my heart, beloved / My heart is burning with fire'.

4 See Patricia Parker (1993), '*Othello* and *Hamlet*: Dilation, Spying, and the "Secret Place" of Woman', *Representations* 1 (44): 60–95.

5 I would like to thank Ayanna Thompson for pointing this out to me.

6 Most editors of *Othello* read 'medicine' to mean 'drug or poison' in Iago's 'Work on; my medicine, works' (IV.i.43–4). See for example, *Othello* (1997), London: Arden Shakespeare, 257; *Othello* (2016), Oxford: Oxford University Press.

7 Sunjoy Shekar's translation, 'shower you with kaleidoscopic illusions', also captures Gulzar's emphasis on visual deception (2009: 77).

8 For a full discussion of the '*kamarband*' in *Omkara* see Diana E. Henderson. 'Magic in the Chains: *Othello*, *Omkara*, and the Materiality of Gender Across Time and Media' in Valerie Traub

(ed.), *The Oxford Handbook of Shakespeare and Embodiment*, 673–93, Oxford: Oxford University Press, 2016.

9 I would like to thank Varsha Panjwani for pointing this out to me.

References

Bhardwaj, Vishal. Interview. *Wild Films India*. 5 October 2017. Available online: https://www.youtube.com/watch?v=OvdrXWl0eSw (accessed 5 June 2020).

Cotgrave, Randle. *A Dictionarie of French and English Tongues*. London: Adam Islip, 1611.

Gulzar. *Autumn Moon*, translated by J. P Das. New Delhi: Rupa & Co, 1999.

Gulzar. *100 Lyrics*, translated by Sunjoy Shekar. New Delhi: Penguin Group, 2009.

Gulzar. *Neglected Poems*, translated by Pavan K. Varma. New Delhi: Penguin Group, 2012.

Gulzar. Interview with Vishnupriya Bhandaram. *The Hindu*, 7 January 2012. Available online: https://www.thehindu.com/books/Lost-in-translation/article13369705.ece (accessed 5 June 2020).

Gulzar. Interview with Priya Gupta. *Entertainment Times*, 28 September 2014. Available online: https://timesofindia.indiatimes.com/entertainment/hindi/bollywood/news/Our-films-captured-only-geography-of-Kashmir-earlier-Vishal-has-captured-its-history-in-Haider-Gulzar/articleshow/43626105.cms (accessed 5 June 2020).

Henderson, Diana E. 'Magic in the Chains: *Othello, Omkara*, and the Materiality of Gender Across Time and Media', in *The Oxford Handbook of Shakespeare and Embodiment*, ed. Valerie Traub. Oxford: Oxford University Press, 2016, 673–93.

Khamoshi (1970), [Film] Dir. Asit Sen, India: Eros.

Macchis (1996), [Film] Dir. Gulzar, India: Eros.

Makdee (2002), [Film] Dir. Vishal Bhadwaj, India: Percept Picture Company.

Milton, John. 'Theorising *Omkara*', in *Translation and Adaptation in Theatre and Film*, ed. Katja Krebs. London: Routledge, 2014, 83–98.

Morcom, Anna. *Hindi Songs and the Cinema*. Hampshire: Ashgate, 2007.

Omkara (2006), [Film] Dir. Vishal Bhardwaj, India: Eros.

Oxford English Dictionary, http://www.oed.com. 7 June 2020. Web.
Parker, Patricia, '*Othello* and *Hamlet*: Dilation, Spying, and the "Secret Place" of Woman'. *Representations* 1, 44 (1993): 60–95.
Shakespeare, William. *Othello*. 1623. Reprinted with notes and introduction. London: Arden Shakespeare, 1997.
Shakespeare, William. *Othello*. 1623. Reprinted with notes and introduction. Oxford: Oxford University Press, 2016.
Shakespeare, William. *Romeo and Juliette*. 1623. Reprinted with notes and introduction. London: Arden Shakespeare, 2012.
Thornton Burnett, Mark. *Shakespeare and World Cinema*. Cambridge: Cambridge University Press, 2013.

11

A Pair of Homotextual Lovers: Bhansali's *Ram-Leela* and Shakespeare's *Romeo and Juliet*

Amritesh Singh

Introduction

The critical reception of Bollywood song-and-dance sequences in the West falls firmly in two camps. The first camp regards them as redundant to the film, an annoying interruption to the narrative flow, and an unfortunate capitulation to economic demands that override artistic integrity.[1] Somewhat differently, the other school of thought takes a more enlightened view of Bollywood music and choreography in extricating them from Western semantics and in according them the status of a culturally specific mode of storytelling and filmmaking.[2] Irrespective of whether they are met with derision or fascination, Bollywood song-and-dance sequences are consistently characterized within the taxonomies of difference and, frequently, non-diegesis. The binaries between the governing sensibilities in Hollywood and Bollywood that interest film studies widen when scholarship directs its attention to Bollywood's engagements with Shakespeare where song-and-dance sequences are regarded as removed from the text. *Omkara* (2006), an adaptation of *Othello*, has 'the usual Bollywood songs' (French 2006), notes a reviewer with studied patience for cultural differences. For another reviewer, the usual Bollywood songs in *Goliyon ki Ras-Leela: Ram-Leela* (2013; hereafter *Ram-Leela*) confound the narrative outcome: 'for much of its length [the film] is such a brightly colored song-and-dance entertainment that audiences may wonder if it's working toward a revised, happy Bollywood ending [of *Romeo and Juliet*]' (Chute 2013). On the rare occasions when the resonance of such sequences with Shakespearean dramaturgy is acknowledged, it is conjoined with surprise, thereby normalizing difference – 'There's *surprising sense* in staging the Mousetrap and gravedigger scenes as musical numbers [in *Haider*, an adaptation of *Hamlet*]' (McCahill 2014, emphasis mine).

Critical paradigms neglect the concordance between Shakespeare and Bollywood, an oversight which I will correct in this chapter through the prism of queer theory. Queer theory, which 'names an ontology of connectedness between and a crossing of temporalities and cultures' (Tuhkanen 2009: 98), opens new prospects for the field of Global Shakespeares where the 'available theories of postcolonialism or current discourses about globalization cannot adequately deal with the issues of multiculturalism, multilingualism, diaspora, and identity' (Huang 2013, 287). In particular, the concept of 'homohistory', as nurtured by Jonathan Goldberg and Madhavi Menon (2005, 1609), is vital to my interpretive apparatus, which is 'invested in suspending determinate sexual and chronological differences while expanding the possibilities of the nonhetero, with all its connotations of sameness, similarity, proximity, and anachronism'. Homohistory turns away from the epistemological imperative of regarding historical and cultural specificity as a marker of difference and separation. Instead, the critical lens of homohistory helps observe the similarities between late-Elizabethan dramaturgy and Bollywood imaginary, which I illustrate through presenting *Ram-Leela* as a case study in this chapter.

Early modern plays and Bollywood films share a highly collaborative mode of textual production even as they evidence striking affinity in terms of their narrative trajectories – they are both punctuated by songs; are not always focused in their narrative progress; require a suspension of disbelief to reconcile to the fantastic logic of their resolution; and typically have subplots and comic interludes that may sit uncomfortably with the purported *genre* of the piece. The hybridity of popular drama in the early modern period was a source of much contemporary concern, most memorably recorded by Sir Philip Sidney (1595: sig. Ir-I2v):

> howe all their Playes bee neither right Tragedies nor right Comedies, mingling Kinges and Clownes, not because the matter so carrieth it, but thrust in the Clowne by head and shoulders to play a part in majesticall matters, with neither decencie nor discretion, so as neither the admiration and Commiseration nor the right sportfulnesse is by their mongrell Tragicomedie obtained.

While the irreverent mingling of genres in the early modern period led to popular drama being regarded as 'mongrell', the impure mixture of elements in the Hindi film industry is best represented by the epithet *masala* that has been theorized as 'a formal reflex of the Bollywoodization of Hindi film' (Gopal 2011, 2). Bollywood *masala* pitches melodrama to orchestrate a fugue state of emotions – an effect that does not harmonize with the composed rendering of verisimilitude, the register in which cinematic achievement, *pace* the anglophone tradition of filmmaking, is meant to be articulated. Yet, if melodrama is about the frisson generated by temporal tension, 'a give and take of "too late" and "in the nick of time"' (Williams 1998, 69), many Shakespeare plays, including *Romeo and Juliet*, can justly be designated as spectacles of melodramatic sentimentality even as they exhibit the mongrel features that vexed Sidney. Similarly, while putative understanding of dance sequences confines them to the status of the zaniest ingredient in the Bollywood *masala*, they were just as integral to the early modern experience and expectation of the theatre – '[d]ancing in Shakespeare's public theater was multifarious: the common player might be called upon to perform with equal aplomb an expert galliard, a dignified measure, or a vigorous morris' (Howard 1993, 326). The points of resemblance between Shakespeare and Bollywood are so numerous and wide-ranging that they are beginning to demand countenance in reflections such as Jonathan Gil Harris's *Masala Shakespeare* (2018).

Homohistory thus helps lean into the propinquity that exists across 'a body of travelling cultural texts' (Huang 2013, 286), which collectively make Global Shakespeares, and untether Bollywood from the critical stake in ascribing difference. Instead, my close readings of the song-and-dance sequences in Sanjay Leela Bhansali's *Ram-Leela* (2013), along with Shakespeare's *Romeo and Juliet*, carry a torch for homotextuality – textual intimacies that are predicated on sameness. This chapter is invested in accruing cultural capital within Shakespeare Studies for Bollywood's song-and-dance sequences, which, like the musicians in *Romeo and Juliet*, currently 'have no gold for sounding' (4.5.136).[3] In advocating the recognition of homotextuality between Shakespeare and Bollywood, I celebrate what is pretty and witty and gay about them even as I critique critical axioms that make one a pattern of lyricism and mar(k) the 'other' as an 'extravagant and wheeling stranger'[4] for its 'excess'. With homotextuality, I aim to create 'a praxis of interpretation ... to arrive at a responsible grasp of [non-anglophone] Shakespearean cinematic expressions that cannot be seen as "the other", for the simple reason that they are us' (Thornton Burnett, 2012, 3). Correspondingly, I argue that homotextuality places two critical imperatives upon the current generation of Shakespearean scholars: (a) to arrive at a finer appreciation of the salutary role played by music and dance in early modern theatre through Bollywood, and in the process, prise open possibilities in the performance of Shakespeare; and (b) to contextualize Bollywood song-and-dance sequences as *a part of* than *apart from* a rich tradition of musical renderings of Shakespeare. Here, I must offer two caveats: in claiming affinity, I do not suggest that Bollywood and Shakespeare are identical, nor do I disavow syntaxes of expression specific to an historical moment. Concomitantly, this chapter does not cleave to the fidelity discourse which parses the reproductive logic that inseminates the process of adapting canonical texts, thereby confining intertextuality to a mode of transmission determined by filial deference.[5] In *Ram-Leela*, I do not look for 'the whole matter/ And copy of the father' (*The Winter's Tale*, 2.3.97–8). Instead, in embracing textual intimacies, my gaze deliberately rests upon the palimpsest of similarities (the 'homo' in the texts) on which differences are inscribed. To my approach, 'queerness is a product of literary affiliation and a critical conjecture about specific points of contact between texts' (Stanivukovic 2016, 46).

Song-and-dance sequences in *Ram-Leela*: a case for homotextuality

Critics are aware of the crucial role that music and dance played in creating the experience that was, if not unique to, distinctive about Shakespeare's plays. David Lindley (2015, 61) accords music a primacy that rivals that of Shakespearean verse in arguing that 'music does not simply occupy a secondary role in endorsing dialogue or the visual qualities of the mise-en-scène, but that in important respects it may actively condition or even determine the way in which we see the action'. In *A Midsummer Night's Dream*, '[the] play itself constantly invites us to conjoin speech, music and dance to render its narrative wholly legible' (Hiscock 2018, 44). The diffuse but decisive effect of music can also be measured in the way it moulded the very text that would be used for performance. The first quarto (Q1) of *Romeo and Juliet*, to cite but one example, has been recognized as one pruned for 'a company with no musicians' (Gibbons 1980, 2). Music, either by its determining presence or conspicuous absence, is an indispensable part of textual and performative histories of early modern plays. Within the early modern playhouse, music co-existed with dance whereby 'allusions to dance, the idea of dancing and the dance itself essentially form part of the dramatic texture of the plays, adding to characterization, illuminating the theme of order and contributing to the structure' (Brissenden 1981, 110). *Romeo and Juliet* not only folds in oblique references to dancing that require editorial clarity,[6] but also plainly embeds instances of actual dancing in its verse. Capulet's behest – 'Come, musicians, play' (1.5.25) – segues so naturally into the stage direction in the second quarto (Q2), 'Musick playes and they dance' (Shakespeare 1599, C3r), that the sparseness of explicit clues to early modern theatregoing experience may not be readily recollected. On stage, the celebrated sonnet sequence (1.5.92–109) lies in abeyance until the measure (a then popular dance form) in which Juliet is participating draws to a closure. Romeo sees in Juliet 'a snowy dove trooping with crows' (1.5.47) and bides his time until the dance ends ('the measure done, I'll watch her place of stand/ And, touching hers, make blessed my rude hand' (1.5.49–50)), which signals how the measure at the Capulet ball simultaneously stays and sharpens Romeo's desire. Later in the play, Peter's request for a country-dance, 'Heart's ease' (4.5.10–101), even as 'solemn hymns to sullen dirges change' (4.5.88), is regarded as malapropos by the band of musicians on the stage. However, it is also indicative of the various effects – in this instance, tragically ironic – that dance and associated ideas can produce in the theatrical experience of *Romeo and Juliet*. The routine omission of Peter's encounter with the musicians from the productions of the play suggests that modern-day ears are not fully attuned to the complex functions of music and dance in Shakespeare.

In a manner akin to their Shakespearean antecedents, song-and-dance sequences in Bollywood's engagements with the

Bard also flummox Western audiences. In part, the difficulty lies in parsing their 'dense and intricate configuration of semiotics from several fields of the literary, visual, and auditory' (Trivedi 2014, 346). Tellingly, the translation of the screenplays of Vishal Bhardwaj's celebrated Shakespearean trilogy into English, as published by Harper Collins India, does not include the songs that thread through the individual narratives. More generally, 'there has been comparatively little written on [the Hindi] film song... because it is difficult to separate the music of film song from the intertextual discourses that circulate along with it' (Beaster-Jones 2015, 7). The individual readings of the song-and-dance sequences in *Ram-Leela* that I present below are an initiative to address the critical lacuna. I pay close attention to the hermeneutics of Bollywood song-and-dance sequences to illuminate how *Ram-Leela* consorts with *Romeo and Juliet*. While the homoerotic charge in the musical metaphor of 'consort' unleashes the irrevocable acts of violence in the play,[7] I bend it here in the service of queer desire to trace textual (be)longing and create an index of homotextuality.

Tattad Tattad: textual congress

The first song-and-dance sequence in the film, '*Tattad Tattad*', introduces Ram, Romeo's counterpart in *Ram-Leela*, and makes ample use of Bollywood conventions. The numerous extras that people the set of a crowded marketplace, attired in ethnic garb, establish the milieu of a village in western India. There are scores of background dancers who dance in synchronous beauty with the lead actor on whose lissome body the languorous gaze of the camera lingers. The music is quintessentially Bollywood, making polyphony out of a medley of musical traditions that range from folk music to Western scores.[8] The dancers, including the actor playing Ram, lip-sync the lyrics to the song, honouring the compact into which audiences enter with Bollywood sensibilities that ask them to cheerfully accommodate a voice that is distinctly different to that of the actor. The lyrics of the song and the enactment of them through choreography elide the differences between Lord Ram, the hero of the Sanskrit epic *Ramayana* who is regarded as divine by Hindus, and Ram who is Bhansali's creation. Simultaneously, the musical interludes that string the chorus and the stanzas together create a striking pot-pourri of the sacred and the secular by making a ribald Ram thrust his crotch in time to the music, eliciting shrieking admiration from besotted girls.[9]

At first glance, a Romeo that courts attention in such bawdy a manner appears to be wide of the mark of Shakespeare's protagonist who, at this point in the play, '[steals] into the covert of the wood' (1.1.123). For Gil Harris (2018: 81) such representation of Romeo can be attributed to the appropriation of the name in the Indian vernacular as 'a synonym for a swaggering street Casanova' and a code for uninhibited and indiscriminate desire. Yet, this representation may not necessarily be appropriation but an extension of *Romeo and Juliet*'s exploration of the limits of (male) licentiousness. Significantly, in admonishing him for forsaking Rosaline for Juliet, Friar Laurence labels Romeo as a 'young waverer' (2.3.85). A Romeo who does not hesitate from following Benvolio's counsel in 'giving liberty unto [his] eyes' (1.1.225) has been presented in the theatre, most notably by Garrick who included Capulet's 'fair niece Rosaline' (1.2.69) in his 1748 production. The vertigo induced in the audiences at the sight of Romeo's fickle desire was so strong that it was not until the nineteenth century that Rosaline staged a comeback.[10]

Equally, the spectacle of a dancing Romeo that *Ram-Leela* showcases, albeit absent from the text, brings into view early modern understanding of dancing as constructing and consolidating gender. In *Orchestra or A Poeme of Dauncing* (1596), John Davies (sig. B6r) singles out the Galliard as a 'gallant dance, that lively doth bewray/ A spirit and a virtue Masculine'. The features of the dance – 'loftie turns and capriols in the ayre,/ Which with the lustie tunes accordeth fayre' (Davies, 1596: sig. B6r) – transpose easily onto the boisterous energy of the music and dance in '*Tattad Tattad*'. Ram himself alludes to the congruity between dance and gender directly after '*Tattad Tattad*' ends. When mocked for not being virile enough, for he professes no interest in the illicit trade of arms and ammunition his family runs, Ram crows '*meri mardangi ke bare mein aap gaon ki kisi bhi ladki se puch sakte ho, <u>report</u> achi hi milegi*' [You can ask any girl in the village about my manhood, you are bound to get a great report; underline emphasis mine]. The pun on the word 'report' – at once the result of the investigation into his masculinity that Ram is proposing and the sound made by firearms from which he intends to stay away – juxtaposed with the fresh visuals of '*Tattad Tattad*' where girls were swooning at Ram's gyrating pelvis, gives the audience a glimpse into the symmetry between dance and gender that the early modern world comprehended.[11]

In conjoining Bollywood imaginary with Shakespearean verse, '*Tattad Tattad*' not only sports with the Bard but also plays with Bollywood norms. The refrain – '*tattad tattad*' – is a nonce-word, a linguistic sleight of hand that works in tandem with the aesthetics of the song, which are both a tribute to and a lampoon of Bollywood *masala*. At one point in the song, the camera goes into soft-focus and then zooms in on Ram who winks at it. Ostensibly, the wink is directed at the bevy of beauties around the character; yet, in that moment, Ranveer Singh, the actor playing Ram, is also puckishly winking at the audience, soliciting their tongue-in-cheek indulgence of the 'weak and idle theme' (*A Midsummer Night's Dream*, 5.1.414) of the moment. In citing and mocking Bollywood conventions, the song self-reflexively draws attention to the arbitrary placement of such sequences in the previous generation of films. Such techniques are often used by contemporary Bollywood to 'historicize its own emergence out of [Old] Bollywood' (Gopal, 2011, 14) and meet the same discursive challenge that *Romeo and Juliet* faced vis-à-vis trite Petrarchanisms.[12] The confluence of these various literary and cultural flows occurs at the moment where Ram flexes his torso (Figure 11.1). Ram's biceps recall both Romeo's 'agile arm' (3.1.168) and the storied strength of Lord Ram's arms. The mural of Lord Ram sits in the same frame as the smartphones

FIGURE 11.1 Film still: *Hand-in-hand*: Ramayana *and* Romeo and Juliet, Goliyon Ki Rasleela: Ram-Leela, *directed by Sanjay Leela Bhansali* © *Eros International 2013. All rights reserved.*

capturing Ram's brawn, chronicling the profusion of texts and technologies in play from *Ramayana* to *Romeo and Juliet* and from Ramleela, a form of folk theatre that dramatizes the life of Lord Ram, to *Ram-Leela*. While each body of texts draws upon a separate reservoir of cultural meanings, in 'cumming' together, they spawn a literary identity that is too protean and polysemous for (hetero)normative epistemologies. There is little wonder that the resistance to neat taxonomies put forward by such literary endeavours would be read in the terms of 'excess' or worse. For *Time Out*, *Ram-Leela* was 'loud, camp, violent and ultimately soulless' (*Time Out* 2013), the comminations that syntactically create parity between camp and soulless make clear that there is no place for the queer in the great chain of being. 'Bhansali also composed the film's ten energetic songs, but he sure ain't no Bernstein [who scored *West Side Story*]' (*Time Out* 2013) the review concludes.

Lahu Muh Lag Gaya: is it wholly palmers' kiss?

'*Lahu Muh Lag Gaya*' ['I have tasted blood'], the song-and-dance sequence that follows '*Tattad Tattad*', serves as the backdrop for the first meeting of Ram and Leela, mirroring the Capulet masque in *Romeo and Juliet*. Ram's smitten looks in the sequence recall Romeo's 'I ne'er saw true beauty till this night' (1.5.52). Similarly, Romeo's rhapsody that Juliet 'doth teach the torches to burn bright' (1.5.43) casts light on the otherwise inexplicable presence of *diyas* [lamps moulded out of clay] in a song choreographed during Holi, a festival celebrated during the day. The festival itself, where people smear each other with colours, is an apt substitute for the disguises afforded by Elizabethan and Jacobean masques. The sestet that unfolds the song introduces the film's running avian motif where culturally resonant peacocks chirp for their Shakespearean brethren: larks and nightingales. Simultaneously, the lyrics of the sestet position desire as transcendent and transgressive – '*Man ure/ Par lage/ pag bhade, teri ore bhade/ jag chod bhade*' ['My heart soars,/ I feel wings on me./ My feet inch towards you,/ Thus I leave the world behind'] – bringing forward Romeo's impassioned contempt of boundaries: 'With love's light wings did I o'erperch these walls,/ For stony limits cannot hold love out' (2.2.66–7). The use of the word *lahu* (blood) in the chorus yokes passion and violence together, foreshadowing the tragic progression of 'violent delights' to 'violent ends' (2.6.9).

While '*Tattad Tattad*' made sly use of Bollywood conventions, '*Lahu Muh Lag Gaya*' subverts them, and in the process provides a key for its homotextuality to come out of the closet. Typical Bollywood dance sequences witness the actors synchronize their lips and limbs to the words of a pre-recorded song. The gestures in the dance embody the lyrics and grant a material aspect to the abstract ideas and emotions of the song. The roots of this relationship between words and gestures can be traced back to *Natyashastra*, the founding Sanskrit text on the performing arts in the Indian subcontinent, that stipulates dance as a physical expression of music and verse. However, while the words to '*Lahu Muh Lag Gaya*' are meant to telegraph Ram's feelings and are accordingly sung in a male voice, Ram himself is unshackled from convention. Far from lip- or limb-syncing the words, he comes into his own through dance with a flourish that is reminiscent of Romeo finding his authentic voice through the Petrarchan clutter.[13] The chiastic relationship between verse and dance that is struck by '*Lahu Muh Lag Gaya*' offers an unexpected entry into the early modern period where poesy and dancing existed in a state of fluent symbiosis. In *Orchestra*, John Davies (1596) is effusive about dances that 'on a triple Dactyle foote doe run' (sig. B7v) and those in which dancers with 'their feet an Anapest do sound' (sig. B7v) but notes weariness at dances that stick to 'Spondeis, solemn, grave, and sloe' (sig. B6r). *Orchestra* exemplifies how, in early modern England, dancing 'was sometimes conceived as a kind of writing, the practiced movements of the feet tracing geometric patterns on the floor as they imitated poetic meters' (Howard 1993, 335). The fecund analogies between dance and verse also pullulated spectacles in the early modern playhouse. Andrew Hiscock (2018, 43) notes how 'dance might all too often augment, enhance and/or demarcate the parameters of spoken text in the unfolding narrative representation of human experience onstage ... Such stylized movement may entertain participant and onlooker alike, but in the theatre, it can serve to evoke locale, event or act as a narrative drive or supplement.' The state of fungibility in which dance and writing exist is hidden in plain sight of the etymology of the word 'choreography' that unites the Greek word for dancing (chorós) with that for writing (graphé). The dexterous hand-movements that distinguish the choreography of '*Lahu Muh Lag Gaya*' from the rest of the songs in *Ram-Leela* can thus be read as a somatic re-interpretation of Shakespearean verse that brought Romeo and Juliet together through an extended wordplay on hands.[14] However, the haptics of the piece also flesh out the social anxieties around dance that both the early modern and Old Bollywood imaginaries sought to address and contain.

In the early modern period, the conception of dance as a representation of cosmic order jostled with invectives against its proclivities. If, for Davies (1596: sig. A5v-r), to dance was to 'imitate the starres caelestiall' and to move to 'the musick of the spheares', for Vives (1585) the movements were anything but heavenly. Contemporary dancing, Vives (1585: sig. K7v) agonized, was 'full of shaking and bragging, and unclenly handlynges, gropynges and kissinges: and a very kindling of lecherie'. Elyot (1537: sig. K5r) waxed eloquent on the civic order that dance made tangible – 'In every daunse, of a most aunsient custome, there daunseth to gether a man and a woman, holding eche other by the hande or the arme, whiche betokenth concorde.' Conversely, for Stubbes (1583: sig. Nv), dancing was one of the abuses that inverted social order: 'what filthy groping and uncleane handling is not practiced everywhere in these dancings . . . it is not a thing wherin a Christian Mans heart may take any comfort'. Leontes has Vives's 'unclenly handlynges' and Stubbes's 'uncleane handling' in mind when he sees his wife, Hermione, and his friend, Polixenes 'paddling palms and pinching fingers' (1.2.115). It is within the cultural matrix that fomented fears of the corrupting influence of dance that Leontes' self-diagnosis makes sense: 'I have *tremor cordis* on me. My heart dances,/ But not for joy, not joy' (1.2.110–11). The association between dance and lasciviousness is also present in *Romeo and Juliet*, where a sanctimonious Romeo, wedded to Rosaline, his Petrarchan mistress, primly leaves dancing to those literally directing their desire to the base and earthly: 'Let wantons light of heart/ Tickle the senseless rushes with their heels' (1.4.35–6).[15]

In Old Bollywood, dance sequences that focused on a couple in love served as a placeholder for other forms of intimacy that were regarded as obscene for actual visual representation. Until the millennium, even on-screen kissing was practically a taboo, which is why songs were designed in a way to 'provide the affective intensities of the on-screen kiss' (Gopal 2011, 29). In her character study of Leela, Varsha Panjwani (2018, 116) notes that:

> Kissing is a risqué act in India both on-screen and off-screen in public. The Central Board of Film Certification (CBFC),

India's unofficial board of censors, regulates lip-locks rather stringently...Even in 2015, CBFC insisted on editing a kiss to half its length in the James Bond film, *Spectre*, before it could be screened in India.

Situating *Ram-Leela* in this context allows Panjwani to highlight how the initiative Leela takes in kissing Ram in '*Lahu Muh Lag Gaya*' is transgressive. By extension, the song (and the film) is renouncing the grammar to which Bollywood semiotics adheres (Figures 11.2 and 11.3). Further, in becoming the site of – instead of a substitute for – kissing, the song conveys the thrill that early modern playgoers would have

FIGURE 11.2 (ABOVE) AND 11.3 Film stills: *Not kissing by the book*, Goliyon Ki Rasleela: Ram-Leela, *directed by Sanjay Leela Bhansali* © *Eros International 2013. All rights reserved.*

experienced on witnessing Romeo and Juliet share a full-frontal kiss, which, was a rare occurrence in the Elizabethan theatre.[16]

'*Ram Chahe Leela*': the rigour of severest law

Instead of rushing into the inevitable tragedy, *Ram-Leela* swerves from the Shakespearean template and wrenches the lovers apart in a (melo)dramatic manner to anatomize the pernicious hold of filial and civic obligations on their bodies with the song-and-dance sequence '*Ram Chahe Leela*' ['Ram desires Leela'] embarking on the excursus. '*Ram Chahe Leela*' is of a species so unique to Bollywood artistry that it has warranted a coinage in Indian English: item song. Typically, item songs feature a prominent artist in a cameo, are known for their lush production values, and are integral to the marketing of the film. Yet, more often than not, an item song 'has no relation whatsoever to the film, and the "item girl" [the actress in the cameo appearance] plays no role elsewhere in the diegesis' (Gopal 2011, 40). '*Ram Chahe Leela*' is a paradigmatic Bollywood item song, not the least in its choice of Priyanka Chopra Jonas, a (now global) superstar, as its 'item girl'. The lyrics advance the plot to the same degree as the prolix speeches in *Romeo and Juliet* that either recount the action (2.0; 3.1.154–77; 5.3.229–69) or impart 'good counsel' (3.3.107–57; 159). Yet, '*Ram Chahe Leela*' is anything but redundant to *Ram-Leela*. For *Ram-Leela* to go retrograde as Ram and Leela regress into the roles that their families expect of them is a studied choice. Subscribing to the conventions it had once mocked or waived, through '*Ram Chahe Leela*' *Ram-Leela* offers a meta-commentary on the teleological forces closing in on the lovers: neither *Ram-Leela* nor Ram and Leela can escape their inherited (Bollywood/Shakespearean) destiny. In the process, it also establishes a homohistorical nexus with early modern conceptualization of dancing.

In *The Boke Named the Governour*, Sir Thomas Elyot conducts a sustained analysis of the various styles and effects of dancing. Although in accounting for the forms that have 'corrupted the myndes of them that daunsed and provoked synne' Elyot (1537: sig. K4r) gives credit to the anxieties of his contemporaries, his enterprise values dancing as 'a soveraygne and profytable exercise'. Elyot (1537: sig. K4r) argues that through 'apte and proportionate meuynge' a dancer is able to at once embody and embrace virtue. The pun on the word 'meuynge', a vestigial remain of middle English that encompasses the meanings of mewing (the moulting of feathers) and moving, is crucial to my argument here, bolstering as it does the relationship between bodily transfigurations and movements within a socially approved sphere of human activity. Elyot's emphasis on 'meuynge' and 'the crafty disposition and facionynge of the body' contextualizes the stylized posturing that sets apart the choreography of '*Ram Chahe Leela*', which is performed when Ram is forced into presiding over his family's mafia. The affective politics of '*Ram Chahe Leela*' are a surreal echo of Elyot (1537: sig. K4r) who contended that when 'dilygentely beholden', dancing served as an 'intimation of sondry vtues' that range from prudence to circumspection, facilitating the smooth governance of the polis. Elyot's precept is also in tandem with *Orchestra*'s praise of dancing as 'the finest pollicie/ To plant religion and societie' (Davies 1596: sig. B8r).

Dancing in the early modern period was thus viewed as 'a material practice disciplining both mind and body in a requisite manner for acceptable engagement in the body politic' (Hiscock 2018, 52). Strikingly, '*Ram Chahe Leela*' configures the 'meuynge' of Ram's (and Leela's) body within the social schemata of Ranjhaar on similar terms. The shift from the fluid moves of previous song-and-dance sequences to the contortions of '*Ram Chahe Leela*' renders palpable the forces at work that bend Ram and Leela against their will. Towards the end of the song, Chopra Jonas strikes several *mudras* or poses that defer to the conventions of Indian classical dancing as detailed in the *Natyashashtra* (Figure 11.4 and 11.5). The decorousness of the *mudras* is proportional to the extent to which the body is twisted in unnatural ways: the dialectic augmented by the aesthetics of an item song that revel in artifice. Casting bodies in rigid moulds controls their unruliness and, in turning supple bodies statuesque, '*Ram Chahe Leela*' holds up a mirror to Ram of the symbolic violence to which he must submit his self. The sequence achieves what it desires, for *Ram-Leela* no longer has a Ram dancing with exuberance; he turns still and joins the ranks of the rest of his clan who never dance. Even more disturbingly, the bodily violence hinted at in '*Ram Chahe Leela*' is not merely symbolic. Between this dance

FIGURE 11.4 (ABOVE) AND 11.5 Film stills: *Apt and proportionate 'meuynge'*, Goliyon Ki Rasleela: Ram-Leela, *directed by Sanjay Leela Bhansali* © *Eros International 2013. All rights reserved.*

sequence and the final one, her mother amputates Leela's ring finger when she refuses to take her wedding ring off – a grisly climax to Capulet's threats at Juliet's 'chopped logic' (3.5.149–57 and 3.5.176–96).

'Nagade Sang Dhol': fearful passage of death-marked love

'Nagade Sang Dhol' ['kettledrums and drums resound'], the final song-and-dance sequence, perfects the notion of dance as determining social identity and defining one's participation in the body politic. In its preference for a folk dance, *Garba* (over spirited or fluid choreography), the sequence consolidates the idea of civic bonds being reinforced via bodies collectively going through their paces. Premised on the pact between form and function made in *'Ram Chahe Leela'*, *'Nagade Sang Dhol'* has all the trappings of a stereotypical (Old) Bollywood song-and-dance routine to signify the inexorable tragic forces tightening their hold on the lovers. The sequence occurs at a tense moment when Ram goes over to Leela's house to end the blood-feud between their clans. He is unaware of the trap he is walking into where Leela's family intends to murder him and, in the process, end the male line of his family. The plan is kept a secret from Leela who anticipates the brokering of peace as a renewal of their marriage vows. While lacking in a point of congruity with *Romeo and Juliet*, *'Nagade Sang Dhol'* coheres with other parts of the Shakespearean corpus. In winding its way through *Macbeth*, *Ram-Leela* establishes the inheritance of Juliet's 'O serpent heart with a flowering face' (3.2.73) in Lady Macbeth's 'look like th'innocent flower,/ But be the serpent under't' (1.5.65–6), patterning itself after the pastiche that is frequently found in intercultural Shakespeare.[17]

In addition to celebrating intertextuality, *'Nagade Sang Dhol'* also revels in homotextuality. The sequence stands in contrastive focus to *'Lahu Muh Lag Gaya'*, which was the last time Ram was in Sanera (Capulet) territory. *'Lahu Muh Lag*

Gaya', Bhansali's version of the Capulet masque, diverges from Shakespeare for Romeo does not dance at the assembly. Wearing the cloak of melancholy, for he is pining for Rosaline at that point in the play, Romeo declares: 'I am not for this ambling ... you have dancing shoes with/ nimble soles, I have a soul of lead/ So stakes me to the ground I cannot move' (1.4.11–16). His abstinence from dancing is singular enough for Juliet to use it as a pretext to enquire into his identity: 'What's he that follows here, that would not dance?', she asks of her Nurse (1.5.131). Romeo's forbearance and his ominous reason (being staked to the ground) would have been regarded as a confirmation of the tragedy – promised in the prologue – by the play's first audience. Bhansali saves these sinister strokes for '*Nagade Sang Dhol*' where, notwithstanding Leela's invitation, Ram declines to dance. The moment captures how, in early modern drama, the response to an invitation to dance could provide 'an alternative and dynamic mode for diegesis for the stage' (Hiscock 2018, 50). The reference to *lahu* [blood] from '*Lahu Muh Lag Gaya*' spills over to colour the costumes and visuals of '*Nagade Sang Dhol*', which are bathed in red, to arrive at the *denouement* of 'the two hours' traffic of (Shakespeare's) stage' (Prologue, 12).

The cinematography, choreography and acoustics of '*Nagade Sang Dhol*' give a keen edge to the imminent tragedy. The grandness of the set and the wide shots that Bhansali favours in this sequence dwarf the actors and lay out the cosmic plan for the 'star-crossed lovers' (Prologue, 6) that is being executed. With frenetic energy, Leela and the background dancers take dizzying spins that are juxtaposed with crane shots, creating a vortex of dramatic tension into which the protagonists (and the audience) are sucked (Figure 11.6). Set during *Navratri*, the religious period that serves as the herald for Diwali, the burden of the refrain sounds like a chant and augments the association between tragedy and ritual with the sombre *dhai* [an onomatopoeia for pistol shots] in the refrain '*dhai-dhai dhum-dhum dhai*'. In addition, '*Dhai-dhai dhum-dhum dhai*' employs *anupraas alankar*, a figure of rhetoric

FIGURE 11.6 Film still: *A story of woe*, Goliyon Ki Rasleela: Ram-Leela, directed by Sanjay Leela Bhansali © Eros International 2013. All rights reserved.

from Sanskrit literary theory that conjoins alliteration with onomatopoeia, for a singular purpose. The alliteration produced through the aspiration of a voiced consonant 'dh' (a phonological phenomenon unique to Indian languages) aurally denotes the lovers' dying breath. The onomatopoeia for the beating of the drums, '*dhum dhum*', is bookended by '*dhai dhai*': the mark of rhythm, which stood for order and harmony in the early modern period, is preceded and cut off by shrill violence. '*Nagade Sang Dhol*' ends with a salvo of bullets, reaching the crescendo of 'the fearful passage of (Ram and Leela's) death-marked love' (Prologue, 9).

Coda: '*Mor Bani Man Thangat Kare*'

The configurations of textual and performative codes as limned by homotextuality not only bring Shakespeare and Bollywood together but also illuminate aspects of Shakespearean corpus, early modern culture, and Bollywood lexicon that are obscure or strange. Concomitantly, homohistory shines a light on the unacknowledged genealogical links between Bollywood song-and-dance sequences and musical reincarnations of Shakespeare that range from Henry Purcell's *The Fairy Queen* (1692) to the 'extra dances and songs which characterised many nineteenth-century Shakespearian productions' (Lindley 2015, 62). The etymology of Bollywood also intimates consanguinity with Hollywood, soliciting a reappraisal of its song-and-dance-sequences within the tradition of the 'integrated musical'[18] of which *La La Land* (2016) is the most recent example. To be a homotextual reader is to sing from the hymn sheet of the modes and mores of textual dissemination where a *Ram-Leela* (2013) is the merry companion to *West Side Story* (1961; dirs Robert Wise and Jerome Robbins), *Romeo and Juliet* (1968; dir. Franco Zeffirelli), *Romeo + Juliet* (1996; dir. Baz Luhrmann), and *West Side Story* (2021; dir. Steven Spielberg). To be a homotextual reader is to be well versed in the interpolations and extrapolations as issuing forth from incontrovertible textual authority: 'Go hence, to have more talk of these sad things' (*Romeo and Juliet*, 5.3.307). To be a homotexual reader is to interrogate the pedagogical and cultural prejudices that eschew certain forms of creativity as the work of 'a crew of patches, rude mechanicals' (*A Midsummer Night's Dream*, 3.2.9). To be a homotextual reader is to draw in a deep breath of the fresh air let in by queer progenies such as *Ram-Leela* that do not identify themselves as adaptations but as '*inspired* by *Romeo and Juliet* by William Shakespeare' (emphasis mine). To be a homotextual reader is to grasp the gestalt of texts such as *Ram-Leela* that combine the poesies of Shakespeare and Jhaverchand Meghani: one an erstwhile envoy of imperialist pedagogy and the other a freedom fighter. To be a homotextual reader is to key into the notes of decolonization that are plucked in Meghani's '*Mor Bani Man Thangat Kare*' ['My heart dances like a peacock'] when it serves as the background score to the balcony scene and opens the film. To be a homotextual reader is to further the methodology for Global Shakespeares, which 'constitutes a postnational space' (Huang 2013, 281). Finally, to be a homotextual reader is to let go of ancient grudges and further the gay agenda of 'bringing out and celebrating "the homo" in all of us' (Bersani 1995, 10). Be homotextual. Be fabulous.

Notes

1. See, for instance, *Cassette Culture*, where song and dance sequences are deemed as 'more-or-less gratuitous insertions into the plot to be enjoyed for their own sake' (Manuel 1993, 41). In his monograph that gives a cultural context to the production and reception of Bollywood songs, Jayson Beaster-Jones (2015) attributes the paucity of scholarship on the subject to critical aversion to their 'unapologetically commercial aesthetic' (7).

2. In one of the pioneering studies that adopted this line of thought, Anna Morcom (2007) makes a case for song-and-dance sequences as 'positive expressions of Indian identity by filmmakers' (241) that stem from conventions that are intrinsic to the creative process. She observes that 'Hindi films have always had songs means that their narratives are designed for the inclusion of songs. They pause for long enough to incorporate a full song on one emotion, and audiences are used to this' (52).

3. René Weis, ed., *Romeo and Juliet* (London: Bloomsbury, 2012).

4. E. A. J. Honigmann, ed., *Othello* (London: Bloomsbury, 1996), 1.1.134.

5. In a slightly different context, Carla Freccero (2011: 303) argues that the protective zeal and regenerative desire of fidelity discourse stem from a heteronormative impulse: 'Accuracy and authenticity are often disciplinary mechanisms operating in the service of "straightening out" the perversity of other possibilities.' On how the fidelity discourse haunts Bollywood adaptations of Shakespeare, see Sharda (2017).

6. For example, 'mistempered' and 'airy word' are gravid with musical meanings, which spring into action when the 'moved prince' is irate at 'civil brawls' (1.1.85–7). Brawls or *branles* were a particularly rowdy form of dancing imported from France. In fashioning the ideal courtier, Castiglione (1561: sig. M3r) makes allowances for the prevailing trends and begrudgingly lets the courtier 'daunce the morisco [Morris] & braulles [brawls], yet not openlye onlesse he were in a maske'. Amongst other places in the text, these motifs dance in Meructio's disdain of Tybalt's swordsmanship: 'he fights as you sing pricksong, keeps time, distance and proportion', 2.4.20–21.

7 Tybalt goads Mercutio into a fight with 'Mercutio, thou consortest with Romeo' (3.1.44) and seeks to offend Romeo in a similar way: 'Thou wretched boy, that didst consort [Mercutio] here,/ Shalt with him hence' (3.1.132–3).

8 On the syncretic nature of Bollywood music, see Morcom (2007), especially 137–79.

9 The unholy alliance between the profound and the profane caused such a furore in India that the filmmakers had to include a disclaimer at the start of the film that sought to retrospectively remove any association between Lord Ram, the deity, and Ram, the cinematic character, to assuage Hindu anxieties.

10 See René Weis, 'Introduction', in *Romeo and Juliet*, ed. René Weis (London : Bloomsburry, 2012), 1–115.

11 On the complex ways in which various dance forms were gendered, see Howard (1996).

12 At the start of the play, Montague despairs that his son, Romeo, 'private in his chamber pens himself' (1.1.135). The pun on the word 'pens' suggests that Romeo's seclusion wears a literary habit that fashions itself after Astrophil's precept of turning away from 'every purling spring' in favour of an 'inward tutch' (Sidney 1591: sig. Br). Yet Romeo's amative cries for Rosaline want 'inventions stay' (Sidney 1591: sig. A2r), typifying logorrhea instead: 'Feather of lead, bright smoke, cold fire, sick health' (1.1.178). Such declarations that echo 'poore *Petrarchs* long deceased woes' (Sidney 1591: sig. Br) contextualize Mercutio's raillery later in the play: 'Now is [Romeo] for the numbers that Petrarch flowed in' (2.4.38–9). For Martinez (2011), 'Mercutio's mocking mention of Petrarchan verse ... tips us off that the play itself is Shakespeare's bid to outdo Petrarch within the arena of the sonnet and its poetics.'

13 Critics concur that through Romeo Shakespeare rivals and seeks to excel Petrarch, the progenitor of Elizabethan love poetry. Scholarship, however, is less decided on the extent to which Shakespeare's dramatic endeavour is successful if at all. In her magisterial study, Heather Dubrow (1995: 265) arrives at a qualified assessment: 'at some points [*Romeo and Juliet*] holds out the hope of replacing Petrarchism with a better alternative, yet elsewhere it challenges that aspiration'. Conversely, more recent critical appraisals erect their arguments on the foundation

of desire consummated in the play that unfolds 'the triumph of English sonnet form and formalizes the supersession of Petrarch, just as on the level of content Shakespeare's married Romeo outperforms Petrarch's chaste lover' (Martinez 2011).

14 At the Capulet masque, Romeo woos Juliet with his 'unworthiest hand' (1.5.92), seeking 'a tender kiss' (1.5.95). Juliet's arch reply, 'palm to palm is holy palmers' kiss' (1.5.99), sets the stage for verbal fencing between the two until, 'want[ing] wit to cease' (Sidney, 1591: sig. E3v), *Romeo and Juliet* enacts Astrophil's fantasy: 'Stop you my mouth with still still kissing me' (Sidney, 1591: sig. E3v).

15 Straw rushes were used in affluent Elizabethan households to keep the floor dry. On festive occasions, such as the Capulet masque, they would be strewn along with herbs that would release a faint but pleasing aroma when trod upon (Woodward 1998: 68).

16 Weis, ed., *Romeo and Juliet*, 175.

17 There is a burgeoning practice of combining Shakespearean texts in intercultural productions such as the National Centre for the Performing Arts, Mumbai's *Reth* (2016) which combined *Merchant of Venice* with *Macbeth* or Tribal Arts' *Darokhand*, a bricolage of six (!) Shakespearean plays. For a discussion of the latter, see Panjwani (2017).

18 Mervyn Cooke (2015) defines an integrated musical as a film whose 'musical numbers could be justified by plot and character' (152) and in which dances could signify 'an expression of a character's individuality . . . [or] articulate romantic plots in a dynamic and thoroughly modern manner' (157).

References

Beaster-Jones, J. *Bollywood Sounds: The Cosmopolitan Mediations of Hindi Film Song*. New York: Oxford University Press, 2015.

Bersani, L. *Homos*. Cambridge, MA: Harvard University Press, 1995.

Brissenden, A. *Shakespeare and the Dance*. London: Macmillan, 1981.

Burnett, M. Thornton. *Shakespeare and World Cinema*. Cambridge: Cambridge University Press, 2012.

Castiglione, B. *The Book of the Courtier*, trans. T. Hoby. London: Wyllyam Seres, 1561.

Chute, D. 'Ram Leela Review', *Variety*, 16 November 2013. Available online: https://variety.com/2013/film/reviews/film-review-ram-leela-1200841506/ (accessed 24 July 2020).

Cooke, M. *A History of Film Music*. Cambridge: Cambridge University Press, 2015.

Davies, J. *Orchestra or A Poeme of Dauncing*. London: J Robarts, 1596.

Dubrow, H. *Echoes of Desire: English Petrarchisms and its Counterdiscourses*. Ithaca: Cornell University Press, 1995.

Elyot, T. *The Boke Named the Governour*. London: Thomas Berthlet, 1537.

Freccero, C. 'Romeo and Juliet Love Death', in M. Menon, ed., *Shakesqueer: A Queer Companion to the Complete Works of Shakespeare*. Durham, NC: Duke University Press, 2011, 302–8.

French, P. 'Omkara Review', *The Guardian*, 30 July 2006. Available online: https://www.theguardian.com/film/2006/jul/30/philipfrench2 (accessed 24 July 2020).

Gibbons, B., ed. *Romeo & Juliet*. London: Methuen & Co., 1980.

Gil Harris, J. *Masala Shakespeare: How a Firangi Writer Became Indian*. New Delhi: Aleph, 2018.

Goldberg, J., and Menon, M. (2005) 'Queering History', *PMLA* 120, 5 (2005): 1608–1617, esp. 1609.

Gopal, S. *Conjugations: Marriage & Form in New Bollywood Cinema*. Chicago: Chicago University Press, 2011.

Hiscock, A. 'Come, now a roundel and a fairy song: Shakespeare's *A Midsummer Night's Dream* and the early modern invitation to dance', *Cahiers Élisabéthains* 97, 1 (2018): 39–68.

Howard, S. 'Hands, Feet, and Bottoms: Decentering the Cosmic Dance in *A Midsummer Night's Dream*', *Shakespeare Quarterly* 44, 3 (1993): 325–42.

Howard, S. 'Rival Discourses of Dancing in Early Modern England', *Studies in English Literature, 1500–1900* 36, 1 (1996): 31–56.

Huang, A. 'Global Shakespeares as Methodology', *Shakespeare*, 9, 3 (2013): 273–90.

Lindley, D. 'Sounds and Sweet Airs': Music in Shakespearian Performance History', *Shakespeare Survey* 64 (2015): 59–73.

Manuel, P. *Cassette Culture: Popular Music and Technology in North India*. Chicago: University of Chicago Press, 1993.

Martinez, R. L. '"Francis, Thou Art Translated": Petrarch Metamorphosed in English, 1380–1595', *Humanist Studies & the Digital Age* 1, 1 (2011); DOI: 10.5399/uo/HSDA.1.1.1196.

McCahill, M. 'Haider Review', *The Guardian*, 2 October 2014. Available online: https://www.theguardian.com/film/2014/oct/02/haider-review-a-hit-in-any-language-vishal-bhardwaj (accessed 24 July 2020).

Morcom, A. *Hindi Film Songs and the Cinema*, Aldershot: Ashgate, 2007.

Panjwani, V. 'Not Minding the Gap: Intercultural Shakespeare in Britain', *Multicultural Shakespeare: Translation, Appropriation and Performance* 15, 30 (2017); DOI: 10.1515/mstap-2017-0004.

Panjwani, V. 'Juliet in *Ram-Leela*: A Passionate Sita', *Shakespeare Studies* 46 (2018): 110–119.

Shakespeare, W. *The most excellent and lamentable tragedie of Romeo & Juliet*. London: Thomas Creed, 1599.

Sharda, S. 'Black Skin, Black Castes: Overcoming a Fidelity Discourse in Bharadwaj's *Omkara*', *Shakespeare Bulletin* 35, 4 (2017): 599–626.

Sidney, P. *Sir P.S. his Astrophel and Stella wherein the excellence of sweete poesie is concluded*. London: Thomas Newman, 1591.

Sidney, P. *The Defence of Poesy*. London: William Ponsonby, 1595.

Stanivukovic, G. (2016), 'Beyond Sodomy: What is Still Queer About Early Modern Queer Studies?', in V. Nardizzi, S. Guy-Bray, and W. Stockton, eds., *Queer Renaissance Historiography: Backward Gaze*. London: Routledge, 2016, 41–66.

Stubbes, P. *The Anatomie of Abuses*. London: Richard Jones, 1583.

Time Out. '*Ram-Leela* Review', *Time Out*, 18 November 2013. Available online: https://www.timeout.com/london/film/ram-leela (accessed 24 July 2020).

Trivedi, P. 'Singing to Shakespeare in Omkara', in M. Procházka, ed., *Renaissance Shakespeare/Shakespeare Renaissances: Proceedings of the Ninth World Shakespeare Congress*. Newark: University of Delaware Press, 2014, 345–54.

Tuhkanen, M. 'Queer Hybridity', in C. Nigianni, and M. Storr, eds., *Deleuze and Queer Theory*. Edinburgh: Edinburgh University Press, 2009, 92–114.

Vives, J. L. *A verie fruitfull and pleasant booke, called the instruction of a christian woman. Made first in Latin, by the right famous cleark M. Levves Viues*, trans. R. Hyrde. London: Robert Waldegrave, 1585.

Williams, L. 'Melodrama Revised', in N. Browne, ed., *Refiguring American Film Genres: History & Theory*. Berkley: University of California Press, 1998, 42–88.

Woodward, D. 'Straw, Bracken and the Wicklow Whale: The Exploitation of Natural Resources in England Since 1500', *Past & Present* 159 (1998): 43–76.

12

'All the world's a stage': The Participatory Indian Cinema Audience and its Impact on Indian Shakespeare Films

Koel Chatterjee

Indian cinema culture evokes the two main ways in which Shakespeare himself used the word 'audience'. The more familiar usage today of one or more people paying attention to an event is used sparingly in Shakespeare – once in *Love's Labours Lost* when Moth is worried 'if any of the audience [will] hiss' (5.1.129) at the pageant of the Nine Worthies, and once in *Midsummer Night's Dream* when Bottom warns, 'let the audience look to their eyes' (1.2.22). The other usage of 'audience' as Pangallo and Kirwan describes is where, 'Shakespeare frames the granting of "audience" – that is, formal attention to an engagement with another's words and actions – as an active gesture in which the person or people who "give" the audience are the ones empowered with agency'.[1] Commercial cinema in India has evolved in the context of the need to appeal to audiences differentiated by religion, class, regional cultures, caste, rural-urban tastes and differing levels of education and literacy. As Srinivas describes, 'the relationship between filmmaker and audience displays shades of a patron–client relationship; filmmakers are dependent on the audiences' patronage and are willing to compromise and craft the film to appeal to audience expectations' (Srinivas 2016, 57). Filmmakers and critics have spoken about the demands of the public and what they would be willing to pay for. Mishra has described audiences voicing exuberance at the appearance of a favourite film star, or displeasure if the film fails to live up to expectation or if there are technical difficulties, by taking out their frustration on their surroundings and ripping the upholstery with razor blades and knives (59).[2] Thomas notes that filmmakers 'operate with an explicit concept of their audiences' imposing constraints on their filmmaking' and that 'a central preoccupation ... is whether or not the audience will accept certain representations or narrative outcomes' (Dickey 1993, 69). In multiple interviews or discussions of script development with Bollywood directors in the course of my research, phrases such as 'our audiences will not accept' or 'they'll burn down the theatres if we show that' were used.[3] Audience members talk to each other, take on the role of narrators, applaud the resolution of dramatic tension and hiss, boo, or shout advice, providing instant feedback (Srinivas 2016, 60). This relationship between audience and filmmakers in India resonates with Stephen Purcell's observation of the usage of the word 'audience' in Shakespeare where 'audience is something one can give and receive, promise or withhold. It is active. It is processual. It is an item of exchange and part of a transaction ... [It] is the first act in a pact of complicity' (Purcell 2013, xiii). Shakespeare wrote for a theatre in which the audience was understood to be, and frequently invited to be dynamic and participatory, and performances of his plays after his time and in different media sometimes struggle to engage with 'that genetic identity of the plays' (Pangallo and Kirwin 2021, 3). Indian

Shakespeare films, rooted in spectatorship cultures similar to those of Shakespeare's times, can help shed light on Shakespeare's plays by highlighting that the Western conventional view of the filmmaker as the 'giver' and the audience as the 'receiver' is too unidirectional and unilateral and that it may be more fruitful to think of the filmmaker as 'receiver', and the consumer of films as the 'giver of audience'.

> NW: We talked briefly about cinema etiquette, we all got used to being lazy, watching films on our sofa . . .
> CS: Or stopping the film and nipping out for a moment for a cup of tea.
> AP: When you go back to the cinema, do me a favour . . . try not to bring in the smelliest food possible . . .
> NW: Or the noisiest . . .
> AP: Or the noisiest. Yes, please. A curry. Please don't.[4]

As the conversation on film etiquette on *BBC Breakfast* quoted above suggests, there is an enormous disparity between film spectatorship in the West and among people from the Indian subcontinent. The generalized experience and expectation of film viewing in public settings at Western cinema theatres is that audiences are silent and immobile; film viewing is seen as an individual experience with the audience attention directed away from one another and towards the screen, the sole source of light and sound. Noise, chatter, interruptions and smelly foods are frowned upon. Most people from a subcontinental heritage, however, remember their parents sneaking in snacks to the cinema; indeed, in my house, where we used to go to the cinema once a month in groups of ten to fourteen people at the very least, a veritable picnic was planned whenever we went, with all the aunties being responsible for different snacks at different points of the run-time. Moreover, cinemagoers in India frequently nip out for a cup of tea, a stretch of their legs, or a bathroom break in between the action of a film just as they would at home or at a performance of *jatra* or *Ramlila* which would traditionally last for four to six hours;[5] ushers in theatres are accordingly equipped with flashlights to seat late arrivals and to help people find their seats during the film. In multiplexes now where a traditional usher is not always present, theatres do not turn off the lights immediately when a film starts and often keep them on for ten to fifteen minutes anticipating a gradual filling up of seats. Chris Matthews, when praising *Argo* (2012) on Hardball, wondered at the spontaneous applause at the end of the screening, given that it was a film and not a live performance.[6] This reaction too would not seem out of place in India, where cinema is embedded in performance culture. The culture surrounding film reception in India is social and participatory, more like outdoor theatre audiences in the West, for instance, in spaces such as the Yard in Shakespeare's Globe in London, which invites audience participation as part of the production.

> People talk throughout the film; piercing whistles, yells and cheers from boisterous 'front benchers' punctuate the screening ... Young men shout out improvised dialogue, make 'catcalls' and lewd comments, people sing and hum along with the songs, and some may even dance. Audiences are known to import ritual practices of (Hindu) worship to the cinema hall as they propitiate the stars on-screen with incense ... and throw coins and flowers at the screen in appreciation.[7]

Several chapters in this collection discuss the uses of song-and-dance in Indian cinema, and how adaptations of Shakespeare on film have embedded this cultural tradition within their iteration of Shakespeare's plays in innovative and effective ways. Indian film culture is not restricted to within the theatre but permeates outside to everyday spaces. Popular cinema is a national obsession in India and influences every aspect of public life. Film music, designed to be appropriable, is heard in shops, restaurants, taxis, and at festival celebrations and political rallies; *filmi* dialogue inserts itself into the vocabulary of the people with famous dialogues being used in everyday speech in India as well as in advertising and media. Public walls are plastered from top to bottom with colourful (frequently hand drawn) film posters, huge billboards dominate the city skylines, and cutouts of stars garlanded by worshipful fans loom above the city streets. New releases are celebrated like festivals with *band baaja* [music band in a procession], flowers and fireworks in theatres decorated like temples or wedding sites. Films influence fashion and trends and provide content for television shows, talent competitions, cultural programmes, radio programmes and magazines.[8] The impact of a film, therefore, is shaped by the broader ways in which the film enters everyday life and is consumed and appropriated by its audiences. This is an area of Global Shakespeare scholarship that is not given much attention; considerations of the Indian Shakespeare film, for instance, frequently focus on reception as interpretation and meaning-making and the absorption of Shakespeare within traditional forms of indigenous performance styles and genres rather than on how audiences shape Indian films. Christine Geraghty argues that 'studying how we watch films ... is an important part of understanding what films mean within a culture' (Geraghty 2000, 1). This chapter will therefore examine the participatory nature of Indian film audiences and then scrutinize the nature of selective or episodic viewing by audiences in India augmented by the existence of a group of spectators called the 'repeat audience' which shapes a Shakespeare adaptation, or indeed the majority of mainstream films in India.[9] By demonstrating similarities between the Indian cinema audience and the Western theatre audience, or even the Western stage-to-screen audience, I hope to be able to re-code the 'familiar strange' Indian Shakespeare film.[10]

Filmmaking in India is frequently informal and improvised; Emmanuel Grimaud has observed that a film is often launched based on title, independent of script or theme.[11] Actors are approached, and funding is secured based on a story and the people involved in the project, rather than a script. The project is announced to the media only after a music company buys the song rights, after which the writers start working on a screenplay with input from the director or producer. Songs are written while the screenplay is being developed, and recorded before shooting for the film begins as the music is released several months before a film is completed in order to market it.[12] Songs are thus, designed to be 'appropriable' for daily life in India and have an extra-cinematic life on radio, TV, weddings, ringtones, nightclubs and the internet (Morcom 2011, 166). Music is intrinsic to all Indian performance traditions: pre-cinema, recordings of songs from Parsi theatre were made and these circulated independently of the plays (Mishra 2006, 15).

Music from films became socially important with the launch of the Hindi entertainment radio programme *Vividh Bharati* in 1957; the roles of the playback singer, composer and lyricist became significant with films being pre-sold for distribution based on their musical appeal. This meant that the audience expected *paisa vasool* [money's worth] from not only multi-talented actors who could dance, sing and fight, but also music directors who could produce a song for every possible storytelling device, and dialogue writers (different from scriptwriters) who specialized in *dialoguebaazi* [the art of penning/delivering dialogues that are memorable and appropriable].[13] Audiences frequently select a film to watch on the big screen based on its soundtrack and wish to 'see the songs' ('picturized' song sequences). In the pre-digital age, audio cassettes came with songs and dialogue which, as mentioned earlier, are designed to be appropriable in everyday contexts: 'Beedi' from *Omkara*, 'Lahu Muh Lag Gaya' from *Ram Leela* and 'Zingat', the popular song from the Marathi adaptation of *Romeo and Juliet* – *Sairat* (2016) and *Dhadak* (2018, itself a remake of *Sairat*) all became viral and can frequently be heard on television and radio now.

Dialogues are similarly adaptable: when *Ram Leela* was released in 2013, two dialogues were frequently heard in common parlance: *Marne ki sau wajah hai jeene ki sirf ek* [We have 100 reasons to die, and just one to live] and *Jab Ram naam ka raag lagey, Toh paani mei bhi aag lagey* [when one begins to sing Ram's praise, then even water becomes flammable]. *Haider*'s Gandhian message was very popular after its 2014 release: '*Inteqaam se sirf inteqaam paida hota hain*' [Revenge only begets revenge] as were the various iterations and translations of the 'to be or not to be' monologue such as '*Hum hain ki hum nahin?*' [Are we, or are we not?] from the Lal Chowk episode in the film and '*Jaan lu ki jaan du? Main rahoon ki main nahin*' [should I kill or be killed? Should I be or should I not?] when Haider is contemplating his own death with Arshia.

Audiences also go to the cinema to see a favourite performer, the attraction of the film's plot often being secondary. For instance, the real-life couple Ranveer Singh and Deepika Padukone proved a draw for audiences of *Ram-Leela* with Pinterest boards, chat groups and entertainment news articles dedicated to moviegoers discussing their desire to watch the film in order to view the chemistry between the couple.[14] When audiences went to see Nana Patekar, an actor admired for his 'dialogue delivery', they were disappointed to find him cast as a deaf mute character in *Khamoshi* (1996). According to Sanjay Leela Bhansali, the director who watched the film with the audience at Liberty Theatre, Mumbai, the audience at first implored the actor to speak and then resorted to booing and shouting.[15] Shankuntala Banaji describes of her cinema viewing experiences, how during screenings of *Astitva* (2000) and *Lajja* (2001) 'young women broke into spontaneous and prolonged applause during "feminist" speeches by screen characters.'[16] Indian film audiences thus participate in a film at the point of reception in a way that Western audiences are only familiar with in live performances.

This culture of spectatorship has led to what Madhava Prasad has described as 'a heterogeneous form of manufacture' with regard to film production in India, a process similar to watchmaking in that it involves an 'assemblage of pre-fabricated parts' (Prasad 2000, 43). Rather than being delivered to audiences as a standardized and finished product with a stable set of meanings, films are re-assembled in encounters with audience and at reception. For instance, when *Sholay* was first released in 1975 to an initially lackluster response, the director and writer considered reshooting the tragic ending of the film to revive Amitabh Bachchan but decided not to once business picked up (Chopra 2000, 164). *Omkara* (*Othello*, 2006) was reported to have kept families away from screenings of the film at the beginning because of the non-family-friendly language modelled on Iago's lines from the original Shakespearean text.[17] Robert Hardgrave, having studied the culture of Tamil Cinema, observes that most audiences 'see the film as a sequence of scenes – fights, romance, songs, cabaret' (Hardgrave 1975, 114). At a screening for *Ram-Leela* in 2013 in Kolkata, after the *holi* song sequence, a viewer jokingly told his partner, 'I've got my money's worth, now we can go home'.[18] Similarly, when Jisshu Sengupta (playing Tybalt), who has a solid fan base among young female audiences, died in *Arshinagar* (2015), a group of schoolgirls behind me discussed leaving for a meal now that Sengupta was dead.[19] Sobchak Vivian observes that film, though objectively presented to viewers, 'may be subjectively taken up in a variety of ways, not only in its entirety, but also in its parts' (1992, 252). Accordingly, moviegoers in the Indian subcontinent are drawn to the cinema for various reasons, be it the fights, the spectacles or the costumes. At a screening for the lavishly produced *Devdas* (2002), a woman said she had heard the costumes were very nice, so she came to see the saris and the jewellery.[20] Another moviegoer who had heard the film's music on the radio, volunteered that his sole purpose in watching the film in the theatre was to see how a song was choreographed and where it fit in the story.[21] Appreciating that audiences watch a film piecemeal and that 'selective viewing' is located in a broader aesthetic of watching film as spectacle and amusement, filmmakers invest a great deal in providing the expected ingredients.[22] As early as in 1935, Majumdar listed 'a pretty heroine, a few thrilling and comic incidents, and a few light-hearted tunes to fill the gaps' as the ingredients for a box office success and Shakespearean tropes, plot lines and characters frequently fit this format.[23]

The organization of screenings in India, evolved as they are from longer traditional narrative modes, creates the conditions for such piecemeal viewing. The intermission, for instance, which is unusual to modern film screenings in the West but familiar to theatre audiences and 'Shakespeare on Screen' audiences, lends itself to selective engagement by Indian audiences. Moviegoers also choose breaks in action to 'leave for a bathroom break' or to head out for a snack. They walk in and out of the theatre in an ambulatory viewing style like the spectators of the *Ram Lila* or *Nautanki* performed in the open in North India, *Bhand Pather* in Kashmir, *Tamasha* in west India, *Yakshagana* in the south, or *jatra* in east India. As Srinivas describes, 'using their bodies to carve out routes through the film, ambulatory audiences reinvent the film; their mobility and its 'rhythms and gestures' shape film experience while making visible the ongoing process of constructing a bricolage'.[24] These movements have a similar effect to audiences hitting the fast forward button on the remote allowing them to avoid scenes they think of as optional, thus reshaping their reception of the film. People frequently exit the theatre before a song-and-dance sequence or a dramatic scene and return ten minutes later anticipating a shift in scene. This is similar to Shakespeare's Globe in London where audiences can leave the theatre and return during a performance as long as they have their tickets on them; I observed this myself as a steward in 2014 when a particularly gory production of *Titus Andronicus* left several audience members queasy and in need of fresh air away from the action onstage.[25] Srinivas also describes audiences frequently attending a movie in sections, either arriving late or exiting early to accommodate other commitments such as school timings, meals with friends or family commitments (Srinivas 2016, 171).

This ambulatory style of viewing is, of course, also due to the cultural tendency of watching a popular film more than once with multiple and alternate groups of people: $QSQT$ for instance, had been watched over a hundred times by some teenagers by the end of 1988 leading to its eventual status as a cult classic.[26] The term 'repeaters', used frequently in the field by theatre managers, filmmakers and distributors in India, refers to an extreme type of viewer who sees the same film over and over. These audiences are different from general Indian audiences who also routinely see films they like more than once, which allows them to have a distinctive experience of the film (Kakar 1981; Iyer 2010).

While repeat viewing is a regular practice among Indian audiences, there are intermittent films which capture the audience's attention in an extreme way – these films have become 'superhits' which have remained in theatres for months, sometimes for years by popular demand.[27] *Sholay* for instance, went on to earn a still-standing record of sixty golden jubilees across India and was the first film in India to celebrate a silver jubilee at over 100 theatres.[28] It was shown continuously at Bombay's Minerva Theatre for over five years. It was the Indian film with the longest theatrical run until *Dilwale Dulhania Le Jayenge* (1995) broke its record of 286 weeks in 2001. *Hum Aapke Hain Kaun* (1994) was reported to have been watched by painter M. F. Husain over 60 times.[29] While on an historic 1,274-week run at Mumbai's Maratha Mandir Theatre, *Dilwale Dulhania Le Jayenge* temporarily closed in March due to the COVID-19 outbreak in India but resumed screening in November 2020.[30]

Often repeat viewing comes about through 'word of mouth', as, upon telling a friend or family member about a film one has seen, one sees the film again in the company of that friend. Through repeat viewing, audiences construct cinema as a social experience as they go to the movies with different groups of people such as with family, with friends, and with partners in multiple viewings which varies the experience and the enjoyment of a film from multiple perspectives due to the different company. This may be compared to a theatre spectator who might choose to go to repeat performances to watch a play from different positions in a theatre, or watch a play both in the theatre and in the cinema for its streamed performance as with RSC and NTLive productions. In fact, the National Theatre 2020 production of *Frankenstein* saw Benedict Cumberbatch and Jonny Lee Miller alternating between the roles of Victor

Frankenstein and his creation, which guaranteed several audience members viewing the production at least twice. Repeat viewing facilitates the participatory and interactive style which Indian audiences adopt in their engagement with popular cinema. Repeaters form a relationship with the characters and talk back at the screen, sing along with the soundtrack or loudly 'predict' what will happen next or even carry on a conversation with a character responding to each line of dialogue with their own improvised dialogue. I watched *Arshinagar* at a multiplex with my mother in Kolkata in December 2015. While the rhyming dialogue led to audiences trying to anticipate what characters would say, some of the audience members loudly asked the characters on screen to 'speak like a normal person'. This elicited laughter and comments from other members of the audience who energetically voiced their dislike of the theatricality and 'unrealism' of the film. Overly dramatic scenes are also often mocked, as viewers use ridicule and irony to transform meaning and emotion. In a scene where the hero stands at the edge of a precipice and tells the heroine he will jump into the chasm below if she does not return his love, viewers shout '*Kood ja!*' ['Jump!'] evoking laughter from fellow audience members and neatly subverting the intentions of the film-maker (Srinivas 2002, 170).

Viewers interact with other audience members as well; at a screening of *Kal ho na ho* [If tomorrow never comes] (2003) in my school days when some of the audience started crying atced sound effects which preview the scene for other viewers and make sense to first-timers only after the scene has shifted (Srinivas 2002, 168). The film editor's role may be appropriated in theatres as well, as Srinivas describes an incident when in the course of watching the film *Hum* (1991) audiences created a commotion in the theatre demanding that a favourite song-and-dance sequence be screened repeatedly while they sang along and danced (2002, 171). There are films such as *Titanic* and *Star Trek* which have drawn repeat viewers too, of course, but these films are exceptions in the movie culture in the West, whereas in India repeat viewing is a phenomenon that is fairly routine and one which cuts across age and gender. Engaging with a narrative whose story is known is something Indian audiences have been doing for generations, firstly through the narrative traditions in India, and secondly through the culture of remakes across film industries in India and of non-Indian (usually Hollywood) films. Performances of religious myths such as the *Ramayana* and *Krishna Lila*, dance-dramas whose stories most Indians know from childhood, are constructed for a participatory audience (Booth 1995).

Consequently, an understanding of how audience expectations and behaviour determine the narrative choices of filmmakers can help readers of the Indian Shakespeare film realize that far from being a respectful, attentive and homogenous group, Indian Shakespeare film audiences are akin to the Yardlings at the Globe or the audience of a pantomime who participate, talk back to, and even force change in films and in this way engage with 'that genetic identity of the plays' which Pangallo and Kirwin remind us of that Western productions often find elusive and thus help shed light and make urgent some of the concerns of Shakespeare's plays for current generations.

Notes

1 See Matteo A. Pangallo, and Peter Kirwan, eds., *Shakespeare's Audiences* (New York and London: Routledge, 2021), for a fuller discussion on Shakespeare's varied audiences. My chapter in that collection can be read as a companion piece to this current chapter; many of the ideas and evidence were drawn from the same experiences as an audience member of Indian cinema.

2 This is of course, more difficult in multiplexes which have stricter security checks and bag scanning facilities, but as Srinivas describes of cinemas which cater to a larger population of male viewers belonging to the lower classes, 'theatres

anticipate audience's actions and have made the seats close to the screen out of hard plastic. In one Bangalore theatre, the seats are made of cement.' See Marc Abrahams, 'Indian Cinema – Where the Audience Joins in the Action', *The Guardian* (28 June 2010): <https://www.theguardian.com/education/2010/jun/28/improbable-research-indian-cinema> (accessed 1 July 2020).

3 Discussions with Vishal Bhardwaj, Mansoor Khan and Robin Bhatt in 2012 and 2016, and Aparna Sen in August 2015.

4 Discussion on film etiquette between presenters Nina Warhurst, Charlie Stayt and film critic Ali Plumb, *BBC Breakfast*, 4 September 2021.

5 Most Indian films are three hours long and include an interval whose absence confused me when I first started frequenting film theatres in the UK as Indian audiences usually get a snack or a drink during this interval if they do not want to miss any of the action in the film.

6 See Chris Matthews, '*Argo' Truly was 2012's Best Film*, https://www.msnbc.com/hardball/argo-truly-was-2012s-best-film-msna17775, MSNBC, 14 January 2013) (accessed 13 December 2021).

7 While Srinivas' research was conducted in the 1990s, before the multiplex boom in India, the film culture she describes resonates with my personal experiences visiting both single screen and multiplex film theatres in Kolkata, India and in Wembley, London. Wembley is one of the few places in London to regularly screen Indian films for a predominantly south Asian audience and I would frequent the theatres in Wembley in order to partake of the full cinema-going experience – the shared comments with strangers before, during and after the film, the Indian snacks, and the shared understanding of filmic codes.

8 See, for instance, Tejaswini Ganti, *Bollywood: A Guidebook to Popular Hindi Cinema* (New York and London: Routledge, 2013); Rachel Dwyer, *Bollywood's India: Hindi Cinema as a Guide to Contemporary India* (London: Reaktion Books, 2014), and Ravi Vasudevan, 'The Meanings of "Bollywood"', *Beyond the Boundaries of Bollywood: The Many Forms of Hindi Cinema* (2011): 3–29

9 I have discussed this active and participatory audience in a study of how audiences shape the Indian Shakespeare film in Koel

Chatterjee, 'Indian Shakespeare Cinema and the Active Audience', in *Shakespeare's Audiences* (New York and London: Routledge, 2021), 102–18.

10 I am referring to Viktor Shklovsky's quote: 'Art makes the familiar strange so that it can be freshly perceived. To do this it presents its material in unexpected, even outlandish ways: the shock of the new', in *Theory of Prose* (as quoted in David Shields, *Reality Hunger: A Manifesto*, Penguin UK, 2010).

11 Emmanuel Grimaud, *Bollywood Film Studio: Ou Comment Les Films Se Font à Bombay* (Paris: CNRS, 2003).

12 See Heather Tyrell and Rajinder Dudrah, 'Music in the Bollywood Film', in *Film's Musical Moments* (Edinburgh: Edinburgh University Press, 2006), 196. The title of Bhardwaj's adaptation of *Othello* was decided by a public competition to market the film; the three possible titles – 'Omkara', 'O Saathi Re' and 'Issak' are all songs on the soundtrack ('Issak' being another name for the song 'Namak'). *Omkara* got the most votes, so even though the actor playing Iago (Saif Ali Khan) was against this choice of title, the film was named *Omkara*.

13 For a more detailed description see Diptakirti Chaudhuri's chapter on the history of Hindi screenwriting in *Written by Salim-Javed: The Story of Hindi Cinema's Greatest Screenwriter* (India: Penguin, 2015), 267–76; and Abbas Tyrewala, 'Dialogues and Screenplay, Separated at Birth', *Hindustan Times*, 12 December 2014: <http://www.hindustantimes.com/brunch/dialogues-and-screenplay-separated-at-birth-abbas-tyrewala/story-EfS1ol8YDFZ6dTv6XnyqGJ.html> (accessed 20 April 2016).

14 See, for instance, https://www.pinterest.co.uk/pin/315040936407599548/ (accessed 1 January 2020) or Vedanshi Pathak, *10 Pictures of Ranveer Singh & Deepika Padukone from the Sets of Ram Leela*: https://www.filmfare.com/features/10-pictures-of-ranveer-singh-deepika-padukone-from-the-sets-of-ram-leela-37415.html, 15 November 2019 (accessed 1 January, 2020) which discusses the pairs' growing relationship on set to culminate in marriage on 14 November 2019.

15 Koel Chatterjee, *Interview with Sanjay Leela Bhansali*, 26 March 2013.

16 Shakuntala Banaji, *Reading 'Bollywood': The Young Audience and Hindi Films* (London: Springer, 2006), 44.

17 *Families Stay Away from Omkara*, http://timesofindia.indiatimes.com/entertainment/bollywood/news-interviews/Families-stay-away-from-Omkara-/articleshow/1833494.cms?referral=PM, 1 August 2006 (accessed 4 February 2015).

18 South City, Kolkata, 1 December 2013. Filmmakers incorporate song sequences picturized on national festivals which will then generate more audience interest through radio and TV broadcasts of the song. *Holi* songs are an example of this phenomenon and many popular films use *holi* songs as romantic meet cues in mainstream films. See, for instance, Shikha, *10 Holi Songs for Your Playlist,* https://in.bookmyshow.com/entertainment/music/concerts/10-holi-songs-playlist/, 29 February 2019 (accessed 1 July 2020).

19 See, for instance, 'Jisshu U Sengupta Starrer "Mahaprabhu" to have a Rerun', *Times of India,* 12 May 2020: <https://timesofindia.indiatimes.com/tv/news/bengali/jisshu-u-sengupta-starrer-mahaprabhu-to-have-a-rerun/articleshow/75694595.cms> (accessed 1 July 2020).

20 Sanjay Leela Bhansali's remake of an Indian literary work, *Devdas*, is also a variation of the 'star-crossed' lovers' trope.

21 Priya Cinema, Kolkata, 20 July 2002.

22 See James H. Johnson, *Listening in Paris: A Cultural History*, 21 vols (California: University of California Press, 1995), 23 on the attitude of operagoers in seventeenth century France.

23 Phanibhushan Majumdar, 'Chalachitra o Darshak Samaj', *Cinema and the Community of Viewers' – Nachghar* 29 (1935), 1934–54. Translation from Bengali are my own.

24 Srinivas, *House Full: Indian Cinema and the Active Audience,* 2016, 170.

25 See, for instance, Nick Clark, *'Globe Theatre Takes Out 100 Audience Members with its Gory Titus Andronicus'*, 22 July 2014, <https://www.independent.co.uk/arts-entertainment/theatre-dance/news/globe-theatre-takes-out-100-audience-members-with-its-gory-titus-andronicus-9621763.html> (accessed 13 December 2020).

26 See, for instance, an article about the unforeseen success of *QSQT* by Simran Bhargava, 'Teenybopper Heart-Throb', *India Today*, 15 December, 1988, <http://indiatoday.intoday.in/story/bollywood-dreamboat-qayamat-se-qayamat-tak-makes-aamir-khan-a-teenage-sensation/1/330097.html> (accessed 12 December 2016).

27 See, for instance, Lakshmi Srinivas, 'The Active Audience: Spectatorship, Social Relations and the Experience of Cinema in India', *Media, Culture & Society* 24 (2002): 167

28 See '35 years on, the Sholay fire still burns', *NDTV*, 14 August 2010, archived from the original on 12 June 2013, retrieved 12 April 2013; Haresh Pandya, 27 December 2007, G. P. Sippy, Indian Filmmaker Whose *Sholay* Was a Bollywood Hit, Dies at 93', *The New York Times*, archived from the original on 28 August 2011, retrieved 23 February 2011; '900 not out!', *The Telegraph*, 3 February 2013, Archived from the original on 4 March 2016, retrieved 11 May 2013.

29 See Tejaswini Ganti, *Bollywood: A Guidebook to Popular Hindi Cinema* (New York and London, Routledge, 2013), 98.

30 'DDLJ back in Maratha Mandir', *Deccan Chronicle*, 7 November 2020. Archived from the original on 3 March 2021, retrieved 7 March 2021. https://www.deccanchronicle.com/entertainment/bollywood/061120/ddlj-back-in-maratha-mandir.html

References

Banaji, Shakuntala, *Reading 'Bollywood': The Young Audience and Hindi Films*. London: Springer, 2006.

Booth, Gregory D. 'Traditional Content and Narrative Structure in the Hindi Commercial Cinema', *Asian Folklore Studies* (1995), 169–90.

Chopra, Anupama, *Sholay, the Making of a Classic*. Delhi: Penguin Books India, 2000.

Dass, Manishita. *Outside the Lettered City: Cinema, Modernity, and the Public Sphere in Late Colonial India*. New York: Oxford University Press, 2016.

Dickey, Sara. *Cinema and the Urban Poor in South India*, 92 vols. Cambridge: Cambridge University Press, 1993.

Geraghty, Christine, 'Cinema as a Social Space: Understanding Cinema Going in Britain, 1947–63', *Framework* 42 (2000): https://www.frameworknow.com/journal-archives-posts/42.

Grimaud, Emmanuel. *Bollywood Film Studio: Ou Comment Les Films Se Font à Bombay* Paris: CNRS, 2003.

Hardgrave Jr., Robert L. *When Stars Displace the Gods: The Folk Culture of Cinema in Tamil Nadu*. Texas: Center for Asian Studies, University of Texas, 1975.

Iyer, Pico. *Video Night in Kathmandu: And Other Reports from the Not-so-Far East*. London: Vintage, 2010.

Kakar, Sudhir. 'The Ties that Bind: Family Relationships in the Mythology of Hindi Cinema', *India International Centre Quarterly* 8 (1981): 11–21.

Mishra, Pankaj. *Butter Chicken in Ludhiana: Travels in Small Town India*. Delhi: Pan Macmillan, 2006.

Morcom, Anna. 'Film Songs and the Cultural Synergies of Bollywood and Beyond South Asia', in Rachel Dwyer, and Jerry Pinto, eds., *Beyond the Boundaries of Bollywood: The Many Forms of Hindi Cinema*. Delhi: Oxford University Press, 2011, 156–87.

Pangallo, Matteo A., and Peter Kirwan, eds. *Shakespear's Audiences*. New York and London: Routledge, 2021.

Prasad, M. M. *Ideology of the Hindi Film: A Historical Construction*. New York : Oxford University Press, 2000.

Purcell, Stephen. *Shakespeare and Audience in Practice*. London: Bloomsbury, 2013.

Srinivas, Lakshmi, 'The Active Audience: Spectatorship, Social Relations and the Experience of Cinema in India', *Media, Culture & Society* 24 (2002); 155–73.

Srinivas, Lakshmi. *House Full: Indian Cinema and the Active Audience*. Chicago: University of Chicago Press, 2016.

Vivian, Sobchak. *The Address of the Eye: A Phenomenology of Film Experience*. Princeton, NJ: Princeton University Press, 1992.

AFTERWORD

Sonia Massai

This collection was conceived in the wake of two important events: the 'Shakespeare in Bollywood' conference held at Royal Holloway, University of London, in 2014, and the 'Indian Shakespeares on Screen' conference held at Asia House, Cavendish Street, and the BFI, Southbank, London, in 2016. Poonam Trivedi, a keynote speaker at both events and a contributor to this collection, has played a key role in bringing Indian Shakespeares to the attention of the international community of scholars interested in translation, performance, film and adaptation studies. And it is a testament to Trivedi's critical acumen and passionate investment in the topic that Indian Shakespeares and one of its most popular manifestations, Indian Shakespeare on Film, have generated so much exciting scholarly work and debate in a relatively short time. Telling in terms of the scholarly and commercial appeal recently garnered by Indian films adapted from, loosely based on or inspired by Shakespeare is the relatively limited and marginal amount of space devoted to the topic in an earlier collection of essays on *India's Shakespeare: Translation, Interpretation and Performance*, which Trivedi co-edited with Dennis Batholomeusz. In this earlier collection, only one essay, 'Shakespeare in Hindi Cinema' by Rajiva Verma, was devoted to cinematic responses to Shakespeare in the region. *India's Shakespeare* was published in 2005, only a decade before the two conferences mentioned above took place, galvanizing attention not only on the best-known examples of Indian Shakespeare on film – Vishal Bhardwaj was a guest speaker at the 2016 event – but also on the longue durée of the history of the reception of Shakespeare within Indian cinema.

This collection acknowledges the sheer variety and size of the Indian cinema industry, which, according to a study commissioned in 2015 by the International Confederation of Societies of Authors and Composers (CISAC), is 'the world's largest by production numbers, ahead of Nollywood and Hollywood'.[1] Within it, Shakespeare sets important precedents: as Trivedi points out in the Foreword to this collection, 'the world's first full-length talkie of *Hamlet* (1935, *Khoon ka Khoon*, dir. Sohrab Modi) was produced in India, as also was the first feature film of the *Comedy of Errors* (1963, *Bhranti Bilas*, dir. Manu Sen)' p. xviii. Several contributions in this collection build on earlier studies, including Craig Dionne and Parmita Kapadia's *Bollywood Shakespeares* (2014), by continuing to map out the presence of Shakespeare in Indian cinema.

Crucially, this collection also takes the debate on the topic to a whole new level of critical sophistication by inviting sustained attention to the importance of perspective: the significance of Indian Shakespeare on film will depend very much on who is watching and who gets to write about it, both in reviews and blogs for popular dissemination and in academic studies. The perspective explored here is at the very least double – Indian and Western – if not 'multifocal', as Trivedi puts it. The added value this collection offers to scholars interested in Indian Shakespeares (and Global Shakespeares) is therefore linked to wider issues to do with the dynamics of interpretation, which, while always complex, are especially challenging in a global context.

The multifocal approach embraced by this collection reminds me of one of Umberto Eco's seminal studies about the interplay between the beleaguered notions of authorial and textual intentions, on the one hand, and the dominance accorded to reader-oriented theories in the latter part of the last century, on the other:

> When I speak with a friend, I am interested in detecting the intention of the speaker and, when I receive a letter from a friend, I am interested in realizing what the writer wanted to

say.... [But] when a text is put in the bottle,... the author knows that he or she will be interpreted not according to his or her intentions but according to a complex strategy of interactions which also involves the readers, along with their competence in language as a social treasury.[2]

At least one contribution in this collection asks an 'empirical author'[3] (or auteur), filmmaker Vandana Kataria, to explicate the reasons for setting her *The Merchant of Venice* adaptation *The Noblemen* (2019) in a boarding school and using it to explore tensions around sexuality instead of religion. Another contribution exemplifies a critical response to *The Noblemen* by a scholar based in the West, showing how Kataria's work signifies when her 'bottle' reaches Western shores. Other contributions tackle the question of perspective even more head-on, focusing on urgent questions that are no longer concerned with issues of ownership over Shakespeare in the Indian subcontinent, but rather with 'competence'.

The notion of 'competence' emerges as a central concern for scholars interested in charting the traversing of borders between world regions (and of boundaries between interpretative communities). How does one go about 'recontextualizing Indian Shakespeare Cinema in the West'? And who is ideally placed to do so? This collection is at its most productive when it goes beyond offering either Indian or Western perspectives on the range of Shakespeare films discussed in it, by considering how Indian Shakespeare Cinema forces critics, scholars and students to interrogate their competence as readers and interpreters of these complex cinematic artefacts.

Returning briefly to Eco, one could argue that this competence is not merely linguistic but also cultural and contextual. While discussing the 'difference between interpreting and using a text', Eco points out that

> [one] can certainly use [a] text for parody, for showing how [it] can be read in relation to different cultural frameworks, or for strictly personal ends ([one] can read a text to get

inspiration for [their] own musing); but if [one] want[s] to interpret [a] text, [one] must respect [its] cultural and linguistic background.[4]

My experience of teaching non-English Shakespeares to English speakers within the context of a British tertiary education institution has led me to believe that one certainly needs to raise 'awareness' of (and, ideally, 'respect' for) cultural and contextual difference, if one regards 'interpretation' (as opposed to 'overinterpretation') as an important pedagogical objective.

Thoroughly inspiring in this respect is Jyotsna G. Singh's essay on Bhardwaj's *Haider* and some of the challenges involved in teaching Global Shakespeare to US university students. Singh writes eloquently about the 'danger of eliding the divide between the global north and south, or between Anglo-American classrooms and the "native," "non-metropolitan knowledges" that are intertwined into global Shakespeares as they make their way into the West' (Chapter 8, p. 169). According to Singh, the danger of 'overinterpretation' stems from a flattening of difference, or, paraphrasing Eco, from 'using' rather than 'interpreting' a complex cinematic artefact, such as *Haider*.

Singh recommends pursuing a 'pedagogy of cultural intelligibility' as a corrective against 'overinterpretation'. In practical terms, Singh gets her students to read texts related to the making of *Haider*, such as co-writer Basharat Peer's memoir about Kashmir, *Curfewed Night*, or to its setting, including poetry by Agha Shahid Ali, the Kashmiri poet recurrently quoted by Peer in his memoir. This kind of contextual or background reading compensates for 'the dominant imperative in US classrooms, among all students, irrespective of their colour, race or ethnicity, [to] cast ["familiar strangers" like *Haider*] in domestic, US-centred terms' (Chapter 8, p.172). The rewards of the additional preparation that 'recontextualizing Indian Shakespeare cinema' involves for students in Singh's class are twofold: Singh's students learn about the long and bloody territorial conflict between India and Pakistan over the Kashmir region through which Bhardwaj relocates Shakespeare's tragedy, but they also return to *Hamlet*, bringing a more politically and historically mindset to it. Overcoming a tendency to interpret Hamlet's demise as the personal tragedy of a flawed but sympathetic character or revenge as a psychological mechanism rather than a politically motivated act or loaded model of statecraft, Singh's students become more alert to the historical and political context within which *Hamlet* was originally written, read and performed.

Retaining, rather than flattening, difference is also the recommendation that emerges from Varsha Panjwani's essay, 'Chutzpah: The Politics of Bollywood Shakespeare Subtitles'. Panjwani's discussion of the re-translation of Indian languages back into English subtitles exposes a similar tendency to 'domesticate otherness', which echoes Singh's account of how US students are likely to approach non-English Shakespeares. Focusing on the DVD and Netflix subtitles for *Maqbool* – Bhardwaj's 2003 adaptation of *Macbeth* – Panjwani, for example, suggests retaining Hindi/Urdu key words that do not easily translate into English, including '*chikne*', '*sharara*', '*Abbaji*' or '*seviyan*', in order to encourage viewers to look into the linguistic meanings and cultural connotations associated with them. Multilingual Shakespeare has certainly proven to be an effective, if not unproblematic, format for productions conceived to be 'put in a bottle' and to travel to far-flung, foreign shores, where they get re-interpreted by local communities of film and theatre goers. Whether such productions can thrive beyond the context of international 'Festival Shakespeare' mega-events, such as the World Shakespeare Festival in the UK in 2012 and the commemorative seasons organized worldwide to mark the 400th anniversary of Shakespeare's death in 2016, or without significant amounts of public funding, as was the case with Tim Supple's British Council-sponsored Indian multilingual 2006 production of *A Midsummer Night's Dream*, is a moot question. Whether multilingual Shakespeare, even when limited to a few key words that are retained untranslated from the original language spoken on screen as part of English subtitles, can work as a corrective against the flattening of difference when Indian Shakespeare cinema travels West is another open-ended question, but one worth bearing in mind, as its appeal, marketability and pedagogical opportunities continue to be on the rise.

In fact, the increasing popularity of Indian (Shakespeare) cinema would seem to have narrowed the gap between the source and the recipient cultures that produce and consume it. According to Trivedi, 'a newer generation of directors targeting a multiplex stratified audience is creating shorter, "content driven" films, with socially relevant themes and fewer, more integrated, songs which have found favour at the box-office' (Foreword, p. xviii–xix), thus departing from the established artistic conventions and commercial model that inform the Bollywood film industry. The increased traffic of Shakespearean exchanges between Indian filmmakers and their audiences (popular and scholarly) in the West is bound to improve mutual intercultural intelligibility. As, indeed, does the interpretative work carried out by the scholars included in this collection. However, while the act of critically 'recontextualizing' Indian Shakespeare cinema leads to increased familiarity, it is also important to heed Singh's and Panjwani's appeal to remain alert to, and to value, cultural difference, even when it remains impervious to translation or interpretation.

I would therefore like to conclude this brief Afterword by invoking a stalwart supporter of cultural difference, Indian critic and theatre-maker Rustom Bharucha, who reminds us to 'be a little wary of those intercultural encounters where differences do *not* surface, because it could mean that the differences have already been resolved within a hegemonic frame that cannot be questioned'.[5] Combined with Eco's emphasis on the desirability of distinguishing between appropriation (or use) and interpretation of a text (or artefact) that respects or shows awareness of (cultural) difference, Bharucha's appeal serves well as an endorsement of the work carried out by this collection, which invites us to mind (and be mindful of) the interpretative gaps that separate source and recipient cultures in the production and consumption of Indian Shakespeare cinema in the West.

Notes

1. https://en.unesco.org/creativity/sites/creativity/files/cultural_times._the_first_global_map_of_cultural_and_creative_industries.pdf.
2. Umberto Eco, 'Between Author and Text', in S. Collini (ed.), *Interpretation and Overinterpretation* (Cambridge: Cambridge University Press, 1992), p. 67.
3. Eco, p. 73
4. Eco, pp. 68–9.
5. Rustom Bharucha, 'Foreign Asia / Foreign Shakespeare: Dissenting Notes on New Asian Interculturality, Postcoloniality and Re-Colonization', in *Shakespeare in Asia: Contemporary Performance*, ed. Dennis Kennedy and Yong Li Lan (Cambridge: Cambridge University Press, 2010), 253–81, at 257.

References

Bharucha, Rustom, 'Foreign Asia / Foreign Shakespeare: Dissenting Notes on New Asian Interculturality, Postcoloniality and Re-Colonization', in *Shakespeare in Asia: Contemporary Performance*, ed. Dennis Kennedy and Yong Li Lan. Cambridge: Cambridge University Press, 2010.

Eco, Umberto. 'Between Author and Text,' in *Interpretation and Overinterpretation*, ed. S. Collini. Cambridge: Cambridge University Press, 1992, 67–88.

Dionne, Craig, and Parmita Kapadia, eds. *Bollywood Shakespeares*. New York: Palgrave Macmillan, 2014.

Trivedi, Poonam, and Dennis Bartholomeusz, eds. *India's Shakespeare: Translation, Interpretation, and Performance*. Delaware: University of Delaware Press, 2005.

INDEX

Page numbers: Figures are given in *italics*. Notes as: [page number] n. [note number]

1942: A Love Story (film) 124

Abba-ji character (*Maqbool*) 187–8, 189–91, 193–4, 199
'abusive' subtitling 150
adaptation
    of becoming 95
    dialogue and 86
    language and 204
    movement within 80
adult certification 103–4, 115, 117
Afro American Association 33
AFSPA (Armed Forces Special Powers Act) 147
Aguecheek, Andrew 57
Ali, Agha Shahid 176, 274
alliteration 244
ambulatory viewing style 261
American classrooms *see* US classrooms
American film festivals 117
Anglo-Indian social class 60–1
Argo (film) 256
Armed Forces Special Powers Act (AFSPA) 147
Asia House screenings 44, 45–6, 271
assimilative subtitling 138–40, 149
Astitva (film) 259
audience
    Bhardwaj's films 158
    diversity of 164
    'giver of' 253, 255
    impact on films 253–77
    knowing 108
    reasons for film-going 109
    as 'receiver' 22, 255
    Shakespeare's framing of 253–4
    subtitles' invisibility 148
avian motif 235

Bachchan, Amitabh 193, 260
Baker, Robin 157, 163
Balfour, Ian 136
Banaji, Shankuntala 259
band baaja music 257
Banerjee, Dibakar 101, 111
    Oye Lucky! Lucky Oye! 111
Bans, Shani 5, 20–1
'bardolators' (*bhakts*) 123
Batholomeusz, Dennis 271
becoming, adaptation of 95
Behar, Henri 145, 148
Bengali culture 58–9

INDEX

Bengali language 65
Bernstein, Leonard 234
'betrayal' 71
BFI Southbank *see* British Film Institute Southbank
Bhabha, Homi 39
Bhandaram, Vishnupriya 208
Bhansali, Sanjay Leela 259
   Ram-Leela 21, 142–3, 144–5, 225–51, 258–60
Bhardwaj, Vishal 11, 45–6, 122–3, 163–4, 231, 271
   Haider 4, 13, 18–20, 137–8, 141, 146–8, 157–8, 167–82, 187, 226, 259, 274–5
   Maachis 210
   Maqbool 4, 18–20, 39, 139–41, 157–8, 172, 183–202, 275
   Omkara 4, 15, 19–21, 39, 41–2, 157–8, 172, 187, 196–7, 203–23, 226, 258, 260, 266n12
Bhargava, Simran 267n26
Bharucha, Rustom 276
Bhatia, Uday 143
Bhatt, Robin 45, 157
Bhul Bhulaiyan (film) 56
Biden, Joe 48, 50n5
Black Lives Matter Movement 170–1
boarding school settings 110, 116–17
bodily violence 241–2
Bollywood 40, 184
   audience understanding of 165, 254
   'crosshatched Shakespeare' 2
   dialogic telling 16, 79–97

heroines 197–8
masala 227–8, 233
musicality 69
romantic tones 69
Shakespeare pairing with 122–3, 127
song-and-dance sequences 5, 21, 87–90, 225–51
subtitles 18, 135–54
'Bollywood Shakespeare' 172
Bollywood Shakespeares collection 2
Bond films 238
The Book of Sir Thomas More (play) 6–7
Boose, Lynda 33
Booth, Gregory 88
border-crossing 10
Branagh, Kenneth 39
   Henry V 38
   Much Ado About Nothing 34
brawls (*branles*) 246n6
Brecht, Bertolt, *The Good Person of Szechwan* 74
Brexit 160
British Film Institute (BFI) Southbank 18–19, 44, 45–6, 157–66, 271
British imperialism 58–9
'Britishness' 160
Bruno, Giuliana 16, 80–1
Buckley, Thea 43
bullying theme 115–16, 118, 125, 128–30
Burnett, Mark Thornton 3, 13–14, 16, 41, 159
Burt, Richard 39–40, 124
Bynes, Amanda 65

INDEX

Calcutta, imperial past 58–9
camera work 86
canonical Shakespeare 168, 170
Carroll, William C. 200n3
Castiglione, B. 246n6
casting methods 114
centre-and-periphery perception 162
Chak De! India (film) 66
Chakravarti, Paromita 39, 58–9, 132n2, 159
characters–plot parallels 124
Chatterjee, Bonila, *The Hungry* 44
Chatterjee, Koel 1–26, 43, 46, 83, 87, 95, 164–5
Chaudhry, Lubna 40
childbirth 186–7, 194–5
children, religious importance 195–6
choreography 225, 231–2, 236, 240, 260
choric function 93
Chowk, Lal 259
Chute, David 144–5, 148
'chutzpah' culture 18, 146–8, 150
cinema, complexity of 161
'cinema of interruption' 88
Civil Rights Act, 1957 32
Civil Rights Act, 1964 30–1, 48, 50n2
class conflict 89
class differences 102, 124
classroom dynamics 19–20, 128, 167–82
Cleage, Pearl 10
Clifford, James 16, 80
clouds as 'ocular proof' 217–20

code-clashing 5, 10
Cole, Nicki Lisa 138
colonial history, language 127
comic effects
    36 Chowringhee Lane 63
    She's the Man 70
Common Market Referendum, 1975 32
'competence' concept 273
'COVID brain' 29–30
COVID-19 Hate Crimes Bill 48
COVID-19 pandemic 29–30, 42–3, 48
cricket 66, 68, 70–3
cross-dressing 65–73
'crosshatched Shakespeare' 2
Crowl, Samuel, *Shakespeare and Film* 39
Cuaron, Alfonso 100
cultural assimilation 140
cultural difference 276
cultural imperialism 141
cultural intelligibility 19–20, 170–6
'cultural literacy' 175
Cumberbatch, Benedict 262–3
curation, BFI programme 157–66

dance
    as cosmic representation 236–7
    disguise 69
    gender construction 232–3
    gestures in 235
    homohistory 239
    invitations to 243
    lasciviousness association 237
    'meuynge' pun 240

music coexisting with 230
social order subversion 237
verse analogies 236
violence in 241–2
writing and 236
Danish adaptations 86
Darokhand (play) 248n17
Das, Sangeeta, *Life Goes On* 45
Davies, John 236–7
  Orchestra 232, 240
Dawson, Anthony 40
'*ḍasane*' association 216
de Palma, Brian, *Scarface* 184, 194
de Witt, Helen 4, 18–19, 157–66
deceipt 203–23
Della Coletta, Christina 9, 80
Devasundaram, Ashvin Immanuel, *India's New Independent Cinema* 100
Devdas (film) 260
Dhadak (film) 258
dialogic telling 16, 79–97
dialogue
  adaptability 258
  everyday influence 256–8
  subject matter of 9
  text/adaptation 8
dialoguebaazi 258
'digital humanities' 167–8
Dil Bole Hadippa! (film) 15, 55, 65–74, 76n16
Dil Chahta Hai (film) 198
Dilwale Dulhania Le Jayenge (film) 262
Dionne, Craig, *Bollywood Shakespeares* 172, 272
director–writer collaboration 104

discrimination, women 72
disguise 69, 70–2, 74
distance 212
Diwali 243
Dolly character (*Omkara*) 203, 211, 212–17
Donaldson, Peter, *Shakespearean Films* 38
Doshi, Sunil 105
double translation 136
dubbing 143
Dudrah, Rajinder 81
Durandy, Francois-Xavier 143, 149
Dutt, Utpal, *Bhuli Nai Priya* 87
DVD format, subtitles 137–8, 149–50

Eco, Umberto 272–4
Egoyan, Atom 136
Ek Duuje Ke Liye (film) 87
Eleftheriotis, Dimitris 16, 96
Elyot, Thomas 237, 240
  The Boke 240
engagement rituals 190–1
English–Indian cultural differences 73
English language 57, 62, 127, 138, 140, 147, 208
epics 91, 92–3
Era Uma Vez (film) 84
Errors, Bhul Bhulaiya (film) 56
eyes, deceipt 203–23

'familiar strangers' framework 5–10, 257, 266n10
family dramas 72, 174
fantasy 88
female chastity 190
female protagonists 184

Ferleman, William C. 191–2, 194–5
Fickman, Andy 65
fidelity discourse 246n5
film festivals 117, 160
filmmaker–audience relationship 254–5
firearms 192–3
folk theatre 69, 234
'foreign' category 158–9, 162, 200n1
'foreign' subtitling 140, 150
Frankenstein (film) 262–3
Freccero, Carla 246n5
freedom 179
Fulbright, William J. 32

Gadamer, Hans-Georg 8–9
Gandhi 34–5, 201n8
Gandhi, Indira 72
gangster film traditions 194
gender
　authorial figures 47
　character changes 200n2
　classroom dynamics 128
　cross-dressing 67–8, 69
　dance constructing 232–3
　mobility 83
　photography 83–4
　sex and 68
　song-and-dance sequences 90
Geraghty, Christine 257
gestures 142–3, 144, 235
Ghosh, Rituparno, *The Last Lear* 127
Gil Harris, Jonathan 57, 228, 232
　Masala Shakespeare 132n2
Gilbey, Ryan 146, 147, 148

global frames of interpretation 121–33
global interchange, Bollywood 16, 79–97
Global Shakespeare
　audience and 257
　generalizations 3
　queer theory 226
　subtitles 136
　US classrooms 19–20, 167–82
Globe theatre 256, 261
'glocal' 100
The Godfather (film) 194
Goenka, Tula 4, 101–9, 110–18, 123
　Not Just Bollywood 17
Goldberg, Jonathan 226
Goliyon ki Rasleela: Ram-Leela see *Ram-Leela*
Gopalan Harris, Kamala 33, 34, 48
Gopalan, Lalitha 88
Gopalan, Shyamala 32–3
grassroots work, US 32, 34–5
Grimaud, Emmanuel 257
Group for Early Modern Cultural Studies 43
Gulzar 20–1, 203, 208–11, 214–17, 219–20, 221n7
　Khamoshi 214
Guy, Randor 56

Hall, Kim, '*Things of Darkness*' 171
Hanuman (monkey-god) 91
Hardgrave, Robert 260
Harris, Donald 33
Hart-Celler Act 30–1
hatred 128–9

Henderson, Diana E. 3, 5, 14–15, 146, 208, 218
heteronormative masculinity 130
Hindi films
  music numbers 88
  Shakespeare pairing with 121–2, 131n1
  songs inclusion 246n2
  subtitles 143
Hindi language
  10ml Love 107–8
  36 Chowringhee Lane 65
  'foreign' category 200n1
  hum expression 188–9
  subtitles 138–9, 141, 144
Hindu fundamentalism 103
Hindu marriage rituals 143
Hinduism, children 195–6
Hiscock, Andrew 236
Hispanic populations 35
Hitchcock, Alfred 100, 115
Hoaglund, Linda 150
Hobak Nair (film) 82–3, 85, 86
Holi festival 235, 267n18
Hollywood song-and-dance sequences 245
Homer, *The Odyssey* 92–3
homohistory 21, 226–8, 239
homotextuality 21, 225–51
Huang, Alexa 12–13, 19, 169
Hum Aapke Hain Kaun (film) 262
hum expression 188–9, 199
Hum (film) 263
humanities project 167–8
Hussain, Tassaduq 21
Hutcheon, Linda 8
hybridity 100, 101, 227

IAST (International Alphabet of Sanskrit Transliteration) 221n1
identity politics 167, 168
Immigration Act, 1924 31
immigration policy, UK 36
immigration reform, US 30–1, 32, 49–50n2
imperialism 58–9, 141
imperialist violence 185
improvisation 106–7
In Othello (film) 124
independent cinema 99–119
India–Pakistan conflict 179, 275
Indian–English cultural differences 73
Indian film industry, birth of 122
Indian identities, locality 45
Indian immigrants 31
'Indian Shakespeares on Screen' conference 14–15, 157–66, 271
'Indianness' 80
India's Shakespeare collection 1–2, 271–2, 276
integrated musicals 245, 248n18
intelligibility, use of term 175
intercultural subtitles 5, 18, 141–2, 149–50
interculturalism 11, 141, 149, 161
intermission/interval 261, 265n5
International Alphabet of Sanskrit Transliteration (IAST) 221n1

interpretation–text difference 273–4, 276
interval/intermission 261, 265n5
Islam, children 195–6
item songs 239, 241

James VI 6
Jarman, Derek 160–1
Jarrett-Macauley, Delia 36, 37
   Shakespeare, Race and Performance 36, 51n7, 171
jatra performance 255, 261
Jayaraj, Harris, *Kaliyattam* 44
Johnson, Lorraine 34
Johnson, Lyndon B. 30
Julie et Roméo (film) 82–3
Junoon (film) 40
Just One of the Guys (film) 66

Kabir, Nasreen Munni 145
Kal ho na ho (film) 263
Kalra, Brjendra 107
'*kamarband*' 218–19, 221–2n8
Kanenas (film) 92–4
Kannadasan (composer) 56
Kanniyin Kaadhali (film) 56–7
Kapadia, Parmita, *Bollywood Shakespeares* 172, 272
Kapoor, Rajat 101, 104, 132n3
   Raghu Romeo 104
Karim-Cooper, Farah 142
Kashmir civil conflict 146–7, 172–7, 179, 180n5, 275
Kataria, Vandana 99–119
   Noblemen 4, 14, 17–18, 100, 110–18, 121–33, 273
Katariya, Sharat 99–119

10ml Love 17, 44, 100–9, 118n6-7, 123–4, 132n2
   Dum Laga Ke Haisha 106, 107–8
Kattak, Saba 40
Kendal, Geoffrey 57–9
Kendal, Jennifer 59, 61
Kendall, Felicity 44, 45
Khamoshi (film) 259
Khan, Irfan 179
Kirwin, Peter 253, 264
kissing 237–9, 248n14
Kolodny, Annette 33
Kozintsev, Grigori
   Hamlet 163
   King Lear 163
Krishna Lila myth 264
Kubrick, Stanley 100
   A Clockwork Orange 113
   The Shining 115
Kurosawa, Akira 38, 39
   Ran 161
   Throne of Blood 149–50, 161, 184, 195, 201n7
Kyd, Thomas, *The Spanish Tragedy* 178

La La Land (film) 245
Lagaan: Once Upon a Time in India (film) 66
'*Lahu Muh Lag Gaya*' song-and-dance sequence 234–9, 242–3, 258
Lajja (film) 259
Lamb, Charles and Mary, *Tales from Shakespeare* 123
language
   abuse of power 147
   assimilative subtitling 139
   film adaptation 204

manifestations 135
modalities of 144
of song lyrics 209
Lanier, Douglas 81, 86, 87, 95, 122–3
lasciviousness–dance association 237
Lean, David, *Hobson's Choice* 45
Lincoln, John 7
Lindley, David 229
literary–popular culture connection 121–2, 127, 167
local dimensions, race studies 171
local readers 169, 175
locality, Indian identities 45
Loomba, Ania 39
love, use of term 183
love heroines 190–3, 195, 197, 199–200
love songs 197
love tragedy 184–5, 189
low budget films 105–6
Lubitsch, Ernst 100
    To Be or Not to Be 103
Luhrmann, Baz, *Romeo + Juliet* 161, 245

MacDougall, David, *Transcultural Cinema* 149
McKellen, Ian 161
Majumdar, Phanibhushan 260
mang bharai ritual 143
Marathi cinema 258
Maré, Nossa História de Amor (film) 94
marriage rituals 143
Martin, Daniel 150

Masaan (film) 143
masala, Bollywood 227–8, 233
'Masala Shakespeare' 57, 118n6
mass emigration 36
Massai, Sonia, *World-Wide Shakespeares* 2
Matthews, Chris 256
medicine as poison 216–17, 221n6
Meghani, Jhaverchand, '*Mor Bani Man Thangat Kare*' 245
melodrama 227–8
memorization 128
Menon, Madhavi 226
Merchant–Ivory, *Shakespeare Wallah* 36, 39–40, 44, 58, 62, 65, 121, 124, 127
metanarratives 94, 210
metonymy 176–7
'meuynge' pun 240, *241*
Middleton, Thomas, *The Revenger's Tragedy* 178
Miller, Jonny Lee 262–3
Milton, John 204
Minh-ha, Trinh T. 148–9
Mishra, Pankaj 254
mobility 83, 92
Modi, Sohrab, *Khoon ka Khoon* 272
mongrel features, melodrama 227–8
monstrosity 209
Mookherjee, Taarini 4, 14, 17–18
'*Mor Bani Man Thangat Kare*' song-and-dance sequence 244–5
Morcom, Anna 210, 246n2

More, Thomas 7
'motion pictures', definition/
 method 80–1
mudras (poses) 240–1
multiculturalism 168
multifocal approach 272–3
multilingual Shakespeare 275
multiplex theatres 99, 256, 263,
 264n2, 265n7
murder scenes 187–8, 189–90,
 191, 193
music
 appropriability 256–8
 Bollywood 225, 228
 dance's coexistence with 230
 early modern plays 228,
  230
 of film song 231
 primacy over verse 229
 Shakespearean reinvention
  89, 232
music director role 210
musicality, Bollywood 69
muttering device 112

'*Nagade Sang Dhol*' song-and-
 dance sequence 242–4
'*Nainā ṭhaga leṃge*' (song)
 20–1, 203–23
Nair, Mira, *Monsoon Wedding*
 107, 132n3
Naked Tango (film) 85
narrative in Indian cinema
 210–12
narrative meaning 8
nationalism 72
Natyashastra 235, 240
Navratri 243
Ng-Gagneux, Eleine, 'Reading
 Interculturality' 13

Nimmi character (*Maqbool*)
 20, 183–202
Nornes, Abe Mark 136, 140,
 150
 Cinema Babel 140
Nunn, Trevor 57

'ocular proof' 205–7, 215,
 217–20
onomatopoeia 244
Orkin, Martin 169
Oroonoko (play) 171
over-the-top (OTT) streaming
 platforms 100
'overinterpretation' 274

Pakistan
 creation of 146
 Indian conflict 179, 275
 Kashmir civil conflict
  177
Pangallo, Matteo A. 253,
 264
Panjwani, Varsha 1–26, 43,
 161, 163, 165, 237–8,
 276
 'The Politics of Bollywood
  subtitles' 275
 'Shakespeare and Indian
  Independent Cinema'
  118n7, 132n2
participatory audience 22,
 253–77
'particular' category 159
Partition of India 36, 66, 173
passion–violence relationship
 235
Patekar, Nana 259
patriarchalism 72
patron–client relationship 254

pedagogy
  of cultural intelligibility 19–20, 170–6
  of revenge 125, 128
Peer, Basharat 138, 173–4
  Curfewed Night 146, 175–6, 274
'pens' pun 247n12
performance culture 256
performance movement 37
Persons, Robert 6
Petrarchism 233, 236–7, 247n12-13
photography 83–4
piecemeal viewing 260–1
Pierce, Kimberley 100
  Boys Don't Cry 113
pilgrimage songs 191
play-within-the-film genre 124
plot–characters parallels 124
poetry 211–12, 220
poison 216–17, 221n6
Polanski, Roman, *Macbeth* 161, 163
politics, subtitles 18, 135–54
popular cinema
  audiences 256
  literary culture connection 121–2, 127, 167
popular drama, hybridist of 227
Prasad, Madhava 259
pre-marital sex 59
pregnancy 194–5
profound–profane alliance 247n9
'proof' (medical instrument) 206
Purcell, Stephen 254

Qayamat se Qayamat Tak (film) 16, 79–97, 261, 267n26
queer theory 226
queerness 228–9
Quince, Peter 107
quotations 85–6

'race', plays about 171–2
race studies 171–2
race-thinking ++ 168
racial analysis 10
rain, 'ocular proof' 217–20
'*Ram Chahe Leela*' song-and-dance sequence 239–42
Raman, Tara 41
The Ramayana epic 91, 102, 145, 190, 232, 234, 264
Ramlila (dramatic tradition) 102, 107, 255
Ramnoth, K. 56
Rankin, Deana 46
Rattansi, Ali 141
Ray, Satyajit, *Jalsaghar* 38
recitation, of play's lines 128
Refskou, Anne Sophie, conversations with 4, 18–19, 157–66
religious diversity 102
religious interpretation, children's importance 195–6
religious tolerance 73
remakes 264
Remember the Titans (film) 34
repeat viewing 257, 261–4
Reth (play) 248n17
revenge 125–6, 128, 129, 178–9

reviews, subtitles and 148
rhizome thesis 81, 87, 90–1, 95
rights, worldwide sales 109
ritual–tragedy association 243
Robbins, Jerome, *West Side Story* 161, 245
romantic tones, Bollywood movies 69
Roméo et Juliette (film) 86, 89
Rusk, Dean 31

sacred texts 190
sacrifice scenes 187–91
'*sagī*–'*ṭhagi*' opposition 214
Said, Edward, *Orientalism* 35
Sanskrit literature 234, 235, 244
Sapra, Rahul 196
Sarkar, Abhishek 180n5
'scattering' 205–7
seating in cinemas 264n2
Second Generation (film) 45
seduction 192, 196, 198–9
'selective viewing' 260–1
Sen, Aparna 196
   36 Chowringhee Lane 4, 15, 55, 57–65
   Arshinagar 44, 131, 260, 263
Sen, Manu, *Bhranti Bilas* 272
Sengupta, Jisshu 260
sex
   gender and 68
   '*kamarband*' 218
   songs association 210–11
sexual attraction 68
sexual identity 116
sexuality as manipulation 192
'shakeshifting' 208

Shakespeare, William
   400th anniversary of death 42, 275
   Antony and Cleopatra 172, 185
   The Comedy of Errors 56, 67, 72, 272
   Hamlet 7, 20, 64, 138, 146, 152n27, 170, 172, 173–80, 187, 226, 272, 275
   King Lear 64, 131
   Love's Labours Lost 7, 253
   Macbeth 139–40, 149–50, 172, 184–8, 191–4, 195, 197, 200, 242, 248n17, 275
   The Merchant of Venice 17, 100–1, 110–12, 116, 124–8, 130, 171–2, 248n17, 273
   A Midsummer Night's Dream 17, 100–2, 107, 124, 130, 132n3, 229, 253, 275
   Othello 20–1, 171–2, 187, 203–23, 226, 260, 266n12
   Romeo and Juliet 16, 21, 76n16, 79–97, 124, 131, 142, 145, 152n17, 185, 225–51
   The Taming of the Shrew 38
   The Tempest 171
   Titus Andronicus 131, 171–2, 261
   Twelfth Night 15, 55–77
Shakespeare and Indian Cinemas collection 2, 4, 12, 101

Shakespeare, The Movie 1 and 2 39
'Shakespearean rhizome' 81, 87, 90–1, 95
Shakespeare's Globe theatre 256, 261
Sharma, Ramesh, *Portrait of the Director* 104
Shaugnessey, Robert 14
Shaw, George Bernard 36
She's the Man (film) 15, 55, 65–7, 68–70, 74
Shklovsky, Viktor 266n10
Sholay (film) 259–60, 262, 268n28
shooting styles 106
Sidney, Philip 227–8
sight concept 217
Singh, Amritesh 5, 21
Singh, Anurag 65
Singh, Jyotsna G. 4–5, 19–20, 39, 274–6
Singh, Prashant 113
Singh, Ranveer 259
Sinha, Amresh 140, 150
snake venom 216
soccer 66–7
soliloquies 178, 184, 209
song 210–12
   appropriability for everyday life 258
   audience appreciation 260
   visual uncertainty 20–1, 203–23
song lyrics
   choreography 231–2, 260
   eyes 203, 216
   language of 209
   'ocular proof' 219
   poetry 211–12
   translation 142
song-and-dance sequences 5, 21, 87–90, 225–51
   audience engagement 256, 258, 263–4, 267n18
spectatorship culture 22, 255, 259
Spielberg, Steven, *West Side Story* 245
Spivak, Gayatri Chakravorty 35
sports 66–73
'spotting' 148–9
Srinivas, Lakshmi 254, 261, 263, 264n2, 265n7
Star Trek (film) 264
Stoppard, Tom 45
stories, media/genre of 8
stories-within-stories 94
story boards 115
storytelling 103, 211
'strangers' framework 5–10, 257, 266n10
straw rushes 248n15
streaming platforms 100, 109, 137, 144
Stubbes, P. 237
subalternity 170
subtitles 5, 18, 135–54, 208
'superhits' 262
Supple, Tim 275

Taneja, Preti 43, 46
'*Tattad Tattad*' song-and-dance sequence 231–4, 235
'*ṭhaga*', multiple meanings of 213–14
teaching restructuring 62
'technomasculinity' 33

text
  interpretation difference 273–4, 276
  song-and-dance relationship 231–4
  v. 'performance' 37
textual intimacies 228–9
theatre
  dance in 232, 236
  repeat viewers 262
Thomas, Miranda Fay 142, 254
'thumri' genre 211
Tieber, Claus 79, 81
time, preoccupation with 88
Titanic (film) 264
tragedies of love 184–5, 189
tragedy–ritual association 243
tragic effects, *36 Chowringhee Lane* 63
translation
  gestures 142–3, 144
  problems with 207–9
  song lyrics 142
  for subtitles 136–7, 146, 150
translation theories 136
transnational networks 169
travel culture 80
'travelling' concept 96, 167–82
Trivedi, Poonam 15, 39, 41–2, 46, 127, 132n2, 159, 184, 188, 192, 195–6, 271, 276
Truman, President 31
Trump, Donald 47–8, 50n4
Tyrewala, Abbas 45, 157

uGugu no Andile (film) 85, 94
United Kingdom (UK)
  immigration policy 36
United States (US)
  Bollywood in 40
  Global Shakespeare in the classroom 19–20, 167–82
  grassroots work 32, 34–5
  immigration reform 30–1, 32, 49–50n2
  performance movement 37
  'unsure observance' 205–7
Uran Khatola (film) 57
Urdu films 2, 3, 137, 141
Urdu language 70–1, 93, 138–9, 141, 188, 275
US *see* United States
ushers 255–6

Veer-Zaara (film) 76n16
Ventura, Zuenir, *Cidade Partida* 84–5
Venuti, Lawrence 136
Verma, Jatinder 36
  'Classical Binglish' 51n7
Verma, Rajiva, 'Shakespeare in Hindi Cinema' 271
verse–dance analogies 236
viewing technologies 39
violence
  in childbirth 187
  in dance 241–2
  firearms 192–3
  imperialist 185
  passion relationship 235
virtual communication 42–3
visual design 114
visual uncertainty, song 20–1, 203–23
Vives, J.L. 237
Vivian, Sobchak 260
Vividh Bharati radio programme 258

voiceover language 93
Voting Rights Act, 1965 32

Washington, Denzel 34
Wayne, Valerie 39–40
We That Are Young 131
Weinberg, Ana 4, 14, 20
Weir, Peter, *Dead Poets Society* 130
Welles, Orson, *Chimes at Midnight* 161
Wembley film theatre, London 265n7
West Side Story (film) 89, 161, 234, 245
White, Robert 15
   Shakespeare's Cinema 144
'whiteness' association 168, 171
Wilder, Billy 100, 103
   The Apartment 103
   Kiss Me, Stupid 103
Willet, Andrew 6
Williamson, Doll 7
Wise, Robert, *West Side Story* 161, 245
witchcraft 83, 197–8, 215
Withnail and I (film) 64
women
   Asia House screenings 46
   authority of 47
   in Bollywood 197–8
   change in roles 184
   childbirth consequences 195
   cross-dressing 65–71
   mistrust of 213
   revisions of Shakespeare 131
   in sacred texts 190
   social complexities 197
   sociological texts 189
   two faces of 214
Wonder, Stevie 211
Woolf, Virginia, *A Room of One's Own* 43
words–gestures relationship 235
world cinema adaptations 84, 101
writer–director collaboration 104
writing–dance connection 236

Young, Sandra 3
youth audience 84

Zeffirelli, Franco, *Romeo and Juliet* 38, 161, 245
Zeitz, Josh 50n4

www.ingramcontent.com/pod-product-compliance
Lightning Source LLC
Chambersburg PA
CBHW052149300426
44115CB00011B/1581